CURTIS
LEMAY

CURTIS LEMAY

STRATEGIST AND TACTICIAN

WARREN KOZAK

REGNERY HISTORY

B
LEMAY

First paperback edition © 2011, ISBN: 978-1-59698-769-2

This paperback edition published in 2014, ISBN 978-1-62157-299-2

The Library of Congress has cataloged the hardcover edition as follows:

ISBN 978-1-59698-569-8

Kozak, Warren, 1951-
  LeMay : the life and wars of General Curtis LeMay / Warren Kozak.
    p. cm
  1. LeMay, Curtis E. 2. Generals--United States--Biography. 3. United States. Army--Biography. 4. World War, 1939-1945--Aerial operations, American. 5. United States--History, Military--20th century. I. Title.
  E745.L42K69 2009
  940.540092--dc22
  [B]
                                              2009009412

Published in the United States by Regnery History
An imprint of Regnery Publishing
300 New Jersey Avenue NW
Washington, DC 20001
www.RegneryHistory.com

Manufactured in the United States of America
10 9 8 7 6 5 4 3 2 1

Books are available in quantity for promotional or premium use. For information on discounts and terms, please visit our website: www.Regnery.com.

Distributed to the trade by:
Perseus Distribution
250 West 57th Street
New York, NY 10107

DEDICATION

To the brave young Americans who took to the skies
to protect us all . . . and to my father, Sidney Kozak,
who watched from below, inspired to keep moving forward.

And to Lisa and Claire.

TABLE OF
CONTENTS

. . . .

PROLOGUE

"THE FINEST MILITARY STRATEGIST
THIS NATION HAS EVER PRODUCED."
—ROBERT S. MCNAMARA

"THE SMARTEST MAN I EVER MET."
—JUDGE RALPH NUTTER

"MY LEAST FAVORITE HUMAN BEING."
—TED SORENSEN

HE NEVER FIT THE IMAGE OF THE AMERICAN FLYBOY—DASHING, handsome, and suave. He was, instead, dark, brooding, and forbidding. He rarely smiled, he spoke even less, and when he did, his few words seemed to come out in a snarl. Women seated next to him at dinner said he could sit through the entire meal and not utter a single syllable. Surly, tactless, and with a lifeless, moist cigar constantly locked between his teeth, he was the prototype of the brutal, inhuman militarist. Most people found him frightening.

Yet somehow, Curtis Emerson LeMay, the youngest and longest-serving general in modern American history, rose from obscurity, lacking social graces, old-boy connections, or lineage, to become America's most innovative and—to this day—controversial military commander.

In 1945, LeMay was a national hero, celebrated in victory parades and on the cover of *Time* magazine. Twenty years later, everything had changed. Hollywood and the press vilified him. He was parodied as the mad general in *Dr. Strangelove*, longing for a nuclear exchange with the Soviets. In a searing essay, journalist I. F. Stone labeled him the "Caveman in a Jet Bomber."[1] At best he was considered a brutish thug; at worst, he was portrayed as demented. Oddly, LeMay never refuted his detractors and even seemed to encourage his negative reputation. "Many people you come up against in the world are all form and no substance," observed Judge Ralph Nutter, who flew with LeMay throughout the war. "LeMay was the opposite . . . he was all substance and no form."[2]

Curtis LeMay's career spanned an extraordinary time in America. He began flying bi-winged, open cockpit planes in the 1920s, commanded America's postwar fleet of giant B-52 bombers, and ended his career in an age of intercontinental nuclear missiles. During World War II, LeMay helped turn the bombing effort over Europe from an ineffective and costly failure into a success. He was also the architect behind the firebombing of Tokyo and sixty-four other Japanese cities. But his enemy was not just the Germans and Japanese; he also fought complacent bureaucracy, laziness, and stupidity.

For three years, day and night, LeMay concentrated his very capable intellect on the new science of destroying property and killing people with aerial bombing. In his firebombing campaign over Japan, LeMay ordered the deaths of more civilians than any other military officer in American history—well over 300,000 and perhaps as many as half a million. No one else comes close—not Ulysses S. Grant, not William T. Sherman, and not George S. Patton. Yet in the strange calculus of war, by killing so many human beings, LeMay saved millions more by making an invasion of Japan unnecessary. Most people would not want to make that kind of decision—killing vast numbers of human beings in order to save even more. It requires someone with a ruthless sense of realism—and if LeMay was anything, he was a realist.

LeMay accepted his life-and-death responsibility as just another part of his job. From a young age, he had shouldered difficult burdens. When he was eight years old, LeMay surpassed his father as the responsible figure in his family; he realized then that if he did not help feed his mother and brothers and sisters, no one else would. This experience shaped his unusually sober character, while his service in the military strengthened his sense of responsibility and duty.

LeMay was also unusually honest. He never shied away from bad news. He understood he was creating a new science and needed all the information. He would not tolerate falsifying data to cover up shortcomings. The stakes in aerial warfare were too important. But his frank nature could make him appear callous and abrupt. "I'll tell you what war is about," he once told Sam Cohen, the inventor of the neutron bomb. "You've got to kill people and when you kill enough of them, they stop fighting."[3] As Judge Nutter remembered, "Very few people can really tell the truth and most people really don't want to hear it; he did. So did Sherman. People don't want to hear that kind of blunt honesty."[4]

Added to LeMay's blunt honesty, brutal sense of realism, and strong devotion to service and country was an odd combination of personality traits: a highly radical mind wrapped up in an extremely conservative personality. He was a mass of inconsistency. While he hated bureaucracy, he chose a career in one of the largest bureaucracies in the world. He felt at times he was too soft to lead men into combat, yet he was viewed as a very hard man by everyone else. One congressman suggested that he be relieved of his command during the war because he seemed so unfeeling and inhuman. Yet he cared immensely about the men who served under him; he felt no responsibility more keenly than preparing them for battle.

Curtis LeMay had the unusual ability to see all parts of a battle and understand how they fit together. LeMay's achievements were even more remarkable when you consider that he was working with new and highly complex machines that had never been used before, on a battlefield that was 25,000 feet above the earth.

It should be remembered that generals Robert E. Lee and Ulysses S. Grant fought seventeen battles in each of their careers. LeMay fought one almost every day for three years. And unlike any other general in modern times, he did not send his men out on perilous missions, he *led* them. On the most dangerous missions, LeMay insisted on flying the lead aircraft in the formation himself, in the first plane the enemy would target. His men followed him into battle. No other general in World War II did this.

LeMay's involvement in momentous affairs did not end with World War II—indeed, he was a protagonist in some of the greatest foreign policy crises of the middle of the twentieth century. He was the head of the Air Force in Europe at the start of the Berlin Air Lift. In the 1950s, he created the Strategic Air Command, the massive nuclear strike force of B-52s. During the Cuban Missile Crisis in 1962 and the beginning of the Vietnam War, he represented the Air Force on the Joint Chiefs of Staff, advising the president. Finally, in the tumultuous year of 1968, he agreed to be George Wallace's running mate in the most divisive and racially charged campaign in recent times.

If a country is lucky, it will produce a Curtis LeMay in times of extreme danger. Nations need men like LeMay when survival is at stake. But once the nation is safe, these men are often rejected because they become walking reminders of events most people would rather forget. As with Curtis LeMay, sometimes these men contribute to their own downfall by continuing to display the belligerence that was necessary during battle but that does not fit in a world at relative peace.

More than sixty years and three generations after the end of World War II, it is very difficult for anyone born twenty, thirty, or forty years after the event to fully comprehend what it was really like to have the entire world at war. Rather than two or three nations fighting against each other, practically every country on the planet, every individual, and every resource was committed to the conflict. It was a war with huge ramifications for the future of mankind.

This country needed a man like Curtis LeMay in World War II and the Cold War. But a generation after the end of those conflicts, it is hard for many people to remember why.

CHAPTER ONE

SOMETHING STRANGE AND WONDERFUL

ON THE COLD AUTUMN MORNING OF NOVEMBER 7, 1910, FOUR-year-old Curtis Emerson LeMay looked up from his chores, startled by a sound he had never heard before. Contrary to the law of gravity, a flying, motorized machine with a man looking back down at him was passing overhead. "It came from nowhere," he wrote in his memoirs, ". . . and I wanted to catch it."[1]

LeMay had been in the backyard of his parents' home in a run-down section of Columbus, Ohio, picking up kindling wood for his mother's stove, but now he went sprinting after the flying machine. "I just thought that I might be able to grab the airplane and have it for my own, and possess it always."[2]

He ran across lawns, streets, and fields, and when he finally lost sight of it, he had no idea how far he had run; it seemed he had been chasing it for minutes, but it took him hours to walk back home. Not being able to grasp the prize was hard for him to accept. "I had lost something unique and in a way Divine," LeMay recalled. "It was a god or a spook, or a piece of a god or a spook, and I had never seen one before. I wanted it and hadn't been able to catch it, and was filled with a sense of exasperation and defeat."[3]

LeMay was one of those children who are "born old." As a child he had a deep sense of responsibility; as an adult he had an abject fear of failure. Both were linked to his father's bankrupt life. But that afternoon, LeMay—the pragmatist, the realist—behaved as the child he was. He came home in tears, unable to catch the mysterious object. The memory of that plane would deeply influence the course of his life. "He stayed with me and sped beside me many times, later on, when it seemed often that I was trying to catch up with something which moved faster than I could run."[4]

The early years of the twentieth century marked a dividing point between America's frontier and agrarian past and its remarkable technological future. The four-year-old boy, who was very much a part of that past, saw something in that object that sparked his imagination and excited him. This particular machine—a Model B Wright Flyer, flown as a publicity stunt for a local department store—became a fixation for the rest of his life. A century later, LeMay's younger sister Pat remembered, "Mother always said that was what set him off."[5]

•   •   •   •

HOME

As a child, LeMay did a lot of running. He ran away from home at every opportunity. He would stare at the door and then simply bolt out. As an adult, LeMay could not explain this manic behavior, admitting that his life was hard enough and these actions only brought him more problems, along with an inevitable beating. Still, he ran. One possible explanation was his father Erving LeMay's mean temper. "Every day, Curtis got a licking from Dad," remembered his younger sister Pat.[6]

Curtis was the eldest child. Six more would follow: Lloyd, Valma, Methyl, Charles (who died at birth), Leonard, and Patarica, twenty-two years younger then Curtis. "My sense was that Grandma LeMay was always pregnant," remarked Curtis LeMay's daughter, Janie.[7]

The LeMay family was of French extraction, but had come to America in the eighteenth century by way of Quebec. The LeMays who remained in Canada were Roman Catholics, but somewhere along the way, the LeMays of America, settling in Ohio, became Methodists. Though Curtis's parents, Arizona and Erving, met in church, he was not raised in a religious household. Years later, one of the men who served under LeMay in Europe admitted, "I don't remember him ever going to church throughout the entire war. In fact, there must have been a chapel on the base but for the life of me, I don't remember that either."[8]

Arizona Carpenter LeMay, Curtis's mother, came from English stock. The most unique feature of the Carpenter family was its unusual choice of first names. Arizona was named by her father, who suspected she would never meet another (she did, but only once). In turn, Arizona named her three daughters Methyl, Valma, and Patarica. The boys, starting with Curtis, were given more conventional names.

Arizona had no more than an 8th grade education (Erving, even less), but she had a flair for learning, which was enough to secure a teaching job in a one-room school house as a teenager. Although she weighed no more than 105 pounds and was not much older than some of her students, Arizona reportedly held the class in strict order and was well liked. She was a pretty woman. Her husband, Erving, stood 6'2", and had a hard face and pronounced ears.

He was strong and had a talent for fixing just about anything—"good with his hands," as it was called. Curtis inherited that ability from his father, along with a special fascination for gasoline engines, whether they were in a Ford or a B-17.

When Curtis was born on November 15, 1906, in a home on the west side of Columbus, Ohio, his father's work life had begun to unravel. Erving was employed as a brakeman for the railroad, which was considered a good and stable job in that era. "But something happened," Curtis wrote later. What happened was never revealed, but Erving would henceforth lose one job after another, dragging his family with him on a long, strange journey. "We lived like nomads,"[9] Curtis wrote, recalling his childhood. Erving was a migrant worker taking whatever employment he could find . . . painting, carpentry, or odd jobs. Arizona followed along, bringing their growing number of children and always making the best of increasingly difficult situations. When her husband was out of work for longer periods, she worked as a domestic servant in addition to keeping her own household in order. No adversity seemed too great for Arizona to handle.

By the time Curtis was six, his family had lived in five different homes. This meant new friends and later, new schools and schoolyards. "I'd just get set at one school in Columbus—say, when we lived on Dana Avenue or perhaps on Guildford—and then, bang, we'd have to move out of town."[10]

No doubt some of it was due to poverty, but some indefinable quality lacking in Erving's character was also responsible for Curtis LeMay's childhood instability. The economy of Ohio and the rest of the country was booming right up and through the First World War. Immigrants with no English skills were walking off boats and finding jobs. The labor pool was simply not large enough to feed the demands of a country that was growing exponentially.

Later in his life, Curtis described his father as a "dreamer," never satisfied and always wanting to move on to something else. To compensate, Curtis would become the ultimate pragmatist, working in just one occupation for his entire life. To Erving's credit, he always looked for work, no matter how menial, and deposited all of his meager earnings not at the local tavern, but with his wife. By all accounts, Erving and Arizona had a stable marriage. But there was a mean side to Erving.

"I was scared to death of my Dad," Pat remembers. "He was a very strict disciplinarian, like Curtis. Maybe they were too much alike."[11] She remembers having more fun and laughing a lot with her other two brothers, but not with Curtis.

Years later, when Erving was elderly, the nursing home where he lived asked his family to remove him because he was causing too many problems for everyone around him. "When he died," remarked Janie LeMay Lodge, "we hoped that Grandma LeMay could start to have some fun."[12]

Over the years, it was Arizona who somehow kept her growing family fed. All the LeMay children looked to her as the role model for self-sufficiency, moral strength, and grit. She instilled a strong sense of honesty, discipline, and integrity. If they were poor, none of the children ever saw themselves that way—nobody else they encountered in the places they lived was any different. In fact, some people had much less. Hard work was a basic part of life.

Even when Erving tried to play the role of responsible father, he managed to do it all wrong. Once he made a deal with his son that he would match the money Curtis needed to buy a new bike he had seen in a shop window. However, one day, on impulse, Erving bought a different bike than the one Curtis wanted—and ended up taking it for his own use. Later, when Curtis desperately longed for his own rifle, Erving went out and bought an expensive Winchester 95. "I just about fainted when I saw it," Curtis later wrote. But the gun, a 30-caliber rifle, was much too powerful for the young boy and he could not use it. "I would never say that Pop was the most practical man on earth,"[13] Curtis recalled years later. "I felt he was—not exactly on the shiftless side [since] he was working all the time—but he was jumping around too much."[14]

· · · ·

MONTANA

The great adventure of Curtis LeMay's youth came in 1914 when he was eight years old. "Pop had lost his construction job and we were in a pretty sorry situation at home."[15] Erving packed up his family and headed west based entirely on a brother-in-law's comment that jobs could be found in Montana. Jobs were just as plentiful and a lot closer in Chicago, Cleveland, or even in Columbus where they were living. But something about Montana caught Erving LeMay's imagination and the family followed.

Curtis remembered the train trip as a mosaic of "crowded straw suitcases, squashed and wrinkled pillows, lunches packed in shoe boxes with as much food as possible taken from home to start with and as little as possible to be purchased along the way."[16] That memory also included peanut shells on the floor, wailing babies, a car with hard seats that was either too hot or too cold, and a foul smelling toilet. There was also the "news-butcher" with a wonderful basket of candies that "the LeMay children could only dream about."[17]

The family finally arrived in Montana to confront cold the likes of which they had never experienced. A high, dry cold, LeMay remembered years later, that "seemed to take your breath after you bit into it for a while." They moved into a tenement house, Erving got a job, and then they moved again when "Pop got fired or quit."[18] Erving next found work as caretaker for an isolated sportsman's club. Just getting to the club, located on a chain of lakes called the Nez Perce, was an adventure. Arizona and Erving put all their belongings on an open horse-drawn wagon, bundled up the children in blankets, and set out for the camp. The trip took them south of Butte City in a driving snowstorm. The caretaker's cabin was normally for summer use only. Somehow, Arizona made it a home where they sheltered themselves from the fierce winter cold.

In this setting, where the nearest neighbor was twenty-five miles away, Curtis fell in love with the outdoors. He saw bald eagles and hawks for the first time, and he could fish to his heart's content. His father taught him how to shoot and handle a gun. Erving did not quite understand how to maintain the hatchery at the club, but his son seemed to grasp the concept and helped move the fish into the various pools as they grew.

During that first winter when there was barely enough food to feed the family, it was Curtis who discovered that if he took a scrap of meat, put it on a hook, and went down to the lake to a spot where a flume kept the water from freezing, he could catch huge trout. Sometimes it was difficult for the boy to drag the large fish through the snow back up to the house. He would come into the cabin, drop the prize in his mother's sink, and wait just long enough to warm up before he went back out to do it all over again. It never dawned on Erving to even get up. "My father was perfectly willing to sit with his socked feet up against the shiny stove fender while the frost snapped and crackled outside." When Curtis came in with the fish, his father simply shifted his feet on the wood-burning stove to let him pass. "The larder was a vague mystery, which Pop didn't bother to penetrate. He figured that somehow, from somewhere, Mom would be able to conjure up a meal out of thin air. Often he was right."[19] At this very early point in his life, Curtis surpassed his father as the responsible male figure in the LeMay family. He was eight years old.

One cold winter contending with the isolation of the camp was enough for Erving. Now it was California that beckoned. A letter from one of his brothers who lived in the Bay area promised help finding a job.

In the early part of the twentieth century, California was a cauldron of opportunity for anyone with drive and imagination. To the south, the movie industry was just beginning to create itself in Los Angeles. The land was fertile in the central valley and agriculture was booming. Factories were coming to the state and San Francisco was its economic center. But for Erving LeMay, none of this mattered. As soon as the family arrived, they discovered that his brother who promised to find him a job had enlisted in the Army and was long gone. Once again, Erving put his family in a tenement apartment in Emeryville and found menial work, this time in a cannery.

California was a magical place for Curtis, one that he would return to throughout his life. The stop in Emeryville lasted just a year and the LeMay family, caught between Erving's whims and his constant failures, soon headed back East again. This time it was New Brighton, Pennsylvania, northwest of Pittsburgh that beckoned with the promise of a mill job. But within a year, the family was back in Columbus, having come full circle on their trek.

. . . .

HIGH SCHOOL AND COLLEGE

For the first time in Curtis's life, his family would stay in one place; a small three-bedroom house at 511 Welch Avenue in Columbus. Young Curtis took advantage of this stability by building a business. In Emeryville, he shot sparrows (with a borrowed .22 BB gun) for an old woman whose cat only ate sparrows. She paid him five cents a bird. In New Brighton, he had taken on a paper route. Now, at the age of fourteen, he started a newspaper distribution business. Curtis was not merely enterprising; he felt a responsibility to earn money for the family. Responsibility always trumped joy: the joy he could have had playing sports or loafing with his friends. Still, resentment remained. He longed to play football with the other boys, but he had to collect those newspapers every day.

The realities of the LeMay family's poverty, Curtis's extremely sober temperament, and his unreliable father combined to create an abnormal childhood. Curtis's unusual sense of responsibility squelched any chance of happiness. His mother never complained about the work she had to do to help support the family; he followed her lead. He worked hard at his studies. He worked hard after school. Fun was simply a luxury he would have to pass up. From an early age, everything he did was in pursuit of earning money or self-improvement. The extra time he had—and there was little—was spent at the library where he read biographies, history, and travel books, which took him away to different times and places.

At South High School in Columbus, Curtis did allow himself one extravagance in the form of a crystal set,[20] a homemade radio receiver he made with materials he purchased. He was fascinated with radio, a relatively new invention, and stayed up late at night with earphones on, twisting the dial through the static until a human voice came through, speaking live from as far away as Dayton or Cincinnati. "Those were the big things you really worked for,"[21] he remembered. During his high school years, radio was his one distraction. Any other time outside of school was spent working or at the library. As for dating—it was too great an extravagance. LeMay explained much later, "The girl stuff cost money—sodas, sandwiches and all, and I thought my personal cash would be better expended in some other direction."[22]

LeMay admitted that he missed out on a lot but, again, it never came out as a complaint. Whining would have been against his nature. However, in a rare moment of introspection, he admitted in his memoirs that "there may have been nights when I looked up into the darkness and held to the opinion that I was carrying a load which not many other people were carrying."[23] He was usually just too tired to think about it. He also wondered, years later, why no one, neither his parents nor his teachers, ever offered him any advice, direction, or guidance. He was always left to figure things out on his own, to go his own direction. This was a challenge he would encounter throughout his life, handling it in the most responsible way: with hard work.

He did keep one dream in his imagination: flying. When he was sixteen years old, Curtis pooled some money with a friend and went to Norton Field just outside Columbus where a barnstorming pilot (who made his living giving demonstrations of the still-novel ability to fly from town to town) had landed. "Five dollars for five minutes," the pilot told them. He normally took one passenger, but business was slow that day, and the two boys talked him into letting them share the front seat. That first experience amazed the young Curtis: the immediate sensation of lightness on takeoff, the view of the ground from the sky—familiar sights re-created on a miniature scale. He told himself that someday he would be a pilot and he would "fly wherever I please, stay as long as I want to, and just have fun."[24] However, much later, after his retirement and after more than thirty years flying countless planes, he admitted that he never had the chance for that "joyride." Not even once. Work always came first.

·   ·   ·   ·

OHIO STATE

It was the desire to fly that motivated LeMay to go on to college. He knew the only opportunity for him to become a pilot was with the military. A college degree would give him a leg up on other candidates competing for the very limited slots in the Army Air Corps. Although he dreamed of attending West Point, he was too intimidated to seek the nomination by a congressman that every applicant needs.

In the fall of 1924, Curtis LeMay enrolled at Ohio State, becoming the first member of his family to go to college. His goal was a degree in civil engineering, so he joined an engineering fraternity and enlisted in the ROTC program.

During his first term, Curtis got a job at the Buckeye Steel Casting Company. He was hired at the amazing salary of thirty-five dollars a week by a manager who had also worked his way through school and was sympathetic to the hard-working young man. In 1928, when food cost a dollar a day and rent for a good size dwelling was seventy-five dollars a month, an entire family could live well on thirty-five dollars a week. But there was a down side.

The job required six days a week, starting at five in the afternoon and finishing at two or three in the morning. The work was incredibly demanding—setting cores in the molds for truck and railroad car frames for nine hours every night. Though it was dirty and noisy, LeMay liked it.[25]

LeMay was going to bed at three in the morning six nights a week, but he still had to get up early for classes. He also found time during the day to study and drill with his ROTC unit. But he was not getting enough sleep and as hard as he tried, he could not stay awake during his 9:00 a.m. course. "Railroad Curves" was taught by Professor Wall, and LeMay failed it two semesters in a row. Wall was unsympathetic. Still, LeMay was practical. He recognized that if he slept through that one class, he would be able to stay up for the others. Early on, Curtis LeMay absorbed a valuable lesson— sometimes, in order to achieve a greater goal, sacrifices had to be made.

There was one bright spot in this arrangement. In order to get to work, LeMay needed a car. He and a friend put down $12.50 a piece for a 1918 Ford Model T. His "partner" used it during the days and Sundays, and LeMay had it from the late afternoon until morning. LeMay's mechanical ability kept the old car running throughout most of his time at Ohio State.

He continued to live with his family on Welch Avenue. A good part of his earnings went to the family, which was a substantial help to his parents. When Erving left town for work, he took Arizona with him and left Curtis in charge of his younger siblings. It was an arrangement that seemed to be an improvement for his siblings. "Dad was gone so much," his sister Methyl would remember, "and never took that much interest in what we were doing, as far as school was concerned. But Curtis would say, 'Let me see your grade card.' We toed the mark when he was the boss." The three girls and Leonard preferred it when their older brother looked after them. "He was a very serious person," Leonard remembered. "He had a drawing board set up in the living room. He was studying much of the time. He was very dedicated. Knew what he wanted to do."[26]

· · · ·

THE OBSESSION

In the spring of LeMay's senior year, a group of Army flyers came through Columbus on their way east. Word would always spread when Air Corps planes were "visiting," and people would come out to see them. It was a major event. A crowd was already waiting when the olive drab planes touched down in a pasture at the edge of town. LeMay was not about to miss the opportunity and joined his fellow ROTC candidates at the field. His adulation for the pilots was nothing short of hero worship. "We tried not to get in their way too much. There were just about a million questions I wanted to ask any of those intent, serious-faced young men, whenever one walked near. Yet I was tongue-tied."

The college boys "watched every movement they made" and copied every gesture. LeMay stayed very late watching them, until the flyers bedded down for the night under their planes—such were the accommodations available to flight officers in the Army Air Corps in those years. That hardly mattered. Everything they did, even the slightest mannerism, impressed LeMay. He was back again early the next morning to watch the planes take off. If he could have, he would have spent the night in the open field just to be close to them. "Every time I closed my eyes for a long while afterward all I could see were leather flying helmets and goggles; all I could hear was the sound of those Liberty engines."[27]

By 1928, during his fourth year of college, the rest of the country caught up with LeMay's flying obsession. Lindbergh had just made his historic flight to Paris the year before. LeMay knew the odds against his getting into the cadet program were increasing. In that year alone, three thousand young men applied for one hundred openings in the Army Air Corps. Of those, only twenty-five would make it through flight school and emerge as pilots in the U.S. Army. Twenty-five out of three thousand.

Curtis LeMay was now twenty-one. He needed less than a quarter's credits for an engineering degree. He had a reserve commission from ROTC and his compulsion to fly overshadowed everything else. Although LeMay lacked the credits to graduate in June of 1928 due to failing his early morning Railroad Curves class, he was still an ROTC honor graduate, and he heard that honor graduates might have a leg up in the competition for those 100 spots.

That spring, as LeMay tried to figure out how to accomplish his dream, he showed a surprising talent for maneuvering within a large organization. There was absolutely nothing in his background that would have given him this understanding. He had no mentor to guide him. He certainly did not learn it from his father. However, just as a chess master can see an entire board with its infinite possibilities, LeMay could look at a vast bureaucracy and intuitively understand how all of its parts fit together. Like his gift of understanding the components of an engine, along with his intense focus on achieving success in every problem, it would stand him in good stead later in his career.

LeMay began the process of getting into the Air Corps by break-ing down the problem. First, he sought information from anyone with knowledge about the application process. LeMay discovered that candidates were ranked according to their military back-grounds with West Point graduates at the top. But he also learned there were loopholes which, although Byzantine, could help him reach his goal. While his ROTC commission gave him a ranking of seventh in the list of applicants for flying school, in a strange twist of the military bureaucracy, he could jump all the way to the number two position if he was a member of the National Guard. Upon learning this, he immediately went downtown to the state building across the street from the Capitol. There he found an old Brigadier-General by the name of Bush, the head of Ohio's National Guard, sitting behind his desk. LeMay had met the General briefly, along with the rest of his class, at an ROTC social event the year before. To the 21-year-old LeMay, the general sitting at his roll-top desk seemed "as elderly as God, and just about as militarily sophis-ticated as Napoleon."

LeMay introduced himself and told General Bush he wanted to enlist in the National Guard right away. "Why all the eagerness?" asked General Bush. LeMay decided just to tell the truth. He explained that the Guard had a priority on the list for flight school, and that was all he wanted. The General took a liking to the forth-right young man. Bush acknowledged that people walking into his office eager to enlist were few and far between. He gauged LeMay with some amusement. He needed an ammunition officer. This young man seemed like he could handle the job.

"There was now a kind of mist in front of my eyes," LeMay recounted years later in his memoirs, "but through that mist I could see General Bush slowly pulling down the top of his old-fashioned desk. I remember following the sound as the little round pieces went smoothly down through the twin, curved grooves. He reached for his World War campaign hat and gestured to me, 'Come on.'"[28]

The General took LeMay across the street to the State House and commissioned him as a Second Lieutenant in the Field Artillery of the Ohio National Guard, setting off a ricochet of red tape. LeMay first had to resign his commission in the Reserve in order to take the Guard commission. Then he waited.

Spring turned to summer. LeMay continued to work at the Buckeye foundry. He fulfilled his duties with the Guard once a week. And he waited at the mailbox every day in hopes of receiving an acceptance to Cadet School. But nothing arrived. By September 1928, LeMay still had not heard whether his application to the program had been accepted. He had those last credits to complete at Ohio State, and the deadline for registration was approaching, requiring him to make a decision. Consequently, he invested a considerable sum of money and sent a long telegram to the War Department in Washington explaining his dilemma and why he needed to know where he stood. Luckily, the telegram was not filed somewhere or lost in a pile of letters on some low-ranking officer's desk. The response soon arrived. It read simply: "This authorizes you to enlist as a flying cadet at the nearest Army station."

LeMay remembered the moment: "Won't say that I was trembling all over, but I was trembling inside." He immediately headed to Fort Hayes in Columbus—the closest regular Army base. He showed the recruiting sergeant the telegram and told him that he wanted to enlist as a "flying cadet"... a term the sergeant had never heard. The sergeant was only too happy to comply. "A college boy was a real Sergeant York in comparison with the run-of-the-mill volunteer recruits they were getting in those days. Average recruits were really something: the deadbeats on the street, a lot of poolroom drunks...once in a while some fairly decent characters—from the country, usually—farm boys who were eager to get away from the binders and hay-rakes."[29]

But once LeMay had been inducted, the sergeant wanted him in the Army as a private and was all set to send him on to basic training. LeMay protested, again waving the telegram. The sergeant went to his lieutenant who went to his captain, who finally resolved the issue. LeMay then helped his ROTC buddy, Francis Griswold, who was also waiting to hear from Washington, through the process he had followed. Before long, both LeMay and Griswold were ordered to report to March Field in Riverside, California for the November class.

Amelia Earhart had become the first woman to cross the Atlantic just four months earlier, only increasing the public's fascination with aviation and its young, attractive heroes. The country was entering its last year of prosperity for a long time to come. The national election was just days ahead in which Herbert Hoover would handily defeat Al Smith. And a young and wealthy Franklin Roosevelt, who nominated Smith at the Democratic Convention that summer, would become the governor of New York.

Curtis LeMay's great adventure was about to begin as well. He packed the few things he owned and said goodbye to his family. Near the end of October 1928, LeMay headed west for the second time in his life. Only this time, the circumstances were considerably different. LeMay and Griswold boarded the train at the Union and Pacific Station in downtown Columbus. The Army had given them a travel allowance that was just enough for a single upper berth. They managed to cajole the conductor into giving them a second berth, but it hardly mattered—the two young men were too excited to sleep. They were hardly fliers. They both knew that only 25 percent of the class would advance to the Air Corps. But LeMay was still able to comprehend the magic of that moment in time. "We are on a black sooty passenger train which ploughs its way toward Chicago in the nighttime, and bangs across switches, and fills the Pullmans with a bitter smell of coal smoke. And we are two kids, jolting along in our respective upper berths, clinging instinctively to the bed-clothes when the train swerves on a fast curve."[30]

He would look back on that trip through the autumn countryside as a special demarcation in his life: "No crystal ball was included in my meager luggage, so I didn't have any glimpses of the future . . . and Griswold and myself [were] studying and flying and yakking, and working our way into that same future. It was all ahead of us, but we didn't know."[31]

CHAPTER TWO

FLIGHT

As THE TRAIN ROLLED AWAY, LEAVING THE SMALL GROUP OF young men who had joined Curtis and Griswold along the way standing on the platform at 5:30 a.m., there was not a living soul to be seen. They wandered through Riverside's tiny downtown, carrying their luggage, until they finally stopped at the post office—the only building with an electric light on. They chose Griswold to make the nickel phone call to March Field where he was able to reach the officer of the day. Griswold explained who he was, why he was calling, and where he was standing.

"That's fine," the officer told him, "our mail truck will be in there at nine-thirty. After he gets loaded, you get on the mail truck and come out."[1] The eight prospective flyers found a diner where they could get some coffee and eventually, as promised, the truck rolled in. They threw their gear and themselves unceremoniously on top of the mailbags and were on their way in their first taste of the world of the Air Corps.

* * * *

HISTORY

The military was interested in the possibilities created by flight from its earliest beginnings. After the Wrights' historic first flight at Kitty Hawk, the U.S. Army Signal Corps hired them to design a plane and teach some of its officers how to fly. The partnership had a rough start. In his very first demonstration for the Army before a large crowd at Fort Myer, Virginia in 1908, Orville Wright's plane crashed. Lieutenant Thomas Selfridge flew along with Wright as an observer. On that day, Selfridge, who graduated from West Point in 1903 along with Douglas MacArthur, had the distinction of becoming the first passenger ever killed in a plane crash. Orville Wright was hospitalized for months with four broken ribs and a fractured leg.

Although manned flight began in the United States, by World War I the Europeans had surpassed the Americans in plane design and pilot training. After the United States entered the war in 1917, the Army increased the numbers of its planes and pilots by the thousands, but it still lagged far behind the French, English, and Germans, something a brash, overconfident Billy Mitchell, who led the American air force in France, sought to change.

After the war, a huge national debate began, pitting the visionaries of air power like Mitchell against the established institutions of the Army and Navy. While the branches of the military appeared to be struggling over theory—whether flight would be a legitimate part of the future of warfare—in reality, they were fighting over money from Congress. Early twentieth-century Washington was very reluctant to spend tax dollars on its armed forces and had, in fact, drawn down their wartime force to 22 aero squadrons from a high of 185.[2] The country had no plans of ever going to war again—and the oceans were considered sufficient protection from any aggressors.

But there were a few men in addition to Billy Mitchell who foresaw the day when those oceans would no longer provide an adequate buffer and when large, multi-engine airplanes could span them. Henry "Hap" Arnold and Carl "Tooey" Spaatz served with Mitchell in the war and shared his belief that fighting would be radically altered by the airplane, breaking the bloody stalemate of trench warfare that killed millions of soldiers, and smashing not just armies but the enemy's ability to produce weapons far behind the front lines. What that meant in terms of civilian casualties was still undefined. But in the 1920s, the War Department could not even envision another war, nor did it understand how to effectively use this section of the Army. All Washington seemed to understand was that airplanes required huge amounts of money it was unwilling to spend for something that remained more theory than fact.

In 1921, in a highly publicized demonstration designed to prove naval vessels' new vulnerability, a squadron of Mitchell's planes bombed and sank ships taken from Germany after World War I— a surplus German destroyer, a light cruiser, and the battleship *Ostfriesland*. But even though hundreds of people watched Mitchell's bombers sink the ships off the Virginia coast, Mitchell failed to convince the War Department and Congress of the growing strength of air power and the need for an air force. A new day had dawned, but Washington did not see it. However, the implications of the exercise were not lost on one observer. Captain Osami Nagano of the Japanese Navy, in attendance as a diplomatic observer, carefully watched the exercise, grasped its implications, and twenty years later helped plan the defining act of air power over naval vessels in the attacks on Pearl Harbor.

· · · ·

DODOS

When the eight new cadets arrived at March Field on top of the mail truck, they were first sent to the supply depot to draw equipment. At the same time, on the other side of the room, the class that had just graduated was in the process of turning in their things. These select few, now aviators, were moving on to Kelly Field in Texas for advanced training. What impressed LeMay more than anything that day was an argument he witnessed between one of the supply sergeants and a graduate who was short one pair of coveralls. The young pilot explained to the sergeant, or tried to explain, that he had loaned his coveralls to another cadet on the same day the unlucky cadet was killed in a crash. He said he had not wanted the coveralls, which were on the mangled and bloody body of the dead cadet, and he figured no one else would. The sergeant was unmoved. The cadet was given a set of coveralls and had to turn in a set of coveralls. End of discussion. LeMay realized the 25 percent pass rate was not the only obstacle facing these green recruits. Despite the stark lesson, whether it was the invulnerability of youth or his own personality, LeMay feared washing out much more than death.

For the next four months, these cadets would be known as *dodos*—ungainly birds, unable to fly, that are easily killed. Until they washed out, were killed, or successfully moved on to Kelly Field, the dodos would spend their time in canvas tents that housed them due to a shortage of barracks. The tents were riddled with holes from flying sparks released by wood stoves that barely worked. Arriving in November, this particular class would be at March Field during the four coldest months of the year.

The first month consisted of ground school and physical training. This was especially difficult for the cadets because they were all eager to fly, and it did not help to constantly march past a row of shining white and gold PT-3s—the bi-wing trainers that were used during World War I, and became the main tool for flight instruction. Instead of flying that first month, LeMay and the others learned about engines, fuel systems, and aerodynamics. "[It] was just about the longest month I ever spent in my life,"[3] LeMay would remember.

LeMay also took note of one particular aspect of life at March Field—the food, which was not very good. Throughout his career and his memoirs, food seemed to play an important role. That may have been due to the fact that during his childhood, it was not always certain that there would be enough to feed the family. Or it could have been as simple as the fact that the man liked to eat. "He fought a weight problem his whole life," one aide would remember years later.[4]

The class was finally divided up, and cadets were assigned to a flight instructor in groups of five. Unfortunately for LeMay and everyone else in his small group, he drew Peewee Wheeler. Wheeler was not mean, ill-tempered, or even difficult. He was a nice man and a great pilot, but he lacked any ability to teach. LeMay saw this right away, but there was nothing he could do

about it. For LeMay, passing on information—teaching others—
was effortless. So he was doubly frustrated to come up against
someone with no such ability. "It is a sad fact that many people in
this life are able to exhibit particular skills—to excel in such skills
sometimes to a degree almost beyond belief—and yet remain
unable to communicate their understandings and procedures to
another," he reflected later in his life.[5] LeMay considered asking
for a different instructor, especially after the other four cadets in
his group quickly washed out, but he was afraid it would sound
like whining. Instead, he made a calculated decision to take his
chances with Wheeler and hoped he could glean enough information to pass his flight tests. LeMay had a certain confidence in his
ability to fly and grasp the basics on his own.

At various levels during those weeks, the instructors would send
their trainees on to "check pilots." It was the check pilot who
would determine whether the cadet would go on to the next level
or wash out. For his final test, LeMay's bad luck continued—he
drew Red MacKinnon, rumored to be the toughest of all the check
pilots. Red was a legend at March Field.

The morning of the final test, LeMay got into the bi-plane, taking the seat directly in front of MacKinnon. The instructor, who
offered no chit-chat, took the controls at takeoff. Soon he brought
the plane down near the ground and told LeMay to "take over." As
soon as LeMay took control of the plane, MacKinnon cut the
power to the engine. LeMay looked for an open field, banked the
plane to the right and headed towards it. This sent the instructor
into a tirade: "God damn it, that's all wrong! Give it to me."[6] After
a while, he gave the controls back to LeMay. Again he cut the throttle, and LeMay responded as he had before. It appeared to LeMay

that MacKinnon might fly right out of the plane in midair, he was so angry.

If a pilot loses his engine at low altitude, he should not bank the plane as LeMay had done, for fear of stalling—losing airspeed—and crashing. Instead, he should keep going straight ahead and hope to find a safe area for landing. But the decision also depends on the plane and the speed it is going when the engines quit, and in both cases, LeMay quickly deduced that they could make the turn. The fact that he was right was irrelevant, though. MacKinnon was interested in the principle. Unfortunately, Peewee had never passed this information on to LeMay.

Next, MacKinnon ordered LeMay to perform a snap roll to the right, a kind of acrobatic maneuver, which he negotiated beautifully. MacKinnon asked for another one, and again LeMay was flawless. Then MacKinnon told him to do a snap roll to the left. Here LeMay ran into another huge problem: he could not do snap rolls to the left. He had tried over and over but just could not master it. When he asked Peewee Wheeler for help, all he got back was, "You just do it a little this way and a little that way." MacKinnon waited and finally yelled: "Go head. Proceed, proceed!" LeMay told him he could not do it. Seemingly disgusted, MacKinnon told him to land the plane. And even here, LeMay's bad luck continued. A strong wind picked up from the desert as he was coming in and he landed long. "Altogether, it wasn't one of my better days, shall we say," LeMay remembered. "And I knew it."[7]

As he sat there in the cockpit after the plane came to a complete stop, LeMay realized that this was it. He had washed out. His career as an officer in the Army Air Corps was over. Everything he wanted hinged on a fateful check mark in a box on an obscure piece of paper. Pass or fail—it was that simple. MacKinnon and LeMay got out of the cockpit and stood there next to the plane. LeMay, unable to breathe, looked at the instructor as he went over his list. MacKinnon just shook his head, not helping LeMay's intake of oxygen.

"Well, son." He said. "By Jesus Christ, I don't know whether to wash you out, or give you a chance and send you on." He paused for the longest moment of Curtis LeMay's young life. And then he broke the interminable silence. "I guess," said MacKinnon slowly, "that I will send you on, after all. But I'll keep my eye on you and see how you do."[8]

In spite of LeMay's mistakes that day, there was something in him that MacKinnon saw—a natural ability, even talent, as a pilot. Years later, LeMay was surprised when one of his early instructors told him that he had only ever had one other student he considered as gifted.[9] Standing next to the plane with Red MacKinnon, he slowly let the reality sink in that he would be one of the 25 percent to advance.

In advanced training at Kelly Field in Texas, LeMay flew the latest, state-of-the-art planes—de Havillands and O-2s. The de Havillands were the bi-plane fighters used in World War I. The O-2 was the first airplane to have a tail-wheel at the back of the plane instead of a skid (a piece of metal that resembled a small runner on a sleigh). Except for a few gauges, there was nothing more complex in the cockpit than a stabilizer, a stick, a rudder, a throttle, and a spark control. There was not even a brake for landings.

LeMay quickly realized just how bad an instructor Peewee Wheeler really was when he encountered his next instructor. "In two weeks, I learned more from Joe Dawson than I had all the rest of the time at March,"[10] LeMay remembered. He became the first in his class to *check off* (qualify to fly) on the DH and again first on the O-2. But LeMay believed none of this was due to any natural gift. LeMay worked at it, day and night. Some of the cadets would go off on joy rides and try to impress girls if they had a night off. LeMay stuck to his training and followed orders, manifesting his mother's influence and his own inner discipline.

But at Kelly, LeMay allowed himself to relax a bit. Things were going well. He had a great instructor, he was flying all the time, and a certain amount of confidence and even pride began to seep into his personality—but only up to a point. He began allowing himself the rare treat of going to a movie, but with another cadet as his companion rather than a date. Though he was still always watching his money, it was not the only reason. He was shy, especially with girls.

Curtis graduated from advanced flight school on October 12, 1929, one week before the stock market crash that began the Great Depression. At the time, the Air Corps was divided into four divisions—Pursuit, Observation, Attack, and Bombardment. LeMay signed up for Pursuit, the predecessor to modern-day fighter pilot training. He was assigned to the Twenty-seventh Pursuit Squadron of the First Pursuit Group at Selfridge Field in Michigan. At Selfridge, the new pilots were divided into three squadrons of eighteen planes each, but there were not quite enough planes to go around. They practiced flying in formations, and in the summer they would fly to Michigan's Upper Peninsula for a week, where they would practice shooting machine guns with live ammunition—their only use of real ammunition in the entire year—and dropping water-filled bombs.

The majority of their time was occupied in a public relations campaign designed to sell the American public on aviation. They would fly at air shows and other public events—even at the opening of new airports. In spite of the Depression that had taken hold of the country, municipal airports were opening up at a brisk rate in cities and towns across the United States in the 1930s. Industry had practically come to a halt in America, but aviation still held financial promise.

Like the population at large, the military was at ease regarding external threats in those days. "There was no war in the offing," LeMay recalled later. "Sure, we work[ed], but nobody work[ed] very hard. There [was] no sense of urgency."[11]

Ironically, during the Depression, life was better for Second Lieutenant Curtis LeMay than it had ever been. With a base salary of $125 plus flight pay along with other allowances, he was earning around $250 a month. This was a very good salary for a single man in 1930. He still sent money home to help his family—something he would continue to do throughout his career—but he had the ability to save money for the first time.

•   •   •   •

HELEN

Advancing in the military prior to World War II was next to impossible. Promotions were based on a system of seniority, not merit. Additionally, slots were limited; a senior officer had to leave the service or die before someone below could move up a rank. LeMay was ambitious and strategic as he sized up his chances in the stagnant hierarchy. He realized that officers with college degrees had a better chance of advancing to those limited posi-

tions, yet he was still short those few credits at Ohio State. Most of
the flyers around him already had degrees, and the West Point
cadets had a leg up on the rest.

There were programs in place that allowed officers to take college credits, but his applications were rejected, so he had to find
another way. By diligently asking around, he discovered he could
take a temporary transfer down to Norton Field in Columbus if
there was an opening. Once there, he could finish his credits at
Ohio State on the other side of town. Norton was much smaller
than Selfridge—it had only one officer and three sergeants. They
were there to supervise civilian mechanics who, in turn, maintained six airplanes for reserve officers in the area. This "Detached
Service" lasted exactly five months and twenty-nine days. If he
timed it just right, he would have just enough time to earn the
credits he needed. He approached his senior officer, Major Brett,
and presented him with his proposal. Brett agreed, and LeMay
reported for duty at Norton Field on October 1, 1931. LeMay was
back at Ohio State and the Air Corps was happy to have an experienced flight officer assist the captain at Norton. Everyone, especially LeMay, was pleased with the plan.

The person who motivated LeMay to do this was not a military
friend or a commanding officer, and certainly not a member of his
family. This guidance came from an unlikely source—a woman.

Herb Tellman, one of LeMay's classmates from Kelly Field, also
at Selfridge in the First Pursuit Group, was engaged to a girl at the
University of Michigan, and he would often fly down to Ann Arbor
to visit her on weekends. Tellman kept trying to get LeMay to
come with him to meet her friends. LeMay's general perception
that he was never quite up-to-snuff socially, combined with

shyness and low self-esteem, meant that he was more than a little behind on the "girl front," as he called it. Until now, he had used his difficult financial situation as an excuse. But by 1931, twenty-four years old and an established pilot with improved finances, his level of confidence began to change. Finally, LeMay surprised Tell-man and took him up on his offer. The two young men, along with another pilot named Vaupre, put on their goggles and leather helmets one Saturday afternoon and flew their bi-planes down to Ann Arbor. LeMay and Vaupre were told about two girls who lived in the same dormitory with Tellman's fianceé, but neither pilot knew which girl would be assigned to whom. As the story goes, the airmen walked across the lawn of Mosher Hall with the girls watching from a window. One of them, Helen Maitland, sized up the two uniformed candidates and announced: "I think I'll take the fat one."[12] With that, the most important and positive relationship in Curtis LeMay's life began.

Helen Maitland's background could not have been more different than LeMay's. Although they were both from Ohio, Helen's father, Jesse Maitland, was a successful corporate attorney in Cleveland and a direct descendent of Mary Queen of Scots. Helen had one sister, and the two Maitland girls grew up in one home their entire lives—a large colonial in Cleveland Heights. She was encouraged to go to college, and her parents hoped she would go on to medical school. Instead, she had graduated from Western Reserve with a nursing degree and attended Ann Arbor for postgraduate work.

LeMay admitted to being attracted to her "right from the start." Helen was ebullient—"bubbling effusion," he called it. It was not unusual for LeMay to be in the company of someone who spoke more than he did. But the secret to Helen's success and her tremendous influence on LeMay was that, right from the start, she put him at ease. And this allowed him to poke out of his armored shell. After dinner, when the two were alone, it was Curtis who began to talk. "Helen inspired in me a desire to try and emulate her frankness of conversation, her honesty of recollection."[13] He found himself telling her an embarrassing story of trying to escape from a one-room schoolhouse when he was a little boy and getting paddled by the teacher.

Instead of just listening, Helen probed further, asking him why he was telling her this story. Letting his guard down even further, LeMay said he was not quite sure, except that perhaps he found himself in the same situation with the Army right now—he wanted to finish his degree and they wanted officers with college degrees, but "it seems I am being punished for some sort of infant misdeed."[14] With almost motherly advice, Helen looked at him in all seriousness. "Then it's up to you," she told him. "You've got to use your best resources, whatever they are. Figure out a way."[15] Completely inspired by Helen Maitland, LeMay came up with the plan that brought him back to Columbus and college the following autumn.

It was a very different Curtis LeMay who returned to Ohio State University in the fall of 1931. He was only required to be at Norton Field in the afternoons and weekends, when Reserve pilots flew. That left a generous amount of free time during the week to attend his classes. With his salary and no expenses other than school, rent (which was minimal), and food (extremely low because of deflation caused by the Depression), his situation was much better than his earlier college experience. "For the first time in my life I seemed to know what it was like to be young and alive, to be intent, and yet at the same time not self-disciplined to the point of crucifixion."[16] The man finally allowed himself to have a little fun.

Even the military work was relaxed. LeMay went to classes in the morning and then changed into his uniform and went over to Norton. Sometimes there would not be enough time to change so he wore his uniform to school. For his thesis, he borrowed a camera from Wright Field and used a plane from Norton to create an aerial mapping sequence of the area. The entire project gave LeMay a better understanding of aerial reconnaissance, which, like almost everything else related to flying in 1931, was completely new.

Although LeMay stayed in touch with Helen Maitland up in Ann Arbor and invited her down to Columbus for the big events, he also dated other girls. But years later, in an insight that seemed to fit his personality, LeMay wrote that the relationship with Helen went beyond a physical attraction. "I stood a little in awe of her. She seemed more advanced as a person than I."[17] Perhaps more telling was his admission that he was excited every time she came down to Columbus. But marriage remained a long way off in his thoughts.

Not wishing to overextend his stay in Ohio beyond the five months and twenty-nine days allotted to him through detached service, LeMay was permitted to take his exams early and get back to Selfridge. His diploma arrived by mail at the end of March 1932. The rest of that year was a continuation of the year before; flying exercises interspersed with classes and drills and seeing Helen whenever possible. But now there was one less worry—he was a college graduate.

.   .   .   .

CCC

In 1933, Franklin Delano Roosevelt became the country's thirty-second president. That same year, Adolf Hitler took power in Germany. Both countries were struggling with economic disasters, but the two leaders had very different solutions to the problem. Hitler put Germany back to work on a program of militarization that would ostensibly restore the country's lost honor while hiding his true aims of world domination and genocide. FDR came up with one plan after another to restart America's stagnant economy within a democratic framework. In 1933, national defense was the least of Roosevelt's concerns.

One of the new president's first projects was the creation of the Civilian Conservation Corps, or CCC. The program put unemployed young men to work in the country's national parks and woodlands. In truth, while the participants did indeed plant trees and build lodges and roads, it was also an effort to feed three million boys who were coming close to starving, while providing a small wage they could send home to their impoverished families.

Somebody had to supervise this massive program. The military was Roosevelt's obvious choice. Germany and the United States in 1933 were in much different places. While the future Luftwaffe, under the direction of former World War I pilot Hermann Goering, began its program of building new fighters and bombers and training pilots for war, America's flyers were sent on a babysitting mission.[18]

In the first nine months of the creation of the CCC, more than 9,000 Army officers and enlisted men were assigned to look after these teenagers.[19] "We were glorified housekeepers,"[20] LeMay recalled. He was second in command of a camp outside of Brethren, Michigan. Most of the Army staff was not pleased about this new assignment, especially LeMay.

But something happened in the middle of the Michigan wilderness. LeMay began to exhibit impressive leadership skills. He found it easy to quickly distinguish the responsible boys in the group from the delinquents. He developed an athletic program to deal with the constant fights that broke out. "It was a good way for them to work off a little steam," he remembered.[21] When fights did break out, LeMay turned them into a lesson. He called for boxing gloves, formed a ring with the others, and let the two miscreants go at each other. When it was over, LeMay appealed to the common sense of the group and asked the logical question, "This actually didn't settle very much, did it?"

Eventually, the boys began to be drawn to LeMay. Though he had no training in this type of endeavor, it seemed to come naturally. He had their respect, and that was all it took. "In a few weeks they were coming along in damn good shape, and we were gratified."[22]

LeMay was more than aware that he and the rest of the pilots were losing valuable flying time working in the camp. As soon as things were in order, he drove down to Selfridge and persuaded the commanding general to let him bring a plane up to the camp so the pilots could fly. Back in Brethren, he found a farmer who allowed them to use his field. Next, LeMay drew up a plan for the approaches and landings. Within no time, he flew up a P-12, but he also set down the rules. Every pilot had to bring the plane back with enough fuel to get back to Selfridge (about an hour and a half in flying time), and they had to make sure the cows were clear of the field so they could land and take off.

LeMay's reprieve from the CCC came in the summer of 1933, when he received orders to report to Communications School at Chanute Field in Illinois. He could not wait to leave. But close to the end of his time in Michigan, he read in the local paper that a fire had burned down a hangar at Chanute Field—the same hangar that housed the Air Corps School of Communications. Already understanding the ins and outs of the military, he told no one and proceeded down to Selfridge where he was supposed to receive his new orders. Sure enough, waiting for him at Selfridge was the cancellation of this order, which had not been relayed to him at the CCC Camp. As his position in Brethren was already filled by someone else, according to schedule, he happily waited at Selfridge for new orders. Two weeks later he was told to report to Langley Field in Virginia for Navigation School. At last he was free of the babysitting detail.

•   •   •   •

A UNIQUE TIME

In the early 1930s, with no more technology available in a cockpit than a compass, it was very difficult for a pilot in the air to figure out how to get where he was going. Consequently, pilots simply followed railroad tracks and roads, just like the Wright plane that had flown over Curtis LeMay's house twenty years earlier. If a plane drifted over water or ran into bad weather, it was dangerous. Since flying was still so new, navigation was not high on the priority list. In fact, there was no such category as *navigator* in the Air Corps—a man whose sole job was to help guide the pilot to his destination—because there was no room for another crewman in any of the planes of that era. Navigating was completely up to the pilot; consequently the navigation school at Langley trained only pilots.

The Army Air Corps hired the leading authority in navigation at the time, an Australian named Harold Gatty, to teach pilots what he knew. Gatty believed celestial navigation—the system that sailors used—could also work for airplanes.[23] However, it was a time-consuming method, taking up to forty minutes to compute. This was problematic in an airplane going over 100 miles per hour. The pilots took their "fixes" and then tried to factor speed, drag, and altitude into the equation. It was a complex mathematical problem, and it had to be done while flying a plane. "It was one of those situations where every time you recognize a problem you come up with a new puzzle," LeMay remembered.[24] But this was exactly the kind of problem that intrigued him.

LeMay was part of a completely new branch of the military, still in the process of inventing itself. Unlike the Navy or regular Army, which had centuries of tradition behind them, the men in the Air Corps were defining their service as they went along. They were not just solving the most basic problems of their craft, but creating their own language and myths that would be passed on to future fliers. The process was complicated, however, by how quickly technology was advancing. New planes were constantly getting larger and faster, and everyone was just trying to keep up with the speed of it all.

LeMay understood that he had entered the Air Corps at a very unique time. And he knew the men around him would be developing the rules. He felt a strong bond with them. In 1931, LeMay heard of a tremendous job opportunity outside the military. The Ford Motor Company was building the Ford Tri-Motor airplane.

In spite of the Depression, new passenger companies like Pan Am and TWA were expanding their routes throughout the country and beyond. Ford developed a package that sold its planes with a pilot, and LeMay was just the candidate they wanted.

On a day off, LeMay flew down to Detroit to look into it and was astounded when Ford offered him a job on the spot at the astronomical salary of $1,200 a month. At the time, he was earning a little over $200 in the Air Corps, which was considered a very good salary. He was torn. Though it was an extremely attractive prospect—a huge salary, as well as the freedom of civilian life, in which he could live and dress as he chose—he knew that he could have a huge impact on the new branch of the military if he stayed in. He also knew there was job uncertainty in the world outside the military. The shadow of his father always loomed over him. Even with the huge salary, there was always the chance that something could happen that might leave him in Erving LeMay's recurring predicament.

After seriously thinking it over, he passed the job offer to another cadet in his class, who eventually became an airline executive. Later, he said he decided to stay because of the way Army officers were respected by the public. But advancement was frozen in the Air Corps—the best he could realistically hope for was retirement after thirty years at the rank of Lieutenant Colonel—and prospects of anything better in 1931 were dim. In addition to respect, job security and camaraderie enticed him to stay in the service.

Some people are drawn to the military because they crave the order that it imposes in their lives. But LeMay's personality was infused with order and self-discipline. He did not need any external rules or artificial means to impose this code on his life.

LeMay's reason for serving was simple patriotism. He had an abiding passion for his country, its history, and its laws. Ever since his childhood, he had felt a deep sense of protection towards those under him—first his younger siblings and later the men who flew with him. He felt this same responsibility to his country as well. And at this place and time, as the United States was just creating its air force, LeMay thought he could have a great impact in shaping the country's future defense. Passing up a larger paycheck seemed like a small trade-off.

• • • •

FDR'S BLUNDER

In 1934, Franklin Roosevelt came up with a plan involving the Air Corps that would lead to a national disaster. The U.S. government used hired civilian contractors to fly the nation's airmail. The first regular route was started on May 15, 1918, between New York and Washington, with a stop in Philadelphia. The first transcontinental service was inaugurated in 1921.[25] It was very popular with the public and highly lucrative for the federal government, but Roosevelt, always short on money for the treasury, wanted the civilian airlines that carried the nation's airmail to do it for less.

The airlines refused to back down. During contract negotiations, FDR called their bluff and fired the entire force. In Roosevelt's mind, he already had an air force that was funded by the government, and with no war on, they were not doing much anyway, so he ordered the Army Air Corps to fly the mail. Military pilots, FDR reasoned, were already up in the air, so they might as well carry the mail while they were flying. In the meantime, it would force the civilian airlines to reconsider the federal government's new contract.

Roosevelt's decision demonstrated an amazing lack of understanding. The Air Corps planes were not equipped to ferry hundreds of sacks of mail. The pilots did not know the routes. And an endeavor on this scale required massive planning. To his credit, FDR would learn much more about air power in the years to come. But because he did not know the basics in 1934, the president's plan backfired.

Today, the modern Air Force has thousands of planes and over 300,000 men and women on active duty to react at a moment's notice to airlift supplies, provide aid in disasters or, if need be, go to war. But in 1934, there were exactly 1,372 officers and men on active duty in the Army Air Corps throughout the world—close to the size of a small high school. Roosevelt issued the order on February 9, 1934, that the Air Corps take over dozens of routes in exactly ten days—on February 19. No money had been allocated for the job, and crews found themselves suddenly sent back and forth across the country with no provisions for food or quarters to live in—absolutely nothing.

"They were eating homemade mulligan and they were sleeping on planks laid across saw-horses in cold hangars. Lucky to be out of the rain. And they were scrounging around for blankets,"[26] LeMay remembered. He told the story of one sergeant who was sent to another city and came back with a pillow given to him by an old lady who ran a hot dog stand outside the field, who was already feeding all the men in his outfit on credit. She took pity on him because he was sleeping on the ground. She told him she did not really need the pillow—it was just lying around on her sofa.

"A wartime psychology ruled. The boys were out fighting and bleeding and dying; generous-hearted folks tried to do whatever they could for them. If one end of your run was—say, Newark, New Jersey—and you had a second cousin living in Newark— Cousin Emily might have a spare bed. Lucky you."[27] LeMay could not suppress his sarcasm as he remembered the entire episode. "It took that Congress until the 27th day of March to appropriate an excruciatingly generous five-dollar per day allowance for our living expenses. Meanwhile, it was hand-to-mouth." But feeding the crews was the least of the problems.

Between February 19 and June 1, 1934 (when the airlines resumed the service), sixty-five Army planes crashed, killing twelve pilots. The problem was compounded by the newspaper headlines and pictures that screamed the news of each accident. When planes ran into trouble that had nothing to do with the airmail delivery, the press did not discriminate. It was an unqualified public relations disaster, which eventually led to a congressional investigation.

The fact is, the Air Corps did not have the planes to do the job, and the planes they had could not accommodate all the sacks of mail. "We'd stuff mail in wherever we could get a sack in: in the small baggage compartment under the rear cockpit, under the cowling, everyplace else."[28] Some mail was lost. Some sacks were not discovered until the plane went in for its regular inspection months later. There was also another problem. The lax nature of the Air Corps had not trained its pilots sufficiently to handle something as seemingly simple as carrying mail. If there was a silver lining in the debacle, it was making Washington aware that it finally had to get serious if it wanted an air force.

LeMay was given a route in North Carolina between Richmond and Greensboro. He flew through driving snowstorms in his open-cockpit plane. There were constant worries about ice buildup on the wings. There were periods when the only food he got was from a pot of stew made by the maintenance crew in the hangar. But the biggest consequence he encountered was having to delay his wedding to one Helen Maitland of Cleveland.

• • • •

THE CHURCH SERVICE

Curtis and Helen had been dating for several years, but he never seemed eager to ask her to marry him. The chief reason, according to his memoirs, was that he felt responsible for his own family financially. He was helping his parents; and after pushing his younger siblings to go to college, he was also helping to pay their way. Marriage, in his mind, was simply too expensive a proposition, one that he could not afford, and there was no one he could turn to for advice on the topic. His mother's response to his question of what to do fit perfectly with the general attitude of the LeMay family: "You're over twenty-one," Arizona wrote back, "and old enough to make up your own mind."[29]

Helen grew tired of waiting and took matters into her own hands. On one of his trips to Cleveland that winter, LeMay was shocked to find out she was engaged to someone else—a doctor working at a clinic in Brazil. That was all LeMay needed to hear. He proposed. The engagement to the doctor was soon broken off, and a date was set for a wedding that spring. However, the delivery of the mail postponed it until Saturday, June 9—nine days after the mail debacle ended.

The wedding itself was a microcosm of the relationship ahead. As forceful as LeMay's personality was, it appeared he had met his match in Helen. LeMay took a ten-day leave and decided to use part of it for the days before the wedding. He wanted a simple ceremony—no one singing "Oh Promise Me" and especially no kneeling. On the day before the ceremony, he was told to be at the church for the rehearsal. "Any stupid person can get married," he told Helen, choosing instead to remain back at the Maitland house and play cards with his future father-in-law. Helen was unphased—she simply went to the rehearsal on her own.

When LeMay arrived at the Maitland's Episcopal church the next day, he found it packed with an overflow crowd waiting outside. It turned out to be a high Episcopal mass, which, of course, began with the singing of "Oh Promise Me." When the priest asked the couple to kneel, LeMay shot a glare at Helen. She responded with a firm kick, and the couple knelt. Later when he complained that he had firmly said no kneeling, she replied: "You didn't come to the rehearsal, you got what you had coming."[30]

The marriage turned out to be a highly successful partnership. Helen was the perfect foil for Curtis's lack of social grace. She was extremely capable and loved to entertain. Her personality could fill a room just as his could darken it. As LeMay would rise up the chain of command, Helen would serve as counselor, helper, and friend. LeMay was devoted to her.

With the marriage, LeMay would be forced to make a break from his family. Helen pushed this. The Maitlands were to become his predominant family. There would be times ahead when outside forces would profoundly disrupt their lives, and the Maitland home in Cleveland Heights would be the place they could return to. LeMay continued to help his family financially and would write letters, but visits became less and less frequent. "This happens in families," explained their daughter Janie. "One family seems to become the dominant one and often it's the wife's family."[31]

The newlyweds decided to forgo a wedding trip and, instead, used their resources to buy furniture and household appliances. After a honeymoon in a downtown Cleveland hotel for two days, the LeMays returned to Selfridge in Michigan, where they set up their home in a little cottage. Given everything that transpired earlier, the young couple seemed to move into marriage with relative ease. Mrs. LeMay was busy creating the household while her husband went down to the base every morning. For a family in the military, life seemed unusually stable. It would not last.

•   •   •   •

WHEELER FIELD, HAWAII

Within ten weeks, LeMay received orders to report to the Sixth Pursuit Group at Wheeler Field in Hawaii. The Army tries to give families about three months' notice for a major move, but there are exceptions. LeMay was given ten days to pack up their belongings and board the Army's largest transport ship, *The Republic*, in New York harbor. *The Republic* sailed down the East Coast of the United States, through the Panama Canal, up to San Francisco (where those heading for West Coast deployments disembarked). From there, *The Republic* sailed across the Pacific to Hawaii.

Housing was extremely limited in Hawaii. Nothing was available on the base and there were not many vacancies outside either, so the couple settled for a small cottage right on the beach, which, although tiny, turned out to be a happy adventure. The house consisted of a small living room, bedroom, and a closet kitchen that opened up directly onto the beach. The shower had no hot water and drained through slats in the wood. But it was also Hawaii, and it was beautiful.

LeMay had a number of extra jobs at the base besides flying. At different times he served as the Communications Officer, Engineering Officer, Mess Officer, and Assistant Operations Officer. He also began teaching a weekly course in navigation. John Egan, who had also taken Gatty's navigation training, was now in Hawaii as well. Both men concluded that little could be taught in one hour a week. They suggested that a real school be set up with more allotted time. The base commander agreed, and soon Egan and LeMay had a dozen students in a full-time course.

In order to stay ahead of the class, LeMay would work into the night in anticipation of questions that might be asked the next day. Every evening after dark, Helen would hold a flashlight on the beach while Curtis practiced his celestial readings and made his calculations.[32]

LeMay was promoted to First Lieutenant in 1934, and with the advancement, secured housing on the base. He and Helen left their beach cottage for the more formal world of the military establishment. The U.S. Army in 1934 had an emphasis on old rules from an earlier era. A strict dress code was in place for dinner—a rule that did not make a lot of sense to LeMay, especially in a tropical setting. "You must be dressed after six p.m., and that was not just if you were dining out, either. If you were sitting at home in your own quarters, you were still dressed after six. A man would usually put on the mess jacket type of dinner coat; those were a lot more comfortable. Still, it was all a damn nuisance," he remembered.[33]

The military in those years was also completely segregated. All officers were white and usually from the same backgrounds with similar religions. Their society was self-contained, and there was not much mixing with the civilian population.

·   ·   ·   ·

"BOMBERS, NOTHING BUT BOMBERS"

Curtis and Helen had arrived in September, 1934. At the end of 1936, they re-boarded *The Republic* for the return trip to the States. They would arrive home in Cleveland for Christmas. The States they returned to had changed very little. The country was still mired in the Depression. Unemployment and general misery were still evident in cities and small towns. But the outside world had changed dramatically between 1934 and 1936. Adolf Hitler was no longer a cartoon character with silly ideas. He had solidified his power in Germany and was quickly rearming his country and breaking every rule in the Treaty of Versailles, while the rest of Europe looked the other way. Japan was arming as well, having learned valuable lessons from the Allies in the last War. It was building a huge naval fleet with an emphasis on what it considered the future of warfare: the aircraft carrier. And it was about to start its conquest of Asia with the invasion of China. For its part, the United States showed little interest in anything outside its borders, with the exception of Edward VIII abdicating the throne of England for an American divorcee. Americans seemed more absorbed with the Depression and big tabloid stories about celebrities than world events.

Before he left Hawaii, LeMay made a course correction that would have a profound bearing on the rest of his career.

He dropped his first live bomb and was exhilarated by the experience: "I still remember the thrill in that moment," he wrote years later.[34] Something in his personality was drawn to bombardment—perhaps the feeling of tremendous power, or the technical question of trying to aim an object at a target that does not fall straight but is dependent on speed, altitude, and wind. Before he left Hawaii, LeMay made the decision to move from fighters to bombers.

The Army Air Corps was already working on a long-range bomber that would allow the United States to leapfrog past every other country in this form of warfare. Given the general attitude of a tight-fisted Congress and an indifferent populace, just getting approval for this project in the 1930s was a stunning feat. The new plane was a marvel—bigger than any other bomber anywhere else in the world. It could fly farther, faster, and carry many more bombs.

LeMay, ambitious as ever, saw the future of the Air Force, and it was all focused on this new plane. "The fighter had evolved as a defensive weapon. How the hell were you going to win a war with it?" he wrote later regarding his decision. "It might have its innings in certain phases of warfare, just as the Attack people might have their innings. But who was it who'd go far beyond the enemy lines and attempt to destroy not only armies in the field, not only supplies and fuel dumps and tank concentrations up near the front; but would go deep into the enemy's homeland, and thus try to eliminate his basic potential to wage war? Bombers, nothing but bombers."[35]

CHAPTER THREE

THE B-17

LEMAY WAS NOTHING IF NOT PRACTICAL. THE AIR CORPS WAS moving its focus towards bombers; if the meager resources allotted by Congress were going to bombers, then fighter pilots would be less valued—and less likely to be promoted. He had no intention of getting stuck in a dead end. But more importantly, he had caught a vision—the next generation of pilots would be leaders of an independent air force dominated by bombers.

During the period of military stagnation between the wars, the leaders of the U.S. Army Air Corps saw the great need to modernize their aircraft. If they could not surpass the Europeans, they hoped at least to keep up with them. They had fallen badly behind in World War I and now, as war grew more likely in Europe, they saw the chasm widen. Germany and Japan already had impressive programs in aircraft design.

In 1934, the Air Corps visionaries, led by Billy Mitchell disciples Hap Arnold and Tooey Spaatz under the command of Major Generals Frank Andrews and Oscar Westover, were able to secure just enough money (with the help of a few friends in Congress) to start the development of a new, modern, multi-engine bomber. They hoped this new bomber would put the U.S. on par with Europe. They set out the following requirements in a competition for airplane manufacturers: the new bomber had to be able to fly at 10,000 feet at speeds of 200 miles per hour with a range of 2,000 miles, meaning the bomber would have to stay aloft for ten hours without refueling. No plane in the United States had that capability at the time.

Three companies entered the competition. The Martin Company offered up the B-12, an updated model of the plane used in the Air Mail debacle. Douglas came up with the new two-engine DB-1. And in Seattle, the much smaller Boeing Company, facing bankruptcy, decided to gamble everything and put its best designers and researchers into the effort. The company filed its proposal for the new bomber on August 8, 1934, a month before LeMay headed for Hawaii.

Under the leadership of the brilliant design team of E. Gifford Emory and Edward Curtis Wells, the first prototype of the B-17 came out of the factory at Boeing Field, amazingly only eleven months later in July of 1935. Taking a plan from draft paper to an actual airplane in less than a year is unheard of, even today with the benefits of computers and advanced technology. The teams of engineers at Boeing were using paper, pencils, and slide rules.

The B-17 went far beyond the requirements of the competition, and jumped light years ahead of every other airplane in the world.

It was the first all-metal bomber with an enclosed cockpit, powered by four 750 horsepower Pratt and Whitney engines. Its sleek lines, futuristic design, and capabilities of flying much higher and faster—235 miles an hour—carrying more bombs, dazzled the procurement officers, who decided immediately after the first flight on July 28, 1935, that the Air Corps should buy sixty-five B-17s. The Boeing plane far outstripped the much smaller and less powerful Douglas and Martins planes. During that first flight, a reporter from the *Seattle Times*, Richard Williams, saw the five 30-inch 7.62 mm machine guns facing out from the plane in all directions and dubbed it a "flying fortress." Boeing saw the value in the name and quickly copyrighted it.

If ever a plane was built that was air-worthy, it was the B-17. While it was more advanced than any other plane, its brilliance lay in a much simpler design and parts. It was easier to build, sturdier to fly, and required less maintenance than any other plane at the time. The new bomber could take a profound battering from enemy anti-aircraft guns and fighters as well as from wind, heat, cold—almost anything—and it would bring back its crews when other planes would have gone down. The B-17 was a marvel. But it had a disastrous beginning.

On its second flight, the test pilots forgot to disengage the gust lock, a brake that holds the plane in place when it is parked on the ground—a forgivable mistake considering it was only the second time the crew had ever flown it. But even simple mistakes by test pilots are unforgiving. The plane went into a stall just after takeoff and crashed, killing everyone on board. Boeing and the B-17 were immediately out of the competition. The Air Corps gave the contract to the Douglas Air Craft company for 133 of its twin engine B-18 Bolos. That should have been the end of the B-17.

But the Air Corps officers who had seen the B-17 could not let it go. They persuaded their congressional friends not to abandon the Boeing project. Generals Andrews and Westover managed to keep Boeing in the game with a limited contract to produce thirteen more B-17s. It was hardly what Boeing had hoped for, but it kept the bomber and the company alive. In the meantime, Boeing's engineers redesigned the B-17 with even more powerful engines and added other improvements. The crash also spurred the institution of the "check list," still used today by all pilots to prevent potential problems before takeoff.

The planes were delivered to Langley Field on March 1, 1937, where they quickly became the hot ticket in the Air Corps. It was the plane everyone wanted to fly. Scuttlebutt about the new bomber traveled as far away as Hawaii, where LeMay heard about it. It would become the predominant plane in the Air Corps after Douglas ran into manufacturing problems and its plane was stalled on the assembly line. Despite that humble initial order of thirteen planes, more than 12,000 B-17s would be built by the end of World War II.

• • • •

RETURN

When LeMay returned to the States at the end of 1936 for his new assignment at Langley Field, Virginia, his reputation as a skilled navigator preceded him. To his disappointment, he was ordered to set up a navigation school. He wanted to fly the new bomber. Once again showing an ability to get his way, he went to his commander, Captain McCormick, and explained why he thought he was not the best candidate to be a professor and why his friend, John Egan, was really better suited for the job. Since Egan already had experience in bombers, LeMay explained, and he had none, it made additional sense to make this switch.

LeMay balanced the nimbleness and maneuverability of a smart negotiator with the brute force of a bull. He was persuasive despite being soft-spoken, which itself played to his advantage—his listeners made a greater effort to hear him, resulting in his receiving closer attention. Throughout his career, his argument style relied heavily on logic and common sense. As a person, he was painstakingly honest while avoiding bluster. There was also something in his personality that made other men trust him.

To LeMay's great relief, Captain McCormick bought his argument. LeMay would be attached to the new bomber. His feelings about this particular plane were immediate and went beyond simple mechanics. He remembered the moment with the fondness of a high school boy who had met the girl of his dreams, later recalling, "I fell in love with the 17 at first sight."[1] His reaction was not unusual.

Almost seven decades after World War II, pilots still talk about the B-17s with a particular fondness. They even insist that the plane had a special smell unlike any other. Later, some crewmembers credited the B-17 with bringing them through the war alive, as if it were a living, breathing being. "Flying the B-17 was unlike flying any other plane. It was a joy," recalled Jacob Smart, who commanded a squadron of B-17s during the war.[2] Jim Pattillo flew both B-17s and B-29s in World War II. "The B-29 was a complicated precision instrument," Pattillo remembers, "but the B-17 was as easy as getting into the family car."[3] General Arnold placed this particular plane in the pantheon of all aircraft: "It had only one predecessor of equal importance in air history"[4]—the Wright brothers' plane.

At Langley, LeMay's lifelong search for a mentor finally ended when he met Lieutenant Colonel Robert Olds. Olds had been in the Air Corps for more than twenty years; he had flown the very first bombers—such as they were—in World War I and served on the staff of General Billy Mitchell. Olds believed in the Mitchell doctrine: that the next war would be determined from the air. He had a huge impact on LeMay's future as a commander by modeling leadership based on common sense, which appealed to LeMay the realist.

More than anything else, Olds shook LeMay out of the quiet ways of the peacetime Air Corps. He was the first commander LeMay had encountered in the Air Corps who articulated why they even existed in the first place—to be ready to go to war. "He was the first man I'd ever come in contact with who really penetrated my thick skull with a sense of urgency in getting things done," LeMay remembered.[5] The days of the Air Corps being a government-paid flying club were coming to an end.

Olds was demanding. He pushed his men to higher levels of efficiency. He expected a constant state of readiness, the same atmosphere that LeMay would pass on to his future commands. There was one more important aspect to Olds's leadership that LeMay took note of and copied. "He and Andrews [Major General Andrews] could do anything and everything which they might have to ask us to do, and they were respected for it."[6] This would become the hallmark of LeMay's leadership. Do not send men into battle ahead of you. Lead them.

Olds made his points in simple ways. He appointed LeMay his executive officer and made it clear that he expected the young lieutenant to be at his desk before he arrived at work in the morning. But just being there did not cut it. The very first day, Olds simply asked for the weather report. LeMay did not have it. "Aren't you the Operations Officer?" Olds asked him. "Suppose you had to lay out an operation today, a mission to Wright Field. What's the weather out there? You'd have to know, wouldn't you?"[7] LeMay never came to his desk again without checking with the weather room first. This quiet but forceful method of getting a point across would be a device LeMay would use often in the future.

At this time the Army Air Corps came into the possession of a device that, along with the B-17, would revolutionize bombing—the Norden bombsight. It would prove to be one of the great inventions and greatest secrets of World War II. The U.S. did not even share the bombsight with the British for fear that it might fall into enemy hands. It was developed by an eccentric Dutch engineer, Carl Norden, who had emigrated to the U.S. in 1904. Norden developed the bombsight for the Air Corps while he worked for the Sperry Corporation.

A bomb does not fall in a straight line from a moving plane. It follows a parabolic trajectory as the various forces of physics—speed, gravity, and inertia—carry it on its long journey to the ground.[8] The bombsight computed all these factors to guide the bomb to its target. It used a series of gears, gyroscopes, and ball bearings that the bombardier would look through over a target. By inputting the speed and altitude, the bombsight could calculate the trajectory of a bomb. The bombardier even controlled the flight of the plane through the site during the time over the target. The U.S. would eventually buy 90,000 bombsights from Norden at a cost of $1.5 billion between 1933 and 1945.[9]

As the pilots, navigators, and bombardiers were grappling with this new technology, the classes LeMay attended reminded him of the school he had set up in Hawaii—the instructors did not know much more than the students.[10]

· · · ·

PUBLICITY STUNTS

By 1937, the military push by Germany and Japan finally caught the attention of the War Department. But because of the isolationists' strong hold in Congress, the Air Corps, along with the rest of the U.S. military, had to go about a buildup in surreptitious ways. The Air Corps understood that it needed to impress the public with the importance of funding its planes and technology. So it set up three air exercises in the late 1930s. By today's standards, they sound simplistic. Back then, they were not.

The first demonstration was really a continuation of a long, simmering rivalry between the Navy and the Air Corps. It was called Joint Air Exercise Number Four, but it became known as the Utah Exercise. It was a competition of sorts. The Navy continued to hold on to its jurisdiction over open water as Washington saw the Air Corps only as a defensive arm of the military. So in theory, the Air Corps existed in case an army invaded the continental United States, which was unlikely. The Army itself saw the main thrust of any future air war only as support for ground troops, but there were those within the Air Corps who wanted to show that the B-17 had significantly changed the paradigm.

The rules of the exercise were simple. The Air Corps was given twenty-four hours to locate a battleship, the USS *Utah*, which would be sailing somewhere off the coast of California between Los Angeles and San Francisco—roughly 120,000 square miles—

and hit it with water bombs. The Air Corps could not conduct its own reconnaissance. It had to rely on position reports from the Navy. Eight B-17s would be used in the drill, along with a larger number of B-10s and B-18s. The Navy was betting its ships were invulnerable to airplanes, and the Air Corps was saying it could destroy ships from the air. Bob Olds, the commander of the Air Corps fleet, chose LeMay as his chief navigator. The B-17s flew across the country in August 1937 and set up their headquarters at the Oakland airport.

At noon on August 12, the Navy sent its position report to the airport, which radioed it to the B-17s already over the Pacific. LeMay quickly made the calculations and determined that they were actually quite close to the ship. The lead pilot, Major Caleb V. Haynes, brought down the planes through the clouds, but to their surprise, they saw only open water. They set up a search—spreading out the planes and looking for the ship—but they were unable to locate the *Utah* before dark, when the exercise ended for the day.

Olds furiously asked LeMay why they had not found the ship. "I don't know, Sir," LeMay responded honestly. "I think we got to where they were supposed to be." After a few more calculations and a celestial reading, LeMay was convinced that he had been right. "We weren't very far off. Maybe two or three miles." Olds asked why he was so sure. "If it's right," LeMay responded, showing his charts, "here's where we are now. And we're headed straight to San Francisco." Olds was not happy and grumbled that they still had tomorrow. But he added, "I want the *Utah*. You'd better find it for me. You were selected to fly lead navigator because I thought you were the best in the group."[11]

LeMay could not have felt good about any of this, yet he remained convinced that he was right. He was so confident about it that he calculated exactly when they would hit San Francisco on their course homeward. When the time came, LeMay left his seat at the navigator's table and came back up to the cockpit where Haynes and Olds sat in the pilot and co-pilot seats. As they came over in the dark, there, as LeMay had predicted, were the lights of the city.

"By God, you were right," Olds said. "Then why didn't we find the *Utah*?"

"Maybe," suggested LeMay, "they gave us the wrong position."[12]

Because of heavy fog, the planes had to bypass Oakland and fly on to Sacramento where they spent the night. LeMay slept under the wing of the plane in the hangar. Early the next morning, Olds, who spent most of the night on the phone, came over to LeMay and woke him. "The Navy now admits they were one degree off on the position they sent us," he said. "One degree! That's sixty miles. No wonder we couldn't find the son-of-a-bitch. Come on, let's have a cup of coffee."[13]

Like the day before, Olds did not wait at the hangar for the Navy to radio in its position. As soon as it was light, he took off so the planes would be out at sea when they received the coordinates. When the information came in, LeMay made his calculations. Then he came back to Olds and Haynes with the bad news. There was no way they could get to the ship before the noon deadline. He figured out that they would be about sixty miles away when the clock struck twelve. Olds was furious. The air seemed to have been sucked out of the plane—everyone on board just sagged. With nothing else to do, Olds ordered the planes to fan out, make sure they were in sight of one another, and fly towards the coordinates anyway. He hoped that the planes could at least locate the *Utah*, even if it was after the deadline.

Then, with about ten minutes left before the deadline, a huge battleship came into sight. They were not completely sure it was the right battleship, so they looked for markings. The sailors on board appeared to be just loitering on the deck and not in any great worry of an imminent attack. When they saw the correct flag, the bombardier asked permission to drop the water bombs the plane was carrying. Olds gave him the OK, and in the ensuing "attack," the B-17s scored three direct hits and several near misses.

As dejected as the men onboard the planes had been just minutes before, they were equally jubilant after the ship was hit. The airmen watched the sailors scurrying around in a frenzy. Then the planes headed back to the coast as LeMay charted a course, this time to March Field in Riverside. Along the way, LeMay figured out why they were able to hit the *Utah* before the deadline. Once again, the Navy had sent out misinformation. For the second day in a row they were off by one degree, which would account for the sixty-mile differential. But this time, the one degree mistake was in their favor. The euphoria of the air crews was short lived, however. An order came out immediately after landing that the entire exercise would remain classified—there would be no publicity whatsoever. The Navy had its way in Washington. The story would stay within the military. The Navy then attacked Olds and the bombers with what now sounds like the weakest possible argument. It said that since the planes came in suddenly out of the clouds, the ship did not have time to perform any evasive maneuvers. "The exercise doesn't prove a thing,"[14] the Navy said. Rather than explain that planes coming in out of nowhere was precisely the problem that ships would face in the future, Olds had another suggestion. He challenged the Navy to one more test on the following day: let the B-17s target the ship from a higher altitude at a prescribed time, allowing the *Utah* to take any evasive action it desired. Boxed into a corner, the Navy agreed. The following day, the B-17s came in at 8,000 feet on what turned out to be a picture-perfect clear day in the Pacific. The ship took evasive action, but to no avail. It was hit again. And again the entire event was kept from the general public.

Twenty-seven years later, LeMay looked up the records of the *Utah* exercise while he was writing his memoirs. All he could find was the following: "The exercise was completed at noon 13 August 1937. A supplementary exercise took place 14 August 1937." That was it. As for the bombing exercise on August 14, all photographs of the damage to the ship were missing. LeMay was not immune to the usual inter-service rivalries; this incident would leave him with negative feelings toward the Navy that would last throughout his life. "The whole thing was too utterly damning," he would remember later.[15]

There is, of course, a tragic postscript to the *Utah* story. A little over four years later, the USS *Utah* was docked in Pearl Harbor on another clear, bright morning. Again planes came out of nowhere, but this time, the bombs they dropped were not filled with water. The *Utah* was hit before most of the men on board could man their battle stations. The ship immediately started to list and went down. Fifty-eight sailors and officers died aboard the ship on December 7, 1941.

Following the *Utah* exercise, the Air Corps realized that, in order to help the American public understand the growing impor- tance of air power, it needed to come up with a public relations campaign. In January 1938, the U.S. State Department announced that as a gesture of goodwill, the B-17s of the Air Corps would fly to Argentina for the inauguration of the country's new president.

Placed in the context of the times, no gesture involving military planes can be seen as a simple diplomatic mission. By 1938, Hitler would annex Austria. In the Pacific, Japan already occupied Manchuria, Korea, and large sections China. The Rape of Nanking, in which Japanese soldiers murdered 369,000 Chinese men, women, and children, was actually in progress when the State Department released its announcement of the tour. Franklin Roosevelt was sending a message to Berlin and Tokyo: the United States had the most advanced, state-of-the-art bomber in the world with a capacity to fly long distances.

As straightforward as it seemed, the mission was still filled with potential hazards for the U.S. To begin with, the Air Corps had never flown its bombers that far and over so much open water. Secondly, it was not clear what kind of mechanical problems might arise or if there would be any service available in South America. And if just one of the planes crashed, that would be the only message received by the world. It had been only five years since the Air Corps had delivered the mail with less than impressive results.

The flight consisted of six B-17s under Lieutenant Colonel Olds, with Major Haynes as the lead pilot. LeMay would serve again as chief navigator. In another indication of just how ill-prepared the military was in 1938 for even the most basic maneuver, LeMay discovered that the War Department did not possess a single map of South America. He had to stop at the National Geographic Society to get what he needed. He had to borrow even more detailed maps from Pan-American Airways. He brought along a standard wind chart used by sailors that gave the monthly averages in various areas around the world. It offered nothing specific, but gave a general idea of what he might expect. With this rudimentary information, LeMay had to chart the longest run the Air Corps had ever undertaken.

To add to the list of potential pitfalls, the airmen knew very little about anoxia, a form of mental fatigue caused by the lack of oxygen at higher altitudes. The B-17 was not pressurized, and oxygen was severely limited at 12,000 feet. At one point during the flight, LeMay could not understand why his calculations were so far off. After he took some deep breaths from his oxygen tank, he realized the cause of his silly mistake. Lack of oxygen was an issue that would come up again as planes became more powerful and flew at higher altitudes. In 1938, these men were the trailblazers. By the time he wrote his memoirs in 1965, less than thirty years later, LeMay observed that 1938 seemed as far off as 1849 in terms of technology.

The flight to South America was an unqualified success. It received a great deal of press coverage, and the people of South America were excited to get anywhere near the planes. The event did not go unnoticed in the Axis capitals. The B-17s had flown fifteen hours over oceans without refueling on their flight from Miami to Lima. Berlin was now in range of England.

By 1938, LeMay was considered the best navigator in the Air Corps. He felt great pride that he was chosen for the top assignments. But almost a decade after entering the training program, he was still a lieutenant. And he desperately wanted to fly the B-17 as a pilot, not a navigator. There were still only thirteen planes, and the pilot's position went only to captains. He was thirty-one years old, and he was realistic. He perceived that if anything were to change, something would have to alter the status quo. He also knew his weaknesses. He was not very social. He did not like to hang around bars with his fellow officers after work—he had never been much of a drinker, and he certainly could not tell a story. He was respected by the others, but he really was not part of the old boy's club which pervaded military society and advanced careers. LeMay spent whatever extra time he had at home. The only form of enjoyment he allowed himself was tinkering with cars in his garage. In 1938, the chances of LeMay rising very far in the Army Air Corps remained extremely small.

In August 1938 there was another "goodwill" trip to South America, this time to Colombia. Again, LeMay served as chief navigator. Just before the trip, he was asked to give his first public speech, to the Propeller Club of Norfolk, Virginia. LeMay had no natural talent as a speaker...not in that first appearance in Norfolk, nor in any later speeches as a member of the Joint Chiefs of Staff, or even as a political candidate. He did not like talking in the first place, even to one person. He knew he was too blunt and that his comments were often misinterpreted as being insensitive at best. Whether it was a form of disdain or shyness, LeMay simply was not capable of changing this dynamic; therefore, standing in front of a group was painful. He retreated to the conclusion that if people disliked him, so be it. And he created a tough, hard shell around his feelings.

He chose to be judged by his work. His reaction to his performance at the Propeller Club event was conflicted. He would later record that he did not disgrace himself nor was he "ridden out of town on a rail," implying he half expected to be. But in a self-deprecating admission indicating he wished he had done a better job, he added: "Come to think about it, I wasn't invited back either."[16]

With everything changing around him, LeMay's family life went through a profound transformation as well. Since he married Helen in 1934, the couple had tried to have a baby. That proved to be more difficult than they anticipated. Helen's first pregnancy ended in the stillbirth of a boy. After that, she lost another baby late in term. Helen required an operation at that time, which meant that any future baby would have to be delivered by Caesarean section. Whenever these crises developed, LeMay tried to be at Helen's side in spite of the demands of his work. Every loss affected him deeply. "Sometimes I'd be so emotionally upset that I feared for the successful completion of whatever job was at hand," he wrote in his memoirs, showing sensitivity many people could not imagine he possessed.

But he also demonstrated an extraordinary self-discipline that would be seen throughout his career, especially during the war, in compartmentalizing personal feelings in order to get his work done. "You might be feeling pretty upset emotionally, but it did not do any good to take the portions of that emotion which had spilled over, and mix them up with exacting elements of the task at hand,"[17] he later explained.

The personal torment ended on February 8, 1939, when Helen gave birth to a healthy baby girl. They named her Patricia Jane, but almost immediately everyone called her Janie. In spite of his well-deserved reputation for being a singularly tough, exacting, and no-nonsense commander, LeMay turned out to be a loving and even doting father. During the war, a pilot in his command remembered LeMay trying to keep his young daughter occupied with hand shadows on the wall. She wanted none of it—she only wanted her father to whistle. LeMay was physically incapable of whistling. Still, this combat commander who sent chills down the spines of thousands

of men, to say nothing of the fear he would later instill in his enemies, ingloriously sat on the floor trying in vain to whistle.[18]

One more publicity stunt would take place before the world
slipped into darkness. In May of 1938, Ira C. Eaker, a senior officer in the Air Corps who had been a journalism major in college,
offered up another exercise—this time in the Atlantic. The
bombers would "intercept" an Italian ocean liner, the *Rex*, as it
sailed toward New York. To help publicize the event, an NBC radio
correspondent would be flying in one of the planes to report it all
live to a national audience, and the venerable naval and military
correspondent for the *New York Times*, Hanson Baldwin, would be
an observer. Eaker decided that the range and capability of the B-
17 could be brought strikingly to public attention, in case Germany or Imperial Japan considered any actions against the United
States. But this exercise also showed the U.S. military's inability to
adjust to new and changing forms of warfare—they were still
preparing for a mighty armada attacking its shores. The last time
that had happened was in 1812.

Unfortunately, when the day arrived, the Atlantic was hit by
one of the biggest storms of the decade with high seas, heavy rain,
and extremely low cloud cover. The *Rex* was supposed to radio its
location the night before, but did not. Before takeoff, the civilian
passengers were issued parachutes and informed of evacuation
procedures. The rain came down in torrents on the runway at
Mitchel Field in Long Island. Before takeoff, C. V. Haynes came
over to LeMay while he was still making his calculations. He
asked him when he thought they might find the *Rex*. LeMay
looked at him, went back to his paper and then said, "I make it
twelve-twenty-five." But he added, "That's provided she's on
course."[19]

This was the chance for the Air Corps to prove that B-17s could find and bomb large ships since no one outside the military knew about the *Utah* exercise. It was also a chance to fail on live radio. As soon as the planes went out over the ocean at 8:45 a.m., they were buffeted by the storm. "Most of the time we couldn't even see the water and turbulence was heaving us all over the sky," remembered LeMay in his memoirs.[20] The plane would periodically drop quickly from huge drafts, sending LeMay's navigational equipment flying into the air. Just as NBC began its live broadcast to millions of listeners, the planes flew straight into a large cold front, and the entire cockpit area grew dark. But about ten minutes later, they came through into beautiful sunshine. Unfortunately, that did not last, and at 12:21 they went back into the storm. Then, at 12:25 p.m., just as LeMay had predicted, there was the *Rex* right in front of them. Right on time.

The trip back proved to be equally challenging because of the weather. LeMay never wrote about adverse conditions any other time, neither in combat nor in any of the thousands of flights he took all over the world. But regarding this one time he wrote, "At times on that return to land we began to wonder whether we'd really make it. It was that close."[21]

· · · ·

THE WORLD AT WAR

When World War II began in Europe on September 1, 1939, the Air Corps was in the process of expanding from 11,000 officers and men to more than 300,000. With that, the stalled promotion system finally came to an end. LeMay was promoted to captain in 1940 and began to fly the B-17 as a pilot. He was assigned to the

Thirty-fourth Bomb Group in February of 1941 at Westover, the new air base in Springfield, Massachusetts, built to be the jump-off point for flights across the Atlantic. The LeMays found a charming New England home not far from the base, and although he had a tremendous workload at the base, he enjoyed whatever free time he had with Helen and the baby. As it turned out, there was very little.

Like all other Bomb Groups in the Army Air Corps at the time, the Thirty-fourth existed on paper only. "We only had a few air-planes and our equipment seemed to have come out of the tool-shed at the Poor Farm," LeMay later wrote.[22] This was typical of the state of the entire U.S. military in 1941. The buildup followed the plans set up by the War Department to expand the Army, Navy, and Air Corps. But the equipment had not yet been produced, nor had the men been trained or even drafted. So regular officers like LeMay were in charge of ghost companies that would have to wait to be filled until the training and manufacturing pipeline produced what was needed, which would take years.

LeMay was made Operations Officer of the Group, but he had hardly settled in when his old friend and commander, C. V. Haynes, ordered LeMay to meet him in Montreal for a new, temporary assignment. Haynes was secretive, giving him no information. He told LeMay to take a commercial airliner and wear civilian clothes.

LeMay had been assigned to the Atlantic Ferry Organization (ATFERO). The Canadians were ferrying American B-24 bombers over the ocean for the RAF with the help of American flyers. Because the U.S. was still technically neutral, any American help for the Allies had to be clandestine. The ATFERO service had been set up by the Canadian Pacific Railroad. The planes would come from factories in the U.S., fly to Canada, and then head out across the ocean to England.

None of the American pilots, including LeMay, had ever flown a B-24. Haynes first took the group back to Wright Field in Ohio. On the first day, he took them up in a B-24 that had just been delivered from the factory. He let each man on board do one landing. Then he announced: "That's enough. We're all right."[23]

Though LeMay perceived the complete inadequacy of this kind of training, he also realized that in unusual times, some rules had to be bent. "So I'd made one landing in a B-24. Next time I saw one of the so-called Liberators, I had been ordered to fly it across the Atlantic Ocean," he recalled.[24]

The North Atlantic route consisted of flying first to Halifax, Nova Scotia. From there they flew to Gander, Newfoundland, and then finally across the North Atlantic for the longest stretch of the journey all the way to Prestwick, Scotland. Bases had to be set up in each of these locations with fuel, food for the crews, and places to rest until they would head off on their next leg.

"Figuratively speaking, we were all feeling our way on this job," LeMay said, remembering how green they all were. "Nobody knew much about flying the North Atlantic, and above all else loomed the question of ice." The crews were also ferrying passengers back to England, often VIPs who had to get back faster than ships could take them. Because they had no oxygen for them, they were forced to fly at about 8,000 feet. And at those levels, ice would often form on the wings.

There was another serious danger—no traffic control. "Sometimes there would be as many as thirty or forty planes ganged up on the ground back in Newfoundland, waiting for halfway decent weather in order to get across." When the weather broke, they would all take off just a few minutes apart. The problem for the ferry pilots like LeMay was that planes were flying in both directions across the Atlantic. There were times when they would suddenly head right into large forces coming the other way. Once, as LeMay headed back to Gander from Prestwick, he was about 300 miles out over the ocean when he saw a huge weather front straight ahead. He had no option but to go forward, when, without warning, he saw a plane popping through the clouds and heading straight at him. "Suddenly I realized that there were about thirty-five more planes back in that front somewhere,"[25] he said later.

Years later, when planes flew the ocean regularly, routes were regulated and different altitudes were assigned for planes flying in various directions. But in those early days, the ATFERO pilots just prayed they would not collide with another plane over the Atlantic. To add one more strange twist to the story, in order to follow the rules of neutrality, the planes had to be flown to the U.S.-Canadian border where the Canadians towed the planes over the line, sometimes by hand. "Everything was cockeyed just then,"[26] was LeMay's summation of the bizarre rules of neutrality.

After several months of ferrying planes across the North Atlantic in the late spring and summer of 1941, LeMay received a new job. The Air Corps needed a route to Africa via South America. LeMay was again chosen, along with veterans C. V. Haynes and C. J. Cochrane. He now belonged to a very small and select group of top pilots in the Air Corps chosen for all the big assignments.

Although now a pilot, LeMay had not forgotten his navigation skills. So when his information came from his own navigator, a man named Kester, for the Africa trip, he questioned it and checked up on him. LeMay did his own calculations and found

Kester to be right on target. After that, he said, "I didn't bother him anymore."[27]

When they arrived in British-controlled Egypt, they had a layover of almost two weeks. The Americans took the opportunity to learn more about combat from pilots who were already fighting the Germans. LeMay and the others went to some of the forward RAF positions to talk to the British flyers. While looking at some damaged planes, the Americans saw blood spattered about the inside of the fuselage for the first time. Combat in the air was suddenly no longer theoretical, and it left a deep impression on them. The return trip home was difficult because most of them had contracted dysentery in Egypt. When LeMay finally made his way home to Westover, Helen opened the door and saw her tanned husband, who had lost fifteen pounds in five days. She thought he looked wonderful. He felt like he wanted to die. LeMay would be plagued by dysentery throughout the fall of 1941.

As the United States inched closer and closer to war, LeMay's advancement, like everything else, suddenly sped up. After being stuck as a lieutenant for eleven years, he jumped from captain to major in fourteen months. He had a solid reputation among the top commanders in the U.S. Army Air Forces—the name had been changed in 1941, although throughout the coming war, most people would still call it the Air Corps. Curtis LeMay's professional future suddenly looked much more promising than it had just a year earlier. The greatest obstacle he faced now was surviving what was to come.

CHAPTER FOUR

"I'LL FLY LEAD"

THE BOMBS DROPPED AT PEARL HARBOR STILL REVERBERATE WITH significance today. But on December 7, 1941, reactions varied. In Tokyo, in spite of celebration over the great victory, wiser minds knew the gamble might bring unintended consequences. In London, Winston Churchill breathed a deep sigh of relief upon hearing the news, and understood immediately that England's position had radically changed for the better. The greatest impact, of course, was on America. Just days before, 80 percent of the population had not wanted to fight either Germany or Japan, in spite of their control over most of Europe and Asia.[1] Within twenty-four hours of the attack, the poll numbers completely reversed themselves.[2]

When the first static-filled radio reports were broadcast from Hawaii, a combustible mixture of rage, indignation, and fear took hold of the population. Every radio bulletin and every "EXTRA" edition shouted by newsboys on the corner only fueled the country's growing anger. It was the only topic at lunch counters from Maine to California. People in offices wrote patriotic messages like "Remember Pearl Harbor!" at the bottom of memos.[3] Flags suddenly appeared on public and private buildings.[4] Americans were united in their anger.

But strangely, not Curtis LeMay.

LeMay was often out of step with conventional thinking. Since his childhood, he had a strange knack for seeing things differently than people around him. Pearl Harbor was no exception. When Curtis LeMay heard that the Japanese had bombed the naval base and that Hickam Field, where he spent two years of his life, was on fire, all he felt was a deep sense of relief.

LeMay was in his car, halfway between Westover Air Force Base and his home in nearby Holyoke, Massachusetts, when the football game on his car radio was interrupted. Unlike his fellow countrymen, he felt no anger, no fear, and, oddly, not even any particular antipathy toward the Japanese. Most of all, he was not surprised. Years later, he would compare learning the news to his search for the Italian ocean liner, *Rex*, three summers earlier. After hunting for the ship over the stormy North Atlantic, "going through a lot of clouds and turbulence, and then breaking out . . . there she was, right in our path," he wrote in his memoirs.[5]

There it is, he thought. We were finally in this war. All the debate, the buildup that still had not accomplished much, had now become relevant. But though LeMay was more invested in this news than most Americans, he did not turn his car around and drive back to the base.

LeMay always worked seven-day weeks, but he tried to spend Sunday afternoons with his family. This Sunday, December 7, was

no different. As he drove through the frozen New England countryside, past farms now shuttered for the winter, LeMay envisioned
the chaos developing back at Westover. He wanted to avoid the
bedlam as long as possible, and he wanted to break the news of the
war to Helen and see their three-year-old daughter, Janie. LeMay
had a relatively normal family life for the military—living off-base
with his family—but between the ferry operation and the Africa
trip, he had been away for long stretches over the past year. And
when he was home, he left before sunrise while Janie slept in her
crib, and returned home after dark when she had gone to bed. He
wanted Janie to remember him, but in her first three years the
opportunities for time together as a family had been limited.
LeMay decided that he would eat lunch with Helen and Janie on
that Sunday and then go back to work. There would be few possibilities for such luxuries in the months ahead, and whatever was
happening at the base right now was probably useless to the war
effort. He knew it would be days or even weeks before a coherent
strategy would be set in place for the Thirty-fourth Bomb Group
at Westover.

He would also be able to spend time with his wife. Helen LeMay
balanced her husband in many of the ways he needed. From the
moment they met, she filed down his rougher edges with her
insight, charm, and teasing humor. Even LeMay's friends admitted
that he could be caustic, but they would always add an addendum
to this assessment: "Helen was a delight."[6] Everyone in the Air
Force benefited when he had Helen near. LeMay depended on her
both for comfort as well as compensation for his spectacular lack
of grace. At this critical moment in his life and the history of his
country, LeMay simply needed to be with her for a brief moment

before he headed into the unknown. Then he could handle whatever came his way.

LeMay felt relief while most of America reeled in the wake of the news from Pearl Harbor because of a nondescript staff meeting he had attended three months earlier. Brigadier General Arnold Krogstad, a matter-of-fact officer with no tolerance for drama—a trait LeMay appreciated—had flown up to Massachusetts from Washington for a routine inspection in September. Afterwards, Krogstad gathered the officers of the Thirty-fourth in a hangar for an informal talk. The men sat on tables, benches, even on the floor around the General. Work on a nearby airplane was stopped so Krogstad could be heard.

Without any emotion, Krogstad told the men that they should prepare for war immediately. He offered no specific time or date, but he made it clear that America's entry was imminent. Instead of a flurry of questions, Krogstad's prediction was met with silence. The General's sober projection hit LeMay like a punch to his solar plexus. He felt sick, not because he feared going to war—concerns for his own safety never bothered him—but because the announcement only confirmed his own chronic worry that war would come before they were ready. LeMay knew just how ill-prepared for war the Army Air Force really was in the fall of 1941.

Earlier that year, President Roosevelt had used all his persuasive powers to push a reluctant Congress to increase defense spending and begin a national draft (which Congress passed by a margin of one vote). But the start of the military buildup in the fall of 1941 hardly relieved LeMay's anxiety. The United States was starting from nothing. It was impossible, he thought, to correct twenty years of neglect in just six months or even a year, and he was right. New crews were arriving steadily, but LeMay was not fooled. "We didn't have a training program," he admitted in his memoirs, "didn't have any range to bomb on, didn't have anything, period. What the hell were we going to fight with?"[7]

The Air Force did not have enough instructors to train the pilots, navigators, bombardiers, and the maintenance crews who were now coming in. The planes they needed immediately had not been built. The War Plans office in Washington had done diligent work and brilliantly put together a massive army, navy, and air force, but everything existed only on paper, from new recruits to barracks to house them in. Everything seemed to be progressing at a glacial place. So, after three months of worry, Curtis LeMay felt relief because he understood that the nation—and especially Congress—would finally be forced to focus on building the war machine the United States did not possess and desperately needed.

Only twenty-four hours after the attack, a radically chastened Congress declared war on the Empire of Japan by a resounding vote of 383 to 1.[8] Suddenly time sped up (in fact, even time had a new name: instead of Eastern Standard Time, it was now Eastern or Central *War* Time). The following day, the *New York Times* reported long lines of impatient young men waiting at recruiting stations throughout the city,[9] a scene repeated across the country.

At Harvard Law School, a young student named Ralph Nutter was trying to study in his room when he heard a great deal of noise in the hall. He stuck his head out the door and asked everyone to quiet down. Then he learned the news. Nutter went back into his room. "I just pushed all of the books and papers off my desk into the trash can and started to pack my bags. I enlisted the next day."[10] Another young man, Mike Kruge, from a mill town in Connecticut, had already been drafted in the first call-up that was supposed to be one year of service. As soon as he heard the news, he realized he would be in longer than that. Though neither had ever set foot in an airplane, before the end of the war, they would log more hours in the air than they could ever have imagined.

· · · ·

A RAGGLE-TAGGLE GYPSY CROWD

Nothing better illustrates the lack of readiness and complete disarray following the attack on Pearl Harbor than the disjointed movements of Major Curtis LeMay. When he returned to Westover Air Base that Sunday afternoon, he was told most existing bomber groups would immediately go to the West Coast because of the threat of a Japanese invasion. In addition to having to move the men and equipment of an entire bomber group across the country, LeMay also had to pack up and move Helen and Janie, along with their furniture, to Helen's parents' home in Cleveland. The large Maitland family home would be their primary residence for the next four years. They were luckier than some. Almost no housing had been built during the Depression, and suddenly homes were needed everywhere—near factories, in mining towns, in large cities, and around military bases.

LeMay flew off to Pendleton, Oregon, with the Thirty-fourth Bomb Group. But no sooner had he arrived than a waiting telegram with new orders sent him doubling back in the opposite direction. The Group would remain in Oregon, but LeMay was ordered to fly directly to Wright Field in Dayton, Ohio. The new B-24 bomber was coming off the assembly line, but it had not been adequately tested. Before the Air Force accepts each new plane, it must be thoroughly checked to make sure it meets the standards promised by the manufacturer. LeMay was one of the few pilots in the entire Air Force with any experience in B-24s, having flown them to England the year before. Now it was the U.S. Air Force that desperately needed the planes.

These movements also began the constant uprooting of Helen and Janie, who quickly made the short trip from Cleveland to Dayton. But there was no housing available there. LeMay ran into an old friend from his training days, Doug Kilpatrick, who put all three of them up until LeMay found two furnished rooms near Antioch College. The LeMay family stayed just long enough for Janie to catch the chicken pox from the Kilpatrick kids. After just one month in Ohio testing B-24s day and night, LeMay was ordered back to Oregon. Helen and Janie returned to Cleveland.

LeMay had barely climbed out of the plane in Oregon the second time when he was reassigned again, this time to Wendover, Utah. He would now be the executive officer of the newly created 306th Bomb Group, consisting of thirty-five crews, but no planes. Shortly after arriving he understood why airmen considered Wendover the lowest point on the planet. "Good place to land and takeoff," LeMay remarked with his usual dose of sarcasm. "There was a rudimentary runway, but no hangars. No barracks. Everybody in tents. And no adjacent civilian residential areas. Hell, Salt Lake City was as close as anything and that was 130 miles away."[11] There were no cooks to feed the men, no office personnel to make sure they were paid. LeMay had to scrounge to find mechanics to service all the planes he had. Many of the men did not even have a change of clothes. "Half their baggage had gone one way and half the other. Very few of them had any records along with them,"[12] LeMay remembered with disgust.

The men in his command presented an even greater challenge. "It had been only a few months since they were lolling on the home farm tractor seat. What do I mean, months? Weeks, in some cases. Here we were, with no airplanes or equipment yet, trying to requisition for the equipment we hoped to get. Trying to build the tar-paper shacks we were supposed to move into . . . everything seemed ephemeral," he recalled.[13] In those early days of the war, LeMay felt that the entire enterprise was so tenuous it could all just evaporate and disappear in a matter of seconds. It seemed that unreal.

LeMay had no idea how long he would be at Wendover, but once again, Helen and Janie made the trip by train to join him. Curtis and Helen understood that he would eventually be leaving the States and might not come back, making the time together even more important. All three of them stayed in a room in the State Line Hotel, a combination bus stop, restaurant, and casino, which sat directly on the state line between Nevada and Utah. There was not much more to the town, and Helen did her best to keep her child and herself occupied. Janie quickly became the hit of the hotel, according to LeMay, and the entire staff spoiled her. As it turned out, LeMay was with the 306th at Wendover for a little more than a month before being transferred yet again. This time, he was ordered across the salt flats to Salt Lake City, where he would take command of a bomber group of his own—the 305th.

The Air Force was building itself rapidly and had great need for any officer with experience. Ten months after becoming a major, LeMay was promoted to lieutenant colonel on January 5, 1942. Just twenty-four months earlier, he had hoped to reach this rank after thirty years of service. But the higher rank only added to his own self-doubt. Nobody had trained him to be the commander of thirty-five crews going to war. If the men under him were inexperienced, so was their commander. While he had been in the service since 1928, he had never been in combat. He had never fired a gun at an enemy plane, nor had he been the target of fire. LeMay was very aware of this. It would always hit him at night—what he called his "soul searching" time. No one taught him how a commander handles this sort of thing. "I wasn't well trained enough myself to do a hundred-per-cent-effective job in that particular slot," he admitted. "I had a pale feeling of inadequacy."[14] But with the sunrise, his strong sense of mission would take over again and mask his feelings, so no one ever sensed them.

The men serving under him never knew quite what to make of LeMay. Coming out of basic training, they were used to being shouted at constantly, but this officer's silence unnerved everyone. He almost never spoke, and when he did his voice was so quiet the men had to strain to listen. But because he was so terse, the few words he uttered had greater impact. Whatever the men did, it never seemed to be enough. The concentration of his message was: "You can do better...do it until you get it right."[15]

"I feared him." That was Mike Kruge's recollection of his commander in the 305th. "He was so severe, he looked like he'd chew you up. But I always respected him. He was honest...no baloney."[16] At first, the men resented LeMay's demand for perfection. And they hated him for imposing constant, unremitting work. They would only appreciate it much later when they understood that his back-breaking insistence on constant training saved lives—particularly their own.

Men in the military, especially those in combat, want commanders who are decisive. LeMay was certainly that, but he was also smart, and the men sensed that immediately. They would overlook the negative aspects of LeMay's character because the positives outweighed them. "[He] had a rough reputation," remembered Bill Witson, a pilot, "but as long as you did what you were supposed to do, everything was alright."[17] Eventually, the men came to revere him.

But the beginning of the 305th was hardly auspicious. At Salt Lake City in Utah, LeMay had only three B-17s available to train thirty-five crews. To make matters worse, the new pilots all came directly from training in small, single-engine planes. They had no experience flying these larger, much more powerful four-engine bombers. The navigators and bombardiers had even less training— they were fresh out of the Air Force's most rudimentary schools. In the entire group, there were only three pilots—including LeMay—who knew how to fly a B-17.

Upon their arrival in Salt Lake City, the men stood together with their gear on the ground and stared at each other and their bleak surroundings. "A raggle-taggle gypsy crowd" was LeMay's less-than-kind description of the whole bunch. But he did not let them loiter for long. He anticipated something they could not; in a short time, more people and planes would be arriving, and within a matter of months, these green, untrained kids would all be in combat half a world away, facing much more experienced German pilots who would be firing very real bullets at their planes.

LeMay had an uncanny ability to spot talent, and he brought together the best people he had come across in his fourteen years in the service. In addition to LeMay, Johnny deRussy and Joe Preston, both talented pilots, taught the men how to fly the B-17s. Ben Fulkrod was a tech sergeant whom LeMay put in charge of all ground support and maintenance. "He was a practical engineering officer to the point of genius," LeMay later recalled. "Heaven smiled on me and on the Group when I got hold of Fulkrod." Fulkrod could foresee precisely what the 305th would need in terms of equipment, and he quietly began to assemble and pack it for shipment to their eventual destination. This was no small feat. Maintenance equipment was nowhere to be found, especially in Utah. Amazingly, Fulkrod found it. When the 305th finally arrived in England, it was the only Group to have something as basic— and invaluable—as a set of wing reamers that allowed crews to cannibalize grounded aircraft in order to get other damaged planes flying again. "We never did receive all of the material which we were supposed to have. But we had stuff that we weren't supposed to have," LeMay explained, acknowledging that the material may not have come through proper procedures. "We can thank Fulkrod for that."[18]

LeMay also spotted Ralph Cohen, a former Marine. Cohen became the armaments officer for the 305th, in charge of acquiring and maintaining the crucial supply of ammunition and bombs. "Come rain, come sleet, come flak, come shortages, Cohen was really tops." Like Fulkrod, Cohen unearthed ordnance not available through regular channels. Again, LeMay never asked where it came from. He was just grateful they had it.

LeMay immediately set up a 24-hour training schedule. The men howled. LeMay tried various ways to impress them with the urgency of the situation, but he was fighting a losing battle. He was not dealing with mature men; most of them were still teenagers. "It hadn't dawned on a lot of these characters that somebody was going to be shooting at them before long. They would rather have gone to town every night and then try to goof off as much as possible the next day," he later explained.[19] LeMay understood they resented the harsh conditions, the relentless training, and their forbidding commander.

But he did not need or even want to be liked. He needed to train his men. And he purposely kept a distance from them, understanding that, as their commander, he could not be a friend. He would eventually have to order them to kill and to risk being killed, and friendships would only make those directives more difficult. He was not more than ten years older than some of the men, but he seemed as old as their fathers. "I wasn't real, I wasn't human. I was a machine." That's the way he believed they saw him. "When I went to the bathroom, it wasn't in the ordinary human process."[20]

Still, no matter how hard they worked, LeMay considered the 305th nowhere near ready for combat. "Most of our navigators had never navigated over water. Most of our gunners had never fired at a flying target from an airplane. How could anyone have the gall to bring rabble like this into battle?"[21]

Earlier that spring, when LeMay had finally given himself a day off, he was awakened at three in the morning when two planes crashed in separate accidents about twenty miles apart. He sent two trucks out to the crash sites to retrieve the bodies and explained in a letter to Helen, who had yet to join him at the time of the accidents, why they occurred. "Both pilots just out of flying school a short time and with only 30 hours on the ship. We will probably have more such things before we're through however 16 people in one day is too many."[22] LeMay was right in his prediction, but he could not even imagine the casualties to come.

LeMay's work at Wendover with the 305th had barely begun when he was abruptly told in June 1942 to pick up everything and move out again, this time to Spokane, Washington. He had been in Wendover less than a month. Intelligence reported, correctly, that the bulk of the Japanese Navy was heading towards either Hawaii or Midway Island.

LeMay's orders were to stop the Japanese fleet from attacking the U.S. shoreline. LeMay still had only three planes to defend Oregon and Washington, and to make matters worse, he was given two different models: two B-17s and a B-24. This meant that he required different mechanics, different ground crews, different bomb racks, and different strategies.

The ludicrous shortages of equipment were hardly just an Air Force problem. Army General Joseph Stilwell, who would become famous in China during the war, was in charge of the defense of the entire coast of California from Oregon to the Mexican border— 840 miles of coastline containing a population of over five million people and almost the entire airplane manufacturing capacity of the United States. Stilwell had enough small arms ammunition for three hours of combat, no artillery, and six tanks—six tanks to defend 840 miles. The rest were out of service. "Good God," said Stilwell, who, like LeMay, was never known for his diplomacy, "What the hell am I supposed to do? Fight 'em off with oranges?"[23]

The Navy's stunning victory at Midway alleviated the need for what would have been a very difficult defense. But instead of going back to Utah, the 305th was next redirected to Muroc (now Edwards Air Force Base) in California on July 4, 1942. Here LeMay encountered his next great challenge as a commander: the facilities at Muroc made Wendover look advanced. There was not a single building for his men, equipment, or planes. The temperatures in the Mojave Desert ranged from 120 degrees during the day to forty degrees at night. As far as the eye could see, it looked like another planet—a vast moonscape. It was clear that the welfare of the men was the last thing on anyone's mind back in Washington. Despite this sense of abandonment, LeMay resumed round-the-clock training. He had no other choice. As he wrote in his memoirs, "This was my outfit. This was what I was going to take to war and fight with."[24] He never lost his focus.

Ralph Nutter, who had enlisted from Harvard, completed navigator school in July 1942 and was immediately assigned to the 305th. As the new contingent of men were driven to Muroc from Los Angeles, the bus driver warned them about the group's tough commander. Upon his arrival, Nutter committed his first offense. Unknowingly, he sat at the table in the mess that was reserved for the staff officers. He sensed he had done something wrong immediately and finished as fast as he could. It was here that he caught his first glimpse of LeMay. "He was about five-foot-ten, full-faced, and stocky, with a broad chest, black hair, and piercing olive-colored eyes. He gave the immediate impression of enormous self-confidence, but without arrogance. It was a look of stern, unflappable strength and indomitability, which in the next three years never changed." Nutter quickly determined that this silent, unglamorous pilot sitting across the table from him was the antithesis of the flyers he had learned about through Hollywood movies. But the calmness that LeMay always displayed was a tremendous asset. He faced everything, from the constant shortages to the stress of combat, with an equanimity that helped those around him. "He was not grim or gloomy that first time I saw him at Muroc mess hall—or ever in the future, no matter what the circumstances," Nutter later recalled.[25]

Major Joe Preston, the chief pilot trainer, set the men straight on their new commander: "When he gives you an assignment, get it right the first time. When he asks a question, get to the point. He doesn't want to hear any bullshit....Performance is the beginning and the end for him. He's fair, but tough as nails."[26]

Bill Witson, a pilot from Texas, was originally assigned to the Doolittle raid that bombed Tokyo and electrified the United States in April 1942 with an act of retribution for Pearl Harbor. But because of tie-ups, Witson had arrived a day late for training, along with sixteen other pilots, and he was reassigned to the 305th. Unlike a lot of the other men, Witson saw his time at Muroc as a vacation, "because we only had those three planes and I couldn't get into the cockpit—maybe once every three days," he remembered. "So we just sat around playing cards and talking."[27]

When one crew landed, another crew took off. The temperature was so hot during the day that the planes could only be serviced at night. "You never touched [a hot] plane more than once," remembered radio operator and gunner Mike Kruge. The men could hardly wait for their turn in the planes. "As soon as we were up about two thousand feet, we'd open the windows. It was the only time we were able to really cool off and be comfortable," he recalled.[28]

The men slept in airless tents in the extreme heat. Because of these conditions, and the fact that the men could not practice unless they were in a plane, LeMay set up a very liberal leave policy. He organized a shuttle flight to Los Angeles and gave the men every other weekend off. But he warned them that this, too, would change. Once all their planes came in, and especially after they left for the war, there would be no leaves. He suggested that if they wanted to raise hell, they get it out of their system now.[29] By this time, Helen and Janie had completed another trip across the country by train. Now they were living in a rented apartment in Santa Monica. But LeMay rarely got away, and the few times he did, it was just for a few hours. He had to focus on flying and preparing his men. "We trained on three airplanes. Seldom more. Our pilots were coming directly from basic trainers right into B-17s. They knew nothing about formation flying. We merely prayed to get 'em off the ground and get 'em down again,"[30] he wrote about the early Muroc days.

Just two months later, in August 1942, with navigators and gunners still drifting in, LeMay received his overseas orders. Barely nine months after the U.S. entry into the War, the 305th began to disassemble at Muroc and pack its gear for the move to Europe. The mechanics went by train to Fort Dix, New Jersey. The pilots were sent to airplane plants in Cheyenne and Tulsa to wait for their planes to come off the assembly line. Everyone seemed to be going in different directions, but they would all come together in Syracuse, New York. Ralph Nutter remembered one touching moment as the train carrying a group of men from the 305th went through the stockyards in Chicago on its way east. It was just after midnight and the train was moving slowly as it passed another crowded troop train on the next track, moving west. "All of the windows were open on both trains. Strangely there was no gallows humor passed between the troops. No one spoke. We put out our hands and slapped the palms of the troops going in the opposite direction, a gesture that would later be called a 'high five.'"[31] No one knew where anyone would end up... silently they wished each other well.

The crews eventually arrived in upstate New York, but nothing ever seemed to work out in the military the way it was planned. Because of delays at the factories, the pilots came to Syracuse without their planes. They would wait there for delivery. To add to the list of problems, the 305th arrived in Syracuse during an early fall cold spell. Most of the men, wearing only their desert clothing, came down with the flu, LeMay included. But there was still too much to do, and LeMay would not ease up. He had to scrounge for cold weather gear for his men, sending trucks all over the Northeast to fill the orders. Heavy woolens were desperately needed—not just for the cold and damp weather of England, but in flight. In addition to not being pressurized, the B-17s had open bays for the guns. At 20,000 feet, the temperatures could drop to forty degrees below zero. LeMay knew no one else had thought of this.

One night in Syracuse, LeMay could not sleep because of a terrible headache. He figured it must be due to either his cold or the constant pressure he endured from flying at high altitudes. The next morning when he sat down in the mess hall, he lifted a cup of coffee to his mouth, only to watch it spill all over his pants. He made his way to the rest room as fast as possible so no one would notice his accident, but one look in the mirror told him something was drastically wrong. The flight surgeon recognized the problem immediately. In civilian life, Dr. Maurice Walsh had done research on Bell's palsy, a disorder that attacks the facial nerves. Walsh told LeMay his immediate diagnosis, and said he thought it was caused by the extreme temperatures in the B-17. (Bell's palsy can actually be caused by a virus.) LeMay, always aware of his limited time, asked about a remedy. Walsh replied that he used everything from heat and massage to shock treatments, but in truth, the doctor admitted, "The cases we didn't treat at all came through just as well as those which were treated."

"You just named my treatment," LeMay abruptly responded. "Goodbye."[32]

LeMay simply ignored his condition. He left the doctor's office and retreated to his basic cure for practically everything: hard work. It was not that LeMay was physically stronger than everyone else, although he was certainly sturdy. Rather, his tremendous focus, his drive, and his unlimited capacity for work pushed him harder than most people around him. The palsy's legacy was the partial paralysis of the right side of his face, which added to the sneering expression that people often commented on.

LeMay continued training in Syracuse. There were navigation exercises to Florida, New Orleans, and flights to Newfoundland. The men found a way to use the flights in a slightly unorthodox manner. If they were flying over a crew member's home town, the plane would sometimes, inexplicably, develop a mechanical problem and the crew would have to land long enough for a quick visit. LeMay was aware of this and, knowing where his men were headed, looked the other way. He ordered as many firing exercises as he could in order to give the men more experience shooting at targets. One plane would pull a flag held by a long tow rope and gunners in nearby planes would take turns shooting at it with live ammunition. A slow moving and relatively static target hardly imitated a German fighter descending at 200 miles an hour, but it was the best they could do. LeMay understood that fire control (shooting accuracy and conservation) could save a plane and its crew and make the difference between a successful mission and a disaster. The training never stopped.

LeMay continued to keep an emotional distance from his men. But the group had now been together for months, and they began to solidify. In spite of himself, there were some men he could not help feeling closer to. He demonstrated this fondness in his own peculiar way. One night, LeMay walked into Bill Sault's room, a pilot from Minnesota. All he said was, "Get dressed Sault, we're going downtown." Sault was sitting on his bunk, reading and comfortable. It was raining outside and the last thing he wanted to do was get up and go downtown. When he saw LeMay's expression, however, he realized the directive was not open for discussion. Sault had no idea why he had to get dressed and leave the base, but he did not ask any questions as they drove silently along. They stopped in front of a downtown hotel where they got out. LeMay took him inside, went to a room and there, to Sault's surprise, were their wives, along with Janie. "He was abrupt, caustic, seldom complimentary. I never saw him smile. But there wasn't anything he wouldn't do for us and he never forgot us,"[33] remembered Sault more than sixty years later.

LeMay also expressed his displeasure in unique ways. Shortly before the group left for Europe, Ralph Nutter asked his immediate superior, Major Preston, for a weekend pass to visit his parents one last time in Boston. He got the go ahead, but failed to ask LeMay. When Nutter returned on Sunday night, he came down the stairs of the American Airline flight and onto the tarmac of the Syracuse airport where he was shocked to see Colonel LeMay sitting in his car alone. LeMay motioned for him to get in. The two drove back to the base without saying a word. Nutter understood he had committed an infraction. The silent, uncomfortable ride seemed to last forever. Finally, when LeMay came to Nutter's quarters, Nutter managed to utter a few words. "I will get out here, sir." That was all Nutter was able to say. "He stopped the car. I opened the door, got out, saluted and turned toward the barracks. He said nothing. He never mentioned the incident to me again. He didn't have to. His meaning was clear. I had committed a serious offense by not obtaining proper clearance for my visit home. His personal trip to pick me up underscored his opinion of my infraction."[34]

By the end of October, the 305th Bomb Group had thirty-five brand new B-17s. Just days before they were scheduled to leave for England, a new problem befell LeMay. Because the situation with Japan was bleak at that time, the 305th was now suddenly—and in LeMay's opinion, stupidly—reassigned to the South Pacific. He heard about the order via rumor, but had not received it in writing. Most of the group's gear had already been shipped to England, and LeMay realized he was about to start on another wild goose chase, looking for a whole new set of supplies and equipment. He stepped in to countermand the order, demonstrating again his shrewdness in dealing with the military bureaucracy.

He persuaded a friend in Washington, Colonel Fred Anderson, to stall the change in orders until the original plan could be implemented. Then he gathered Fulkrod, Cohen, DeRussy, and Preston and ordered them to pack up everything immediately. Within three strenuous days, final alterations to the bombers were complete, and the group left for England.

LeMay's unwillingness to go to the Pacific was not because he desired to fight the Japanese any less than the Germans, or thought they posed a less serious threat. The order was just impractical. With half his unit already on its way across the Atlantic, he understood that stopping everything already in progress would hardly help the war effort. The sooner the 305th got into battle, he reasoned, the sooner they could help win the war and get back home. It was basic LeMay logic. Europe was simply the most sensible place for them right now.

LeMay got his wish. He left just ahead of the change in orders. Now he faced his next great challenge: his pilots had never flown across an ocean. They had no concept of the problems they would encounter over the North Atlantic in late October. Their navigational skills were limited, the weather could be atrocious, and the distance was greater than any of them had ever flown. Just before they took off, LeMay reminded them again of their course— Syracuse to Presque Isle, Maine, to Nova Scotia, to Gander, Newfoundland, to Prestwick, Scotland—and he offered some last bits of flying advice. His concerns ranged from iced-up wings to getting lost over the ocean, or missing England altogether and winding up in German-occupied France. He had done everything he could, but, of course, he considered that inadequate. Now it was up to them. On October 23, 1942, the first bombers took off for England.

Everything they had trained for was about to be tested. And LeMay, never arrogant enough to believe that anything he did was wise or correct, felt his real challenge was about to begin as well. Still, he appreciated the moment. "I suppose any commander worth his salt has always felt proud when he took his people off to war," LeMay remembered. "And I was humanly proud . . . and also delighted that we had managed to squeeze out of that hare-brained scheme to send us to the Pacific minus ground echelon, group maintenance, baggage, et cetera."[35]

In all his letters home throughout the war—and he tried to write one every night, no matter how long the days—LeMay did not wax romantic or even very personal. He would never tell Helen about the real horrors he was experiencing. Instead, he talked about the mundane parts of his day. When he left Helen after her last visit in Syracuse, he came as close to personally opening up to her in writing as he could, but even then, he seemed to qualify it with an upbeat ray of hope. "Saying goodbye the other night was a lot harder than I thought it was going to be in spite of the practice we have had in the past. But this is just another trip and will get the job done and be home soon."[36]

To LeMay's amazement, they all made it, in spite of several mishaps. Many of the planes had propeller problems—some of the propellers actually disconnected from the engines and spun off over the water. One B-17 had to ditch in the ocean. But the pilot performed a perfect water landing and managed to come down so close to the Newfoundland shore that the crew did not even get wet stepping out of the plane onto the rocks. They had to wait there for a replacement plane and join up with the rest of the group later. In Gander, the runways were abnormally wide, and one of the pilots took off sideways rather than down the length of the runway and ran off the edge. That crew eventually linked up with the group as well. Bill Sault's B-17 hit a concrete bunker in Presque Island and waited there for repairs. When he finally rejoined the group and walked into the camp, LeMay looked up and asked, "Where the hell did you come from?" Sault replied: "Do you want me to go back?" LeMay's response: "Naw, we'll find something for you to do here."[37]

After all the efforts and interruptions and difficulties, LeMay allowed himself a brief moment of optimism for the first time upon his arrival in England. "We began to think, 'might be that we could do some good in this war, after all.'"[38]

. . . .

ENGLAND

By late 1942, England had won the Battle of Britain, but it would continue to suffer through terrible German bombings. Americans were arriving by the tens of thousands, and air bases were being built throughout England for both bomber and fighter squadrons. Engineering units, using segregated African-American and Irish laborers, eventually built forty bases for the Eighth Air Force throughout the East Anglia section of Great Britain. The bases were most frequently located outside picturesque small towns, where local pubs were the places crews could relax and mingle with the locals, although London was the hub of all activity and the preferred destination for anyone with a two-day leave.

The English people were charmed at first by the young Americans who swarmed all over their island. They all seemed to be rich, handsome, and fun-loving. "Women? That was never a problem," remembered Mike Kruge. "In the beginning, there were so few of us. Later when the country filled up with Americans, I stopped going to London and went north to Nottingham because there weren't so many of us there." Everywhere the Americans went they were greeted with warm wishes. "Hey, Yank," Kruge remembers strangers would call out, "thanks."[39]

All this masked the reality of a unique type of warfare the airmen found themselves caught up in. This form of battle had never taken place in the long history of human conflict, and it differed from all other fighting in World War II. For the first time, battles were fought on a unique field—the thin, freezing air 20,000 feet above the earth.[40]

As historian Donald Miller described the unusual nature of the air war, "Bomber warfare was intermittent warfare. Bouts of inactivity and boredom were followed by short bursts of fury and fear. Then the men who survived would return to clean sheets, hot food, and adoring English girls. The endless, unfamiliar killing space added a new dimension to the ordeal of combat, causing many emotional and physical problems that fighting men experienced for the first time ever."[41] Unlike ground troops, who, landing on the Continent in 1944, would remain on the ground until they were killed, wounded, or the war ended, the men of the Air Corps would fight ferocious battles with the Germans on a regular basis and then be back at their base to sleep in their bunks by evening.

The 305th's first home in England was a base called Grafton-Underwood, a temporary stop until they could relocate to an R.A.F. base being renovated near Bedfordshire. Grafton had very little pavement and a lot of mud. The men tried to keep it out of their Quonset Huts, but it was a losing battle. Eventually, the mud made its way inside. It was everywhere. "You breathed it . . . it was under your nails, it was in the grooves of your hands," LeMay would remember.[42]

The second and final base for the 305th was Chelveston. The 305th got its first taste of English weather almost immediately, which allowed for, at best, five days of bombing missions a month. As they moved into the month of November, it was constantly cold and damp, which made a shortage of coal even more problematic. Since there was not enough coal, LeMay had to choose which areas of their living quarters would have heat. Knowing the men would be more likely to congregate in public areas, he settled on the dining room.

No matter where they had come from in the States, Americans had never experienced such miserable weather. They were enshrouded in a heavy fog that seemed to hang over them. LeMay recalled being in the control tower one dark afternoon, trying to help a pilot at the end of the runway in a fog so thick it was difficult to see much farther than the nose of the plane. LeMay asked the young pilot over the radio if he could at least see the runway lights as a guide. "Shit," responded the pilot, "I can't even see my co-pilot."[43]

LeMay did what he could to make sure the men were well fed, but in the early days, when the German U-Boats were sinking so many supply ships, everything, including food, was limited. Breakfast consisted of powdered eggs and spam. The only two items in abundance, potatoes and mutton, were provided by the English. Mike Kruge, who came out of a tough situation in the Depression, thought the food was "great. All those different kinds of potatoes... I never ate so good."[44] Ralph Nutter could not stand it, skipped a lot of meals, and by the end of the war weighed 125 pounds.

Cultural differences between the Allies came out at odd times. On one occasion, a local women's group invited the 305th to high tea. LeMay was horrified to see the men descend on a table of small sandwiches and cookies like vultures. Afterwards, he told them what he thought of their behavior and had someone explain the formal rules of tea in England. The lesson was probably lost on the men, who preferred the local pub to high tea. In another instance, an officer pushed LeMay to attend a dinner given by a Lady's Auxiliary Club. Afterwards, the officer saw that LeMay was not at all pleased with the evening. When he asked if he had a problem, LeMay replied, "Couldn't understand a damn word they were saying." Between the constant work and responsibilities of command, as well as the self-imposed pressure, LeMay almost never went to pubs and took very little down time during his entire stint in England.

•　•　•　•

THE RADICAL PLAN

Shortly after he arrived in England, LeMay ran into an old friend, Frank Armstrong, who had been one of the first Air Force commanders to arrive a few months earlier and help set up the Eighth Air Force—the huge umbrella command that included LeMay's 305th. He had been fighting the Germans, so LeMay asked Armstrong to talk to his group and pass along information about his combat experience. Though he was packed and ready to fly back to the States, Armstrong stopped by on his way to the plane to answer a few questions. LeMay listened intently, but Armstrong's assessment surprised him and made him uncomfortable. First, Armstrong warned, the German flak "is really terrific"; and second, he told them, "If you fly straight and level for as much as ten seconds, the enemy is bound to shoot you down."[45]

LeMay did not say anything at the time, but he was troubled by what he heard. This made absolutely no sense to him. But he doubted his instincts—Armstrong had flown against the Germans; LeMay had never even been in combat. Who was he, he wondered, to question Armstrong? But LeMay did know that no bombardier could drop bombs on a target in a ten-second run. It was impossible.

The Eighth Air Force had begun bombing missions just three months before LeMay and the 305ᵗʰ arrived in England. The entire American effort managed just over seventy sorties in August of 1942, compared to later in the war when a vast armada would fly more than 20,000 in a month.[46] These early missions, led by people like Armstrong, were testing and learning rather than doing any great damage. Instead, the damage in those early days was being done to them.

Armstrong had piqued LeMay's curiosity. "I went around making a nuisance of myself, hunting for photographs of bomb damage," LeMay explained. The results of his search brought another stunning realization: there were very few after-mission photos. "These people didn't know where half their bombs fell," he realized, "and most of the bombs didn't hit the target anyway. It was standard operating procedure to use evasive action over the targets. Everybody was doing it. And everybody was throwing bombs every which way."[47] This offended LeMay's sense of logic. "The only point in flying a bomber in this war," he would say much later, "and crewing it up and bombing it up and gassing it up and arming it and spending all the money and all the effort and all the lives—the only point in proceeding on such an operation was to drop bombs where they would do the most harm to the enemy."[48]

LeMay came to a depressing conclusion. The Eighth Air Force was not succeeding at all. Their planes were being shot down at a horrific rate and they were not even hitting their targets. The way it was being done had to change, but swimming against the tide in an organization as regimented as the military is not an easy thing to do. However, since the Army Air Forces was still developing the science of strategic bombing, its leaders were open to new ideas.

This started at the very top with Hap Arnold, and the willingness to listen trickled down the chain of command. LeMay was in the right service at the right time.

. . . .

THE LEMAY DOCTRINE

The British and the Americans disagreed on how to prosecute the air war against Germany. Sir Arthur Harris, the head of Britain's bomber command, favored nighttime saturation bombing of targets and cities, with Winston Churchill's support. The darkness cloaked their bombers, providing better protection against German flak. The ongoing pummeling that the English were taking from the Germans meant that there were few moral compunctions regarding German civilian casualties. However, the Americans, LeMay included, thought that despite higher risks, daylight precision bombing of military targets would work if given enough time to prove itself. But in 1942, the Allied air forces were not winning, and stopping the Germans was imperative.

LeMay knew that what he had to do—what the entire Army Air Force had to do—was destroy Germany's ability to wage war. But he also understood that victory in war is inevitably purchased with the lives of young men. If a country was hesitant to spend this capital, LeMay believed, there was no sense in fighting a war in the first place, a belief shared by William T. Sherman, Ulysses S. Grant, and even Abraham Lincoln. But LeMay now had the ability to take this strategy to new levels with the modern bomber.

LeMay's theory of war—his doctrine—in its most simplified form came down to this: a nation should think long and hard before it makes the fateful decision to go to war. But once that decision is made, then that nation should be willing to hit the enemy with every conceivable weapon at its disposal to end the conflict as quickly as possible. If a nation is not willing to do that, it should not go to war in the first place.

He was pragmatic about it. Since political and military leaders much higher up had already determined that this war should be fought, it was his job to make sure what he was given was used to its maximum efficiency. He might be able to reduce the loss of men if he trained his crews to peak fighting form, but he could never completely stem that loss. It was inevitable that men would die on both sides. As he would bluntly say, in war, you have to kill a lot of people. Once you have killed enough of them, they stop fighting. Therefore, the enemy should be hit with everything available to end the war as quickly as possible to enable both sides to get back to a normal life.

At this point in the war, however, LeMay and the United States did not have a lot to hit the enemy with. LeMay believed his job was to constantly think up newer, more ingenious ways of killing the enemy and undermining their potential to make war. In doing this as quickly as possible, he would ultimately save the most precious variable of his equation: the lives of young Americans. He took that responsibility very seriously.

The LeMay Doctrine developed directly from an understanding of the world that developed long before he ever went into combat. Growing up, he had learned that the world could be a very tough place. There were always other boys in the schoolyard who were bullies. And the only way to keep from becoming a victim was to stand up to them. Nations had the capacity to become bullies as well—Germany and Japan were prime examples. Negotiations with both had proved pointless. There was only one way to stop them in LeMay's mind: complete and utter defeat.

In pursuit of that defeat, LeMay began to create an entirely new
theory that challenged the ten-second bomb run advocated by Armstrong. He gathered the few reconnaissance photos he could find
and spread them out on a table in the mess hall. His men knew him
well enough at this point to understand that his table was off limits—no one came near him, and those who walked in and saw him
there turned around and left immediately. After studying the photos and charts for a long time, he realized his first instinct had been
correct. No one could hit a target using evasive maneuvers—not
even their best pilots. And if the best bombardiers in the Air Force
with years of experience could not hit a target in a ten-second bomb
run, how would these green kids do it with no experience at all?
This question dominated LeMay's thoughts. He was even more
quiet than usual over the next several days, sitting in the mess hall
with other flyers, not talking at all, far away in his thoughts.

LeMay knew that if strategic bombing were to work at all, the
bomb runs would have to be long and straight, no matter how
deadly the German flak. LeMay believed in the B-17. He considered the plane vastly superior to anything the Germans had in their
arsenal. He anticipated that hundreds, even thousands, of the magnificent machines would soon take the fight to the heart of the
German war machine like no other force the world had ever seen.
But how could long, straight runs be executed given what he had
learned from Armstrong?

His answer began to come together after the 305th's first attempt
to fly in formation over England. It did not go well. To no one's
surprise, Curtis LeMay was not happy with what he saw. He had
been flying the lead plane, and no matter how hard he tried, he
could not get the rest of the group into the placement he desired.
That night, as he lay on his cot, he thought, "The top-turret." He

shouldn't be *flying* the lead plane, he should be in the lead plane's top turret—inside the Plexiglas bubble that protruded from the top of the plane's fuselage. There he could see everyone in formation. He jumped out of bed, and as he studied the charts a new concept began to come together in his mind. "Immediately I could see a properly effective formation taking shape," he wrote in his memoirs.[49] The formation offered the maximum fire protection for the entire group. Each bomber would protect the other, but they had to fly together in a tight group.

The next time the planes were in the air, LeMay quickly handed the controls over to his co-pilot, headed for the top turret, and plugged in the radio extension. Now able to watch and communicate with the entire group, he ordered each plane to its proper spot. Mike Kruge was his radio operator on that flight and never forgot the experience. "I can still see him under the glass, spelling it out to the men over the radio: 'Number six further to port'... 'number eleven raise yourself above number 14'.... 'C'mon 12... stay with us... tighter... tighter... tighter... you can do it.'"[50] Like a master choreographer at 20,000 feet, LeMay formed his group. If he could not see them from the turret, he would climb around to the hatch or back to the rear turret and plug in his radio set there. This way, LeMay invented the Lead-High-Low or the wedge-shaped combat box that gave each plane the maximum protection from German fighters. It would soon become standard for the entire U.S. Army Air Forces in the war.

LeMay was still far from pleased. "People roved around for this reason or that, people broke formation," he recalled. Though the formation he was asking these pilots to make was much more sophisticated than their meager training allowed, he kept at it because he knew that German fighters went after the stragglers and sloppy formations. Eventually the men, in spite of their grousing, began to come together. "That second try, when I talked them into position—they could fly that one all right. We didn't go any further. We just concentrated on maintaining a decent form and shape."[51]

Bomber Command began to notice that LeMay consumed much more fuel than other bomb groups used. Word came back to LeMay from above to slow it down and save gas. He simply ignored the order and continued to train.

The first two missions of the 305th took place in November of 1942, a few weeks after its arrival. Both missions were diversionary flights for other bomb groups. LeMay was skeptical that this form of deception would ever fool the Germans. "The GAF (German Air Force) had been fighting this war long before we ever got over there and they had a hell of a lot of experience," LeMay lamented. "They weren't very often caught off base. Unhappily for us." The flying abilities of the Germans impressed everyone. "You knew that they were showing off," recalled one U.S. veteran, "they were trying to scare the heck out of you and they were doing it."[52]

In between those first two missions, the 305th was in the air over England practicing its formation, with LeMay driving home his concept from the top turret. Through it all, the nagging thought of working so hard, losing so many Americans, and having the bombers still miss their targets continued to consume him. It was active in his unconscious as well—ideas often came to him at night in his cot. That is where he was the night after the second diversionary mission when the answer came to him. "I climbed out of bed, closed the windows, pulled the blackout curtains into place, turned on a light, and went prying into my foot locker." LeMay rummaged for, of all things, an old book from his ROTC days back at Ohio State. He did not even understand why he had brought that particular book with him to Europe in the first place. "I don't think it was a conscious act, it was more or less automatic,"[53] he recalled. The book was an old artillery manual.

LeMay had studied under a professor at Ohio State who had been an artillery officer in the First World War. Professor Chester Horn hammered artillery theory into his students. He also told them one anecdote that LeMay remembered: during World War I, a brigade out of Minnesota, a bunch of big Swedes, spent the years before the war cutting down trees in the forests up north, or working on wheat farms. Passing along the artillery shells proved lighter and easier than the back-breaking work they did back home. "Those Scandahoovians, stripped to the waist, would be lined up back from the breech of the gun," he remembered Professor Horn telling them, "and they would pass shells along with lightning speed. Every time the breech came back on recoil, the breech-block rotated and opened; empty shell flipped out, new shell was slipped in as the gun went forward."[54] One day a German artillery battery was captured and marched back behind the lines. On the way, the German POWs begged to have a look at the new artillery pieces the Americans were using. They assumed they were automatic because they fired with such terrific rapidity.

Because Professor Horn had been relentless in drilling every aspect of the 75-millimeter gun used in World War I into his students, LeMay had a fairly good sense of its mechanics. Now, the Germans were using 88s, which were larger than the 75s and deadlier. LeMay got out a notebook and pencils and started working on a problem. He could figure out the difference between the two guns using the textbook. Then he imagined a target the size of a B-17 sitting on an imaginary hill, 25,000 feet away, as far as the B-17s were from the German guns on the ground. It was the type of classic fire problem that he solved back in college.

He had pulled the covers over himself because of the cold damp weather, "but I was too excited to freeze," he remembered. LeMay calculated the lift required to place the shells that high, the target size (seventy-four feet, nine inches from a B-17's forward gun to its tail), the number of shells the German gun batteries could cover, the dispersion of those rounds and, finally, their accuracy. All of this was based on the number of guns he thought the Germans were using, according to intelligence reports. Finally, he had it: 372.

"That was the way the answer came out," LeMay remembered. It would take 372 rounds to hit one B-17. "That was a lot of rounds, even for those busy batteries. I concluded that we could take this... thought it was worth a try."[55] Then he went back to bed. But now he could not sleep because of his excitement. In order to shut off his mind, he did a mental exercise. It was similar to a trick Franklin Roosevelt used during the long nights when the terrible burdens of his office kept him from falling asleep. Both men would think about one moment in their pasts that made them happy and relive it. The crippled president remembered in detail sledding on winter days at his home on the Hudson as a boy. Roosevelt imagined each run down the hill and then the slow walk back up the hill, step by step, dragging the sled.[56] Curtis LeMay's happy memory fit his methodical personality. During the summer of 1927, LeMay and a fraternity brother, Bob Kalb, rebuilt a 1918 Model-T Ford they salvaged from a fire. By rebuilding that car again in his mind, piece by piece, LeMay could finally shake off all the nagging problems that kept him awake. Finally, he fell asleep.

The 305th Bomb Group of the United States Army Air Forces went into combat on November 23, 1942, just shy of a year from the date the U.S. entered the war, and five months since it began to assemble at Muroc. Its targets were the railroad yards and submarine pens across the channel in St. Nazaire.

The morning began with a normal routine. The men were awakened at 4:00 a.m. An enlisted man would come over to a flyer's cot and say, "Captain Smith, you're flying today." The men trudged off to the cold latrine and then dressed. The uniform consisted of long underwear, heavy leather pants with fleece lining, shirts, and heavy bomber jackets. The crews made their way to the mess hall. It was pitch black outside, and the lights and warmth of the mess hall provided one of the few pleasant moments, even if the food had become monotonous. The cooks did their best. They had been up since midnight making sure the men had a hot meal. The menu was, once again, dried eggs and Spam, along with toast and large metal pitchers of black coffee. The men had fifteen minutes after leaving the mess hall to finish assembling their gear and take care of any personal matters. Then they all headed to the auditorium for the pre-flight briefing.

The room was crowded with over 300 airmen in chairs facing the riser. At the front of the room a large map filled the great board, with colored yarn stretching from Grafton-Underwood to the "I.P."—the initial point, where planes headed before making a sharp turn to the "A.P." (the aiming point or target), St. Nazaire, and then straight back to England. The I.P. was set up to throw off the German plane spotters along the coast. The men had heard rumors of LeMay's straight-run plan, but many did not believe it. When they saw the yarn stretched in one long, straight line to the target, the room fell silent. From the back they heard "Ten-SHUN!" and they all jumped to their feet. LeMay walked in at a fast clip and stood in front of the map, picking up a pointer. Then, any semblance of routine ended.

Sixty-four years later, the men who have survived remember it differently, but the impact of LeMay's orders remains. "You heard a moan go up in the room during the briefing," as Mike Kruge remembered it.[57] "A feeling of horror," said Bill Sault. "We didn't think we'd survive."[58] But Bill Witson's recollection of that day had a different twist: "If he said do it, that's where you went."[59]

"They were really howling." That's how LeMay remembered it. "Don't blame them at all for their reaction, it was just about what I expected." LeMay's lack of confidence played against his inventiveness right up until he took the stage. "It seemed a brash thing to decide; especially to have such [a] decision made by a guy who had never been over a target."[60] But LeMay's desire to win overcame his negativism. And any personal ambivalence had disappeared by the time he stood in front of his men.

This was the fifth attack on St. Nazaire. The Eighth Air Force had to return again and again because they had done very little damage to the German rail yards and submarine pens in each previous mission. LeMay was determined that this time would be different. In front of the entire bomb group, he went over the details of the day: the target location, the weather at takeoff, the forecast over the target, the expected enemy fighter attacks, and, of course, the reason for the mission. Then he paused for a moment. He looked out and simply told his crews they would fly straight in— no diversions, no zigzags, no nothing. Just one long, straight run directly into the target in a tight formation. Everyone would stay together, offering each other maximum protection. No one would break formation. If anyone did not like it, they could stay back and transfer to the infantry.

"I told them we were going to put some bombs on the target," LeMay recalled. He also made an attempt to explain his logic. "Told 'em that anyone in his right mind knew you couldn't shoot a qualifying score by zigging around every ten seconds. It was just impossible. Might as well not go. Might as well have remained at Muroc or Syracuse and they might as well have stayed in that old A & P store or Amoco station back home."[61] At this point, a lot of the men probably would not have minded being back at the A&P stocking shelves or pumping gas. It was not as exciting, but it was a lot safer.

Standing on the stage in front of them, LeMay tried to reassure the skeptical crews that this would work because, although the German anti-aircraft guns and fighter planes were effective, they were not that effective. The Germans could not place enough shells in the air at once to knock down all the U.S. planes. And most important of all, this would give the bombardier enough time to put the bombs down the chimney.

The men did not know what to think. On the one hand, they were not pleased with their performance to date. On the other hand, LeMay's plan ran counter to previous strategy and everything they had heard. They were worried and confused, but they were also intrigued. Silence filled the room at first. Then there were murmurs. The murmurs gave way to talk. Finally one pilot stood up about halfway toward the back and suggested, in a most polite way, that it was suicidal and that they'd all be killed. That gave LeMay the opportunity to put it all to rest. LeMay did not castigate the young pilot. He looked directly at him and answered calmly, simply, and with tremendous confidence that it *would* work, that he thought they could take the German pounding. He revealed the magic number he had come up with—372. He reminded them that if they hit the target this time, they would not have to keep going back.

Finally, he laid down his strongest card. To prove it would work, to prove he believed it, he told them, "I'll fly lead." They would all follow their commander.

That quieted everyone in the room down. If this demanding, enigmatic, but smart commander believed in his idea so much that he was willing to fly lead, the first plane in the formation Germans put in their sights, then maybe he was onto something. They were at least willing to try it. They even began to feel it just might work. LeMay's confidence seemed to rub off on them. "Any more questions?" LeMay asked. No hands. As he stepped down from the stage, a voice yelled, "Ten-SHUN!" one more time, and they jumped to their feet. After LeMay passed through the auditorium, the men picked up their gear and followed him out.

Some sat on the hoods of jeeps that ferried them to the flight line. Some walked. The ground crews were waiting at each plane. They had worked all night to fill the tanks and bomb bays, and checked and rechecked every conceivable part of the B-17. The ground crews took their jobs very seriously. They felt tremendous responsibility to make sure that the one thing the fliers should not have to worry about was the condition of their plane.

Years later, a close friend reminded LeMay that they talked about his chances of surviving that day. He said LeMay told him that he fully expected to be killed. LeMay said it was very possible he felt that way, but he did not really have much time to "think about that phase of it: I was too concerned about the revolutionary rabbit I was pulling out of the hat," he wrote in his memoirs. "Course, I wasn't in the same position as the average commander. I'd never been over a target before and I was trying a thing like this!"[62]

On November 23, 1942, Curtis LeMay led his troops into their first battle against the Nazis. There was no place on earth he would have rather been.

CHAPTER FIVE

THE WAR IN THIN AIR

IT WAS A SPECTACULAR SUCCESS. IN HIS FIRST MISSION OVER Europe, LeMay laid the strategy of the ten-second bomb runs and zigzag maneuvering to rest. The results were even better than LeMay expected. The B-17s flew straight and level for 420 seconds without any deviation before passing over the railroad yards and submarine pens at St. Nazaire. Two fortresses and their crews were lost on the mission, both shot down by German fighter planes on the way in. But not one B-17 was brought down by the flak batteries on the ground, and the 305th put twice as many bombs on the target as any other group before. Within two weeks, the entire Eighth Air Force would adopt his strategy. However, although he was pleased that his ideas were recognized, LeMay thought it childish to find any personal gratification in the success, considering the American lives that were at stake.

When the planes returned to Chelveston, the crews were immediately whisked from the airfield for debriefing. As they entered
the mess hall, they were greeted by large pitchers of grayish coffee,
platters of Spam sandwiches, and interrogators at each table waiting with clipboards and pencils.

Each crew sat together for questioning by an intelligence officer. This was always done immediately after a mission while the
event was still fresh, and the men could recall as much as possible.
They discussed it together as a group so details could be confirmed. The questioners would then compile the information and
analyze the data to see if they could glean anything that would
help them change and improve the tactics for the next mission.
LeMay read this data again at night as if it were a puzzle with some
magical formula hidden within. If he could just unlock its secret,
he believed he might save one more crew on the next mission, or
improve the accuracy over the target.

The Germans were no less diligent in studying the Americans,
and they were just as frightened. During the war, they captured a
B-17 and analyzed every aspect of its flight, shooting, and bombing capabilities. "Bit by bit we are able to familiarize ourselves with
every technical detail," wrote a Luftwaffe pilot. Every minute of
their spare time, he wrote, was used to figure out a [counter
defense], until "the spell [was] broken: the myth that these monsters are invulnerable is ended."[1]

Even though he was as exhausted as all the other men in the
room, LeMay moved from table to table, listening to the crews to
pick up the general profile of the mission from different vantage
points. He had been there from start to finish, but he wanted to
know the experience through the eyes of the crews who flew
behind him. His curiosity kept his adrenaline charged. Even

though the initial reports were much better than expected, LeMay's own internal debate continued. Was he justified flying straight in? Should he have done anything differently?

LeMay did realize one mistake he made while still in the air. In the future, he would not fly in the pilot's seat. He would still fly the lead plane, because he understood the importance of having the commander out in front of the men. But he would be in the co-pilot's position on future missions so he could get up and watch the formation behind him. He would learn more that way.

There was one more important and highly personal aspect to this mission that he told no one. Curtis LeMay finally put to rest one worry—the question of how he would deal with his own fears in combat. The men around him who only saw a very calm and supremely confident commander never guessed that he was as nervous as anyone. This was the first time in his entire life that anybody had ever taken a shot at him. He had survived.

LeMay had created his own way of dealing with fear. He found that if he focused his mind on his mission, his many responsibilities, and his men, as well as the cascade of details surrounding the twelve hours in the air, he could sublimate his anxieties. All the way there and back, he kept telling himself one thing: stick to the bombing, that's all that counts. He repeated this mantra to himself over and over. He concentrated on his primary goal—the destruction of the German war machine. Everything else, even his own life, was secondary. A co-pilot who flew with him described an extraordinary transformation that would take place just before each takeoff: "He bites down on his cigar and manages to turn from anxious to angry in just a few seconds."[2] He turned his fear into fury. *Iron-Ass*, his men called him, but never to his face.

When LeMay finally returned to his quarters, satisfied that he had heard everything he was going to hear, he still had one final task. He wrote twenty letters to the families of the men in the two fortresses that did not return. The twenty-first letter went to Helen. He wrote home nearly every night, even if it was only a line or two.

•   •   •   •

DUELS IN THE AIR

Although strategic bombing was an altogether new and modern form of warfare, it had more similarities to past forms of fighting than most people imagined. Though the men flew in fantastic machines high above the earth, this warfare brought back the classic man-to-man duels of the past and the test of strength between hunters.[3]

A mission lasted ten to fifteen hours. The men were on the lookout for German fighters the entire time. The fighters would first appear as tiny black dots in the far distance. As they drew closer, the men in the B-17s could see the cannons on the German planes begin to spit fire as tracer shells darted towards their formation. Yet up until that moment, most missions were quiet, except for the drone of the engines and the air rushing by. Radio silence was strictly observed, and the men were either busy performing their tasks or deep in their own thoughts. The introduction of enemy fighters brought a sudden and jarring sensory overload.

There was an immediate upsurge of chatter over the intercom as various crewmen in different planes brought attention to the fighters in rapid succession. Viewing the horizon as an imaginary face of an enormous clock, the sky turned into a fast moving and constantly changing battlefield. "Fighter at 3 o'clock"... "Two at 9 o'clock"... "Hold your position... Number four pull up... May Day, May Day!" would crackle over the radio channels. These fighter attacks could last as long as twenty minutes. But that was just the beginning. Another ordeal was about to begin.

"We were only in the final run no more than two to five minutes, but it seemed like a year," Mike Kruge recalled.[4] When the bombers neared their targets, the sky ahead of them suddenly filled with small, black, puffy clouds—the explosions from German anti-aircraft batteries—the 88s—that surrounded all valuable targets. There was nothing benign about these dark little clouds, which were really concentrated masses of death sending shards of hot metal through the thin membranes of the plane. Sometimes these hit an unlucky waist gunner or pilot or navigator in the head with a thud, killing him instantly. The most feared wound was a hit in the groin that did not kill. Similar to combat on the ground, there was no logic to who was hit and who was not. Men could be standing right next to each other, and one would live, one would die.

Sometimes, a man would be wounded and in terrible pain. There was a first aid kit on board, and as soon as the attack was over, another crewman came to help as best he could, but the wounded man still had to wait as long as eight or nine hours until the plane returned to its base in England. Often, wounded men died on the way. In one case, a crewman understood that his friend who had lost an arm would bleed to death before they returned to England. He applied a makeshift tourniquet to the stump and then put the wounded man's parachute on him, pulled the cord and pushed him out of the bomber, hoping someone on the ground would take pity on him and provide medical assistance. Sometimes a black cloud scored a direct hit on a Fortress. The other planes around it saw the plane in formation one moment, and then it was suddenly gone, disappeared with a loud bang, leaving a cloud of reddish smoke in the place where ten men had been working moments before.

When the B-17s finally reached the aiming point, the bombardier had one chance to locate the target and unload the bombs. As soon as the bombs were released, the plane would immediately jerk upwards from the sudden loss of weight. Then the planes would bank to the left and start their dangerous trip home, through the same fields of fire they had just survived.

LeMay had actually been incorrect in his earlier calculation. It took an anti-aircraft shell only eight seconds to reach its destination, flying upwards at 180 miles an hour, but it was much more difficult to hit a plane traveling between 250 and 300 miles an hour than he realized. Flak proved to be highly inefficient—it actually took around 8,500 rounds to shoot down one bomber, much higher than LeMay's figure.[5] But flak actually brought down more bombers than fighters—5,400 American planes were destroyed by anti-aircraft guns in the war as opposed to 4,300 brought down by fighters. And flak accounted for almost three quarters of all wounds suffered by the Eighth Air Force during the war.

Beyond these numbers, flak produced one more insidious result which is impossible to quantify. Those menacing puffs of black smoke could reduce men to a state of complete helplessness—passive stress, Air Force physicians called it. Since the source of the problem was actually miles away, there was nothing a flyer could do to protect himself or strike back. Some planes returned with as many as 300 holes in the fuselage, along with dead and wounded crewmen inside.[6]

In one of the many ironies of war, the ten men inside a bomber had a great deal in common with the people huddled in shelters below. Neither group had any real control over their fate. A bomb could fall directly on one's shelter, ending life in an instant. Similarly, one of those dark puffs of smoke could shear a wing off a plane, sending the bomber into a sickening spiral of centrifugal force all the way to the quickly rising ground. Between the fuel and the bombs on board, the men were trapped inside a steel canister that was itself one huge bomb.

LeMay was somewhat dismissive of the entire concept of combat fatigue. On the one hand, he understood that a man could go through a great deal of stress in these terrible battles day after day and come unglued by it. He never punished any of his men suffering from it, as General George Patton famously did.[7] But LeMay ultimately held the science of psychiatry in very low esteem. Air Force psychiatrists were dismissed from his office, sometimes with a bare minimum of patience when they came to talk to him about the problem. It did not fit into his world view because it sounded like whining. LeMay's own childhood had been difficult, but in his mind, complaining about it never improved the situation. Instead, he solved his own personal problems—a failure for a father and terrible poverty—by working harder than anyone else around him to succeed. That did not come from sitting on a psychiatrist's couch, which he wrote about in sarcastic terms. Instead, the remedy came from his own initiative. LeMay was capable, even brilliant, and as the oldest child of a struggling family, he was conditioned from an early age to believe that the weight of the world rested on his shoulders. He worked harder than anyone around him—whether as a child bringing fish to his family in the freezing Montana winter, at the foundry six nights a week in college, or even now, spending eighteen to twenty hours a day trying destroy his targets. Throughout his life he would demonstrate a steely efficiency in fulfilling his responsibilities.

Before a mission, LeMay admitted that his own stomach could do flips, but "once you go chugging down that runway, once you're off to the races—you're not scared. You're busy, you're doing your job. No chance to be scared. If you're going to be knocked down, or if you're going to burn up from a hit in the gas tank—O.K. So that's going to be. There's not one thing you can do about it."[8]

That's what he told Ralph Nutter—do not dwell on the losses. Nutter had seen men blinded and paralyzed by fear. Most men did whatever it took to not think about it. Many of the crews drank themselves into numbness after the missions. But Nutter remembered LeMay giving him a piece of advice one day that was cynical yet almost uplifting in its acceptance of fate. "Nutter, you're probably going to get killed, so it's best to accept it. You'll get along much better."[9] And that, Nutter says, is what he did all the way to his final mission. "If there is no escape," wrote LeMay, "you don't experience combat fatigue."[10] It was unjustified hope, in LeMay's mind, that could undo a man's moorings.

LeMay divided his men up into two groups: the good ones (the vast majority) and the "No-Goods"—those airmen who never should have been in the service in the first place. When someone from the first group (the good ones) demonstrated symptoms of stress, perhaps because of some very difficult missions or losing crewmates, LeMay found remedies that worked more often than not. He allowed the man to save face by explaining he needed help with a "serious problem in supply." He told him he would have to stop flying until this problem could be solved. The man usually

complained, telling him it was not fair, but he would be out of
combat, privately relieved, with the chance to calm down.[11]

In one case, a pilot with an excellent record had seen too many of
his crewmen killed. He was still willing to fly himself, but could not
face losing another man. LeMay compared notes with the flight sur-
geons and understood the distinction. He asked the man how he felt
about fighters. Fighters were fine, the pilot replied. So he was transferred to a squadron of P-47 Thunderbolts. In a fighter, the pilot was
not responsible for anyone but himself. With the huge weight off his
shoulders, the man relaxed and performed heroically. In another
case, a man came into LeMay's office and talked for twenty minutes
about his fears. LeMay sat there and said nothing. He just listened.
After twenty minutes, LeMay looked at him and said simply, "Snap
out of it ... get back to work."[12] The startled pilot looked at him,
stood up, and did just that. It seemed all he needed to do was talk it
out and be told by his commander to come back to reality.

As far as the second group was concerned—the "No-Goods"—
when LeMay spotted them, he quickly got them out of his units,
and sometimes out of the service. He considered these men as dangerous as infections and detrimental to the entire effort. He had no
tolerance whatsoever for stupidity, incompetence, or laziness, and
he was brutal when he witnessed these cardinal vices.

The bombardier in Ralph Nutter's crew was Julius Dorfman
from New Jersey, and one of the door gunners was named Galway.
"Galway was this big All-American football type and Dorfman was
a small guy," Nutter recalls. Galway was also a vicious anti-Semite
and never gave Dorfman, who was Jewish, a break. Nutter finally
heard enough and went to LeMay to tell him about the situation,
which he thought was outrageous and bad for the morale of the
entire crew. LeMay listened and then told Nutter not to say

anything to anyone, he would take care of it. When Nutter asked him what he was going to do, LeMay replied, "Just leave it to me." The next day Galway was gone. They never saw or heard from him again. "LeMay used to say," Nutter remembers, "whoever didn't cut it or didn't like it here could always go to the infantry." Nutter believes that is where Galway probably ended up.[13]

•   •   •   •

ON A MISSION

In an effort to protect the men physically, Bomber Command came up with some ingenious ideas. In a direct connection to England's distant past, Colonel Malcolm Grow, the chief surgeon of the Eighth Air Force, developed body armor for the crews. Dr. Grow worked with the Wilkinson Sword Company to develop the flak suit, which included a steel helmet with flaps to accommodate earphones. It was designed by the curators of medieval armor at the Metropolitan Museum of Art in New York. More than 13,000 of these flak suits were delivered to bases by the end of 1943. The *New York Times* wrote: "A London firm, specializing since 1772 in the manufacture of swords, is now beating its product into something much more useful at the moment. It is making suits of mail for the American airmen . . . . Thus the cycle rolls around again, and American fighters, like the Yankee in King Arthur's Court, find themselves back in medieval armor."[14]

The Germans created the greatest problems for American bomber crews, but there was a long list of deadly challenges from other sources as well. The planes often took off from their bases in the worst kind of weather imaginable. As soon as the B-17s lifted off the runway, they flew blindly through the dark masses of thick clouds that almost always covered the English countryside until they finally reached the clear blue sky above the weather. They were all flying blind. The planes circled above and waited for the others to align themselves into formation at 12,000 feet. With the sky filled with planes all heading for the same rendezvous point, collisions were inevitable. If two planes accidentally touched each other while flying in formation, a mass of fire and bodies could rain onto the ground below.

Every crew member had to be at the very top of his game to avoid simple mistakes—hard to do for pilots who were human, young, tired, and finding themselves under more stress than most people encounter in a lifetime. Mistakes happened, and their consequences were deadly. It was LeMay who had to constantly remind them to stay alert and pay attention.

"He would be so severe." Mike Kruge related it especially occurred when things did not go well. "He kept yelling at the pilots in the briefing after a practice . . . and it was always practice, practice, practice."

There were no bathrooms in the plane. If a man had to relieve himself in the sub-zero temperatures, and over the course of fifteen hours every man did, he had two options. The first was a relief canister into which a crewman could urinate, but the opening to the canister almost immediately froze up. The second option was to urinate on the floor, which would freeze as well. On many occasions, when a crewman was wounded, the interior of the B-17 turned into a horrific scene of frozen blood, urine, and vomit. One of the most unpleasant jobs after a mission was not patching up the holes in the plane, but washing out the interior.

The Americans who arrived in England in 1942 came at the worst point in World War II for the Allies. The Germans were at the apex of their domination, and they completely controlled the skies over the continent. Yet, American bombers would increase at an amazing rate in just under two years: the Eighth Air Force went from just seven men and no planes in February 1942 to 185,000 men and 4,000 planes by December 1943.[15]

The Joint Chiefs in Washington—especially Hap Arnold and George Marshall—understood they were fighting a war of attrition, and they believed the United States would ultimately win it. But those early crews with no fighter escorts, facing much more experienced German pilots, were cannon fodder. The Air Force made a conscious decision to send those inexperienced crews out to wear down the Germans, knowing full well that they would be able to replace their planes and crews, out of reach of enemy bombs, faster than the Reich could replace their own. "They knew [the missions] would be failures," General Laurence Kuter said after the war. "They couldn't hit their damn targets. And if they hit their targets, they wouldn't hurt them. And still they'd take off on every mission."[16] The U.S. command's goal was clear skies over Europe by the time of the Allied invasion. The men in the Eighth Air Force would be sacrificed for this aim. And they knew it.

Beyond these life and death issues, LeMay had a list of relatively mundane problems that took up more of his time than he cared to think about. Due to shortages, the conditions on the ground were so bleak that units started stealing coal from each other to heat their Quonset huts. Food remained a problem. He had to deal with irate Englishmen with pregnant daughters. There were racial problems in the service as well. Though the U.S. Army was still completely segregated, there were hundreds of black units in England doing strenuous work, from air base construction to maintenance. When they were on leave in the local pubs, they were often the targets of white soldiers, especially when both groups were competing for local girls. This was an American problem; the English tended to treat black soldiers no differently than white soldiers. To solve the conflict, the Army divided up the nights of the week and gave black troops at least one night when white troops would be confined to the base.

· · · ·

LEAD CREWS

It was not long after that first mission that LeMay came up with his next big idea. Since navigators and bombardiers saw their targets for the first time on the morning of a run, they were unfamiliar with them. How could anyone, he reasoned, hit a target at 250 miles an hour when he barely recognized the terrain? To solve the problem, he created lead crew schools. He found the best bombardiers and had them concentrate on certain targets, which he knew would eventually be selected for missions. These crews would then be more familiar with the particular targets when they were assigned, so they would lead the entire wing into combat. When they dropped their bombs, all the rest of the planes would follow their cue.

On the second mission, Ralph Nutter was flying in one of the most dangerous positions. He was in the last plane of the group, nicknamed "tail end Charlie," second only to the lead plane in being targeted by German fighters. On the way back to England after the bombs had been dropped, LeMay got on the radio saying, "My navigator got us lost. Does anyone know where the hell we are?" Most navigators let the lead navigator do the work on the way home. This way they could be on the defensive and keep their eyes open for German fighters. Nutter always did both. "Maybe it was because I was a New England type or it was my Harvard training," he says, "but I always followed where we were." So Nutter got on the intercom and told LeMay he thought he knew. LeMay and the rest of the formation followed Nutter's directions and returned to the base. "When I came out of the plane, I saw LeMay driving over to me in his jeep. All he just said was 'All right, you're the new lead navigator.'"[17]

"Well, I told him I was just a second lieutenant and no one would listen to me. He just glared at me and said, 'You tell me if they don't listen to you.'" From that point on, Ralph Nutter was the lead navigator for the 305th. He would chart the course for every mission, and every time LeMay went over his work to double check it. He rarely changed any of Nutter's calculations. One night around midnight, Nutter had his maps spread out on the table and was charting a course for the next day's mission when LeMay approached him. "You gonna fly tomorrow?" LeMay asked. Nutter told him he was. "Go to bed," LeMay ordered. When Nutter asked who was going to do his work, LeMay responded: "I'm not flying. I'll do it. You go to bed."

"That's the kind of commander he was," remembers Nutter.[18] People would ask him over the years how he got along so well with LeMay, knowing LeMay's disdain for lawyers and Nutter's left-leaning political views. "We never discussed politics at 25,000 feet," Nutter would answer. Nutter also believes LeMay was the smartest individual he ever met—"and I knew Supreme Court justices."[19]

Nutter was just the type of person LeMay wanted in his group. Challenges fascinated Nutter, and he never left his work half-done. Like LeMay, Nutter was also intellectually curious, yet not at all imperious. "I'm a little suspicious of the genius," LeMay would advise. "They can be used in proper spots but [are] inclined to forget about the rest of the team, so that as long as they're around everything goes well, but once you lose them, you're liable to really fall to pieces. I'd much rather operate with a group of average individuals that were highly motivated."[20] No one was indispensable. Men were going to be lost. Nothing could prevent that. In LeMay's mind, an individual's life, including his own, was less important than the final outcome.

LeMay tinkered with every aspect of the missions. Once, Nutter complained to LeMay that it was depressing having chaplains waiting on the flight line to offer final prayers and even last rites. He said it set the wrong tone for the day. When a chaplain suggested Nutter join him, he responded: "I'm going to grease my guns ... that's the only religion those God-damn Nazis understand."[21] LeMay saw his point and asked the clergymen to remove themselves from the flight line and take care of their business back in the barracks. On missions, LeMay monitored every position on the plane, and even fired machine guns at approaching German fighters.[22]

After fifteen-hour missions and debriefs, the men would often head directly to the bar on base or the pub in town if they were not flying the next day. If they had a two- or three-day pass, the destination was London. There were other remedies to relieve the stress besides alcohol. Closer to the base, in fact, just beyond the fence, were the Land Girls working in the fields. Land Girls were part of a national agricultural program that brought young women from the cities throughout England to farms to do the work left behind by men who were now in the service. These girls were the same age as the airmen and found the Americans quite dashing. Their work was difficult and often dirty. Both groups seemed to appreciate distractions from their labors. LeMay was realistic about his chances of curbing this behavior and turned a blind eye to the hay stacks that were used, against Army regulations, just outside the fence. He had more important problems to solve.

•   •   •   •

THE WAR OF TERROR

The missions began to run together in 1943 ... L'Orient, Wilhelmshaven, Hamm, Emden, Antwerp, Paris (a Renault plant), Kiel, Rouen, and Vegesack. The targets varied—there were German fighter fields and the factories that produced those planes, as well as ball bearing and synthetic petroleum plants.

The British flew their bombers only at night, and Churchill did his best to talk the Americans out of daylight raids. But Arnold, Spaatz, and Eaker—all disciples of Billy Mitchell—were determined to prove his theory of strategic bombing correct. They were against the idea of area bombing in the early years of the war. LeMay also did not support area bombing at that point in the war, believing bombers should be able to hit military and industrial targets with less collateral damage. He just needed more time, practice, and planes to prove it.

The bombing campaign was a war of reaction before the Americans arrived on the scene, with the stakes growing higher and meaner as the conflict progressed. Germany had bombed civilians in Spain during their civil war back in 1937. At the outset of World War II, the Luftwaffe again was the first air force to indiscriminately bomb civilians throughout Poland. Prior to the Battle of Britain in 1940, England and Germany tried to avoid bombing civilian neighborhoods. But as the fighting escalated, anger and retaliation upped the ante.

At first, this infuriated Adolf Hitler and pushed the terror war to extreme limits. Bombing soon became *punishment* raids. In a speech during the Battle of Britain, when London suffered pummeling nightly, Hitler spoke to the German nation at the Sportpalast (a stadium in Berlin) on September 4, 1940, warning the British of even further destruction:

> And should the Royal Air Force drop two thousand, or three thousand, or four thousand kilograms of bombs, then we will now drop 150,000; 180,000; 230,000; 300,000; 400,000; yes, one million kilograms in a single night. And should they declare they will greatly increase their attacks on our cities, then we will erase their cities! We will put these nighttime pirates out of business, God help us! The hour will come that one of us will crack, and it will not be National Socialist Germany.[23]

For his part, Winston Churchill answered Hitler's rhetoric measure for measure. "We ask no favor of the enemy," the Prime Minister told the House of Commons.

> We seek from them no compunction. On the contrary, if tonight the people of London were asked to cast their votes whether a convention should be entered into to stop the bombing of all cities, the overwhelming majority would cry, "No!" We will mete out to the Germans the measure and more than the measure, that they have meted out to us.[24]

Hitler had a very worthy opponent not just in Churchill, but in Britain's Air Marshall Sir Arthur Harris, known as "Bomber Harris." He became the head of Bomber Command in 1942, and through the end of the war Harris would match Hitler in his determination and anger. Harris was also more intelligent. Proving how crucial a good leader can be in war, the men under him sensed his skills immediately. "When Bomber Harris arrived," said one flyer, Leonard Cherise, "you knew Bomber Command was going to see it through to the end. You felt a push, and we felt at last we were going to have to pull our socks up and get on with it."[25]

Harris turned Britain's Bomber Command into a highly efficient military organization and constantly pushed for more area bombing. These policies were controversial even among his men. Dave McIntosh, a Canadian navigator, did not mince words: "Harris didn't give a damn how many men he lost as long as he was pounding the shit out of German civilians. Butcher was the deserved nickname of the RAF chief of Bomber Command."[26] Harris gave, perhaps, the single strongest defense of area bombing years after the war in an interview with Canadian journalist and military historian Gwynne Dyer. When asked about the morality of bombing civilians, Harris showed he had not lost his aggressive stance: "Tell me one operation of war which is moral," Harris demanded. "Striking a bayonet into a man's belly, is that moral? Then I say, well, of course strategic bombing involves civilians. Civilians are always involved in major wars . . . I don't believe it is right to hit a man in the nose and make his nose bleed. But if he is offensive enough, you hit him in the nose or anywhere else you can hit him in order to stop him. The same principle applies to nations."[27]

One night Harris was stopped by a traffic policeman for speeding on the winding country road near High Wycombe, the headquarters of Bomber Command. When the officer, trying to reprimand him with the utmost respect, suggested that he could kill someone driving like that, Harris responded: "Young man, I kill thousands of people every night!"[28]

Both LeMay and Harris were sent to fight a war with Germany, not to negotiate. Fighting the war meant killing as many Germans as quickly as possible and not waiting for them to come up with better ideas for killing first. Harris immediately recognized LeMay's abilities. After he personally decorated LeMay with the British Distinguished Flying Cross on May 22, 1943, he commented to his counterpart and LeMay's boss, Ira Eaker, "LeMay looks like a man you would like to have with you if you were sent out on a dangerous errand."[29]

Harris also got along well with General Ira Eaker. The general arrived in England in January 1942 to organize the Eighth Air Force at the same time Harris took over. The two men could not have been more different. Eaker opposed area bombing, and unlike Harris, he did not have the killer instinct. But the two commanders would often sit down together in the evenings in Harris' library at the estate that had been given over to Bomber Command and enjoy each other's company.

Even though he disagreed with it, Harris was supportive of the U.S. Air Forces' daylight strategy, and he would help them whenever he could. He figured the U.S. would eventually abandon trying to pinpoint their targets. For their part, Eaker and Arnold never opposed the British night raids out of concern for German civilians. "I don't believe there was any moral consideration among military men," said Ira Eaker in an interview after the war. "When I watched bombs falling and hitting houses and churches I had a distaste for the whole business, but they were shooting at us."

If the atomic bomb had been available in 1942, and he had the authorization to use it, he would have dropped it on Germany with no reservations, Eaker said.[30] Both LeMay and Harris were cut from the same cloth. In describing Harris, Australian war correspondent Murray Sayle could have been talking about LeMay: "[He had] a shrewd mind uncluttered by religion, reflection, military tradition or anything much except the immediate job in hand."[31]

If the lower ranks of the U.S. Air Force had reservations about what they were doing, that seemed to change after just a few missions. As the war dragged on, Ralph Nutter was on a mission when the weather turned bad and made it impossible to find the exact target. "Just drop them in the center of town," he told the bombardier, later recalling, "I had lost so many friends at that point that I just didn't care."[32]

Throughout 1942 and into the first half of 1943, the American "fortresses" concentrated their attacks on France and the occupied countries. In the spring of 1943, the British came up with an ingenious plan to knock out Germany's armament industry by hitting the dams that supplied the hydroelectric power to the Ruhr valley. They developed bombs that would skip over water before they exploded and practiced these runs on lakes in Scotland. On May 13, 1943, Lancaster bombers surprised the Germans and delivered their load. Only one of the dams was damaged, however, and they gave up the plan, thinking it was a failure. What they did not know until the war was over was how close they had actually come to success early in the war. Hitler's Armaments Minister, Albert Speer, put 70,000 slave laborers on a concentrated effort to fix the dam and worried that if the bombers came back, Germany's armaments industry might suffer a devastating blow. But they never returned.

. . . .

MOVING UPSTAIRS

By May 1943, LeMay's days with the 305th were already numbered. It began with rumors. One day, one of his officers said: "Boss, I don't think you're long for—," and then he stopped. LeMay finished the sentence. "Long for this world?" But the young officer had meant the 305th.[33]

LeMay was promoted to Wing Commander. He would now be in charge of four bomber groups. He would not move far, just eight miles from Chelveston to the little village of Thurleigh. But his surroundings seemed a world away. The headquarters of the 102nd Wing was a country estate called Elveden Hall, which had been given to the government by the earl of Iveagh, head of the Guinness brewery family, for wartime service.

When LeMay was shown his personal quarters by Colonel Carl Norcross, which consisted of a bedroom, living room, and private bath—a sharp contrast to his army cot in the small, mud-caked, and drafty plywood room at Chelveston—he said nothing. His only reaction to the extravagance was to order Norcross to start a target study for the entire group immediately. Norcross was put off by this odd commander who only seemed to have work on his mind. It never dawned on him that LeMay might be uncomfortable with the opulence now surrounding him. LeMay believed soldiers in the field—no matter their rank—should live in spartan conditions. "Now I found myself with a copper dome over my head and God knows how much 'richly veined marble' staring me in the face." He kept thinking, "What the hell am I doing here?"[34]

Curtis LeMay's relatively brief time with the 305th at the beginning of the war was unlike any experience he would ever have again. His new quarters marked a shift from being one of the guys to a member of the brass, set apart. The growing complexities of the Air Force, the fast changes in warfare, and his own trajectory in rank had already rendered his intimacy with the men of the 305th a thing of the past. He was emotionally attached to those men in a way he would never know with any groups he would be assigned to in the future. He already missed that closeness.

The period in his life and career as head of the 305th always stood out. He would talk about the little English village of Chelveston— its church spire and green fields—and the men of the 305th with a fondness that is absent from other assignments. When men from the 305th came to visit after the war, he would always make time to see them. If they needed a favor, he would help. Years later in his memoirs he apologized for giving the 305th many more pages than other assignments. "I was close to the people with whom I worked, and I could fly along with them and share their perils. We felt an intimacy of proven human devotion while doing our job together." He may have been uncharacteristically sentimental, but he still managed to sum up this vital experience and dismiss it at the same time in his sardonic best: "You could call it my Big Week."

During his time with the 305th, he had produced impressive results—in the entire Eighth Air Force, the group ranked second in the number of sorties (375), and, though suffering more battle damage, it had fewer than average losses owing to the constant training LeMay demanded.

LeMay's new position lasted less than a month. In June he was suddenly given more responsibility, this time to command an entire division. The command was supposed to go to Nathan Bedford Forrest, the grandson of the Confederate general and LeMay's classmate from cadet school in 1928. But Forrest was killed on his very first mission. Now, at the age of thirty-six, LeMay had the responsibility of a general, although the promotion did not come immediately. As usual, he doubted his qualifications, as he later wrote, "God almighty! I had so little experience. I had commanded a squadron for only a short period of time—certainly not long enough to learn anything much. Next thing I knew, I had a group, and I was still engaged in learning the Commerce and Industry there when I got fired upstairs."[35]

In his first seven months in Europe, he had consistently written to his old commander and mentor, Bob Olds, about the difficulties he encountered. Because of serious health problems, Olds had not come to Europe. Instead, he was assigned the task of creating the Army Air Forces on paper. Although he was an able architect, it proved too much for his poor health. In February, he wrote to LeMay: "Within the last 24 hours I have been relieved from command of the Second Air Force [Training Command] and hospitalized to try to get this damned rheumatism out of my joints. I will let you know what develops in the future."[36] He died of a rare heart ailment on April 28, 1943, in a hospital in Arizona. Now, as LeMay ascended the chain of command, always unsure of himself, he was without the one mentor he had. "I know it irked the hell out of him to have to remain in the States as an organizer and training director. Let no one doubt that he would have made a terrific commander in the field."[37]

CHAPTER SIX

A WAR OF ATTRITION

As U.S. Air Forces grew larger and stronger in 1943, Germany itself became the target. Facing threats to their homeland, the German anti-aircraft defenses became even deadlier. In the summer of 1943, Hitler transferred some of his best fighter squadrons from the Eastern front to protect the homeland in the West. Albert Speer, the able architect and armaments minister of the Third Reich, tried to talk him out of that, thinking the squadrons would be much more effective in the East. But Hitler was irrational in his response to the Allied bombing campaign on German soil. His anger took control, and he ordered greater and more punishing strikes on London, believing that would bring the British to their knees. It had the opposite effect. Yet, oddly, when German cities began to be hit, Hitler refused to visit them, or even receive people from those areas.

By late July 1943, the Eighth Air Force was big enough for the next phase of its air war. They called it "Blitz Week," with one mission scheduled every day for seven days. No longer would they send fifty or sixty bombers on a mission. The U.S. Army Air Forces could now send hundreds of B-17s into the sky. On July 24, in the largest raid since the war began, 324 bombers attacked the harbor installations and factories used by the Germans in Norway. The rest of the raids were directed against Germany proper. On July 25, bombers flew to Kiel, Hamburg, and Warnemunde. Because the clouds were too thick over the primary target, LeMay's Third Division went to the secondary target in Rostock.

The next day, July 26, 1943, 292 Fortresses got into a tremendous air battle with German fighters. Between the fighters and bad weather, only ninety-two planes from the Third Division were able to hit a railway yard and a rubber factory in Hanover. The weather grew worse the next day, and the crews were given the day to rest. On the following day, LeMay sent his bombers out against a Focke-Wulf factory in Oschersleben, hitting the plant and knocking it out of production for a month. On July 29 the bombers split up, with the First Division hitting Kiel, and the Third Division going after Warnemunde for the second time. By the end of the week, the Americans could only muster 186 Fortresses. The Germans had inflicted tremendous damage on the fleet. 100 planes and 1,000 men were lost in just one week. Seventy-five suffered psychological breakdowns. Ralph Nutter found the worst time was coming back to his quarters and seeing the empty bunks. "They quickly moved out their belongings and replaced them with new crews," Nutter remembered, "but those were my friends who had been there. It was very upsetting to see [the new men]."[1]

It was hard on everyone—even the men who stayed behind. One member of the ground crew, William Teitelbaum, was a kid from Brooklyn, New York. His task was putting the bombs in the

B-17s. One of the planes he worked on happened to have a crew who were all from Brooklyn as well. The airman spent all of his time with the crew. They went to the pub together. They went on leave together. They became his best friends. One day, the crew simply did not return. Teitelbaum survived the war, but never made another friend for the rest of his life.[2]

Every airman had a different way of handling the stress. Some men could not attend any of the funerals on the base; it was too difficult. Many tried not to get attached to any of the new crews. Mike Kruge remembered that "old timers" might have appeared to be unfriendly to the new men, but it was really just self-defense. "You just didn't want to get to know them because it hurt too much when they didn't come back."[3]

The name, rank, and date of the last mission of each lost airmen was put up on a wall, which served as a memorial. There were no funerals for most of the thousands of airmen who were killed. Their families received only a notification of their deaths, and months later, a foot locker filled with their personal possessions. An officer always checked the contents before sending it home to make sure there was nothing inside that might upset the families. In most cases, their bodies were never recovered. Sometimes civilians who found the bodies would bury them with temporary markers that later disappeared. The only reminder of these men back at Chelveston was the wall of names, which itself was lost when the barracks was torn down after the war.

· · · · ·

A VERY BAD PLAN

Shortly after Blitz Week, the commander of the Eighth Air Force, Ira Eaker, came to see LeMay at Elveden Hall. That was out of the norm, as officers were usually summoned to Eaker's head-quarters. Eaker had not allowed LeMay to fly on any of the missions during Blitz Week because he needed him to lead the next big planned mission. The target this time would again be German plane factories and the ball bearing production facilities in Schweinfurt and Regensburg. But instead of flying back to England, LeMay's planes would keep flying all the way to Africa. LeMay's group would refuel, rearm, and head back to their original bases, hitting more targets on the way. In football terms, it was a "razzle-dazzle" play, and the planners at Bomber Command hoped their scheme would catch the Germans off guard and confuse them. Eaker was actually against the idea from the start because there were too many variables involved. He also did not believe he had the manpower for it. But the idea came from Washington, and he had no choice. "We were pushed into it before we were ready," he told an interviewer late in his life. "I protested it bitterly." As one of his commanders explained, "It was like lining up the cavalry, shooting your way in and then shooting your way out again."[4]

It was still unclear where in Africa LeMay should land his planes. But if the plan was successful, the U.S. would continue the operation and force the Germans to divide their forces to meet air attacks on two fronts. LeMay made a quick trip to the headquarters of the Fifteenth Air Force in Tunis to find an airfield that could provide bombs, fuel, and service for a large group of heavy bombers. Colonel Lauris Norstad, the chief of staff for General Spaatz, told LeMay he would find everything he required in Telergma, Algeria. However, Norstad's information was old. Although at one point, Telergma had everything LeMay would have needed, the fighting in North Africa had ended by that time, and unbeknownst to Norstad—or LeMay—the U.S. Army had moved on to

Sicily. All the supplies and equipment had gone along with it. That was just the beginning of the misinformation, bad timing, and bad luck that would turn the plan into one of the greatest disasters of the war for the Eighth Air Force.

LeMay worried about the weather. He knew that if his planes were clouded in, they would not be able to coordinate with the other planes. Timing was crucial, and the need to maintain radio silence to hide from the enemy meant they had no way to communicate once the operation began. Planning for the worst, LeMay had his crews practice instrument takeoffs. The instruments available in 1943 were still rudimentary. The pilot on the left side would take off, watching only the instruments in these practice sessions. The co-pilot on the right side would watch and take the controls if anything went wrong.

On the afternoon before the mission, a young officer arrived from the States to discuss a secret new device that would be used for radar flying. The officer, Edward D. Gray, assumed that LeMay would be too busy to meet with him because of the upcoming mission, and they would have to reschedule. But LeMay had everything in place for the Regensburg-Schweinfurt mission, and to Gray's astonishment he was ushered into LeMay's office. Again, Gray assumed LeMay would have his mind on the mission and be unable to focus. For almost an hour, as Gray briefed LeMay on the radar machine that would help bomb targets in bad weather, LeMay offered no small talk. He said nothing throughout Gray's presentation. Then, at the end of the talk, LeMay asked what Gray described as "sharply pertinent" questions.[5]

LeMay then ended the discussion to go to the mission briefing. Gray came along and sat in. LeMay spoke to the crews, answering all of their questions. He gave them some final reminders and warned them, one more time, to stay alert. As he left, he walked over to Gray and asked, "Don't you think it might be better to use a two-group combat wing with each group sixty percent equipped with your gadget rather than a three-group wing with one strongly equipped group unbalancing the other two?"[6] Even though Gray was not flying on the upcoming mission, he had become completely involved in it during the briefing, and LeMay's question caught him off guard. Here was a man preparing to lead a very dangerous combat mission. This could easily be his last day alive. Yet he demonstrated no fear or concern for his own safety; he focused only on the mission and thoroughly briefed his men. And he was still considering the radar device throughout it all. LeMay's suggestion had never occurred to Gray. Only later, after a great deal of thought, did he realize that LeMay was absolutely correct.

On the morning of the actual mission, August 17, 1943, the crews were awakened shortly after midnight. One ominous sign the men saw almost immediately: instead of dried eggs, they were given fresh eggs for breakfast and extra bacon. They called it "the last supper."[7] But when the men came down to the flight line, it was obvious that everything was locked in with the thickest fog they had seen yet. In a complete reversal of typical summer conditions, the skies over the target were unusually clear, while England was covered in fog. So the men waited there . . . and waited. When they received word that the mission had been bumped up two hours, they emerged from the planes and just sat around on the tarmac.[8]

The plan called for LeMay's Division of 150 bombers to head for Germany, along with a larger force of 230 bombers of the First Division led by General Robert Williams. The two wings would fly together as if they were heading for the same I.P., but then they would separate and head for different targets—LeMay to Regensburg and Williams to Schweinfurt, where most of Germany's ball-bearing production was located. After the bombing LeMay would head out over the Alps to Africa, and Williams would head back to England. The plan was brutally simple: LeMay would fight his way in and Williams would fight his way out.[9]

If the mission was postponed, the information could leak, and the Germans would not be caught off-guard. Bomber Command could cancel it altogether, or could go ahead with it and risk losing an untold number of bombers taking off in the thick fog. The decision had to be made within the hour. Because there was so much pressure from Washington to produce "results," and because it was believed that the ball-bearing plants were crucial to Germany's war machine, the bombardment commander of the Eighth Air Force, Frederick Anderson, finally gave the go ahead. The Germans, of course, were aware of the importance of these targets, and both sites were strongly defended.

LeMay, waiting at his headquarters for the "go" from bomber command, came up with the idea that the ground crews hold flashlights all the way down the runways to enable some sort of visibility. When he finally got the approval and the planes started their engines, LeMay dashed from his headquarters to the airfield in Snetterton Heath, where the 96th Bomb Group was about to take off. His car found its way to the lead plane piloted by Thomas F. Kenny. LeMay was to fly as co-pilot. He got out of the car, threw his gear into the plane, and then hopped in himself.[10]

Just getting 146 B-17s off the ground in that severe fog, having them fly through the clouds, and then find each other and fall into formation above England was an amazing accomplishment. The Third Division was now ready to turn and head across the Channel. But something was wrong. The eighteen squadrons of American Thunderbolts and sixteen squadrons of British Spitfires that were to accompany them were nowhere in sight. The entire First Division of bombers was unable to take off as well. LeMay and his planes were in the sky alone. Since they were supposed to fly all the way to Africa, they had to conserve fuel and get there before dark. Instead they were forced to circle while LeMay waited for a second "Go" from Bomber Command. To put it mildly, LeMay was not happy and voiced his disapproval.

"Here we were up in the air, all assembled, and there were no fighters around, and there was not any First Division airborne. Old Fred Anderson down at Pinetree[11] was in severe trouble. He had to decide whether to scrub the whole mission, or send me in alone. So he said Go. We went." LeMay always had a simple way of stating things. But he pointed out that had the fighters and the bombers of the First Division been practicing those blind takeoffs the way he had done, all of those planes would have taken off as planned. Instead, the mission was turning into a fiasco. Years later, LeMay noted that the official Air Force record of the day did not recount the mission truthfully. "The history books will tell you that eighteen squadrons of Thunderbolts (p-47s) and sixteen squadrons of Spitfires were assigned to provide cover for our bombers on that day. And I will tell you that I led that mission, and not a damn Jug (American P-47) or one damn Spit (British Spitfire) did I see. Our fighter escort had black crosses on their wings (the Luftwaffe)."[12]

The fight began with a call over the radio "fighters at two o'clock," when they reached Belgium, and it never seemed to stop.

Whole squadrons of German fighters, one after another, came at the formation, resulting in one of the fiercest air battles of the war. "We got punched all over the ring that day, and sometimes it looked as if we were going to be knocked through the ropes," was LeMay's assessment, but he flew at the front and did not see the worst of it.[13] The Third Division lost twenty-four bombers. Later, when the First Division finally got off the ground, the Germans were ready for them as well. The First lost another thirty-six bombers, bringing the number of losses to sixty, which translated to six hundred lost airmen who were either killed instantly or taken prisoner. Four crews made it to Switzerland, where they spent the rest of the war imprisoned.

There were moments when many of the crews thought not one plane would make it back. Although LeMay was able to drop his bombs right on the target, he had no idea of the full extent of the disaster until he landed. One crew member described the assault in a letter he wrote to LeMay later:

> That's what I still can't get out of my mind. There were two different 17's which went *whuff*. That was it: just *whuff*, and they were gone. We saw debris flying around from one and saw absolutely nothing from the other. The plane and its entire crew and bomb load and everything else, seemed to disappear as if some old-fashioned magician had waved a wand.
>
> There were Forts falling out of formation with bad fires. Then we'd try to count the chutes and then our attention would be directed somewhere else and couldn't count any more chutes. We'd look again, and the airplanes were gone, and also the people with chutes. There were more fighters coming in, with the leading edges of their wings all fiery...

And there was that one airman going down, doubled up, just turning over and over. He went right through the formation, and nobody seemed to hit him, and he didn't collide with any of the airplanes. He just fell fast and furious, over and over, no chute, no nothing. I wondered who he was. Did he come out of a Fort named Lewd Lucy or one named Wayfaring Stranger or the Nebraska Cornball? I had friends flying in crews of Forts like that, and maybe he was one of my friends. But his own mother wouldn't have known him then, and certainly she wouldn't have known him after he hit the ground.[14]

Both LeMay's Third Division and Williams' First Division faced the largest German fighter squadrons of the war—as many as 300 planes. And because of the delay, the Luftwaffe fighters were able to land, refuel, rearm, and regroup in time to hit Williams' Division after they hit LeMay. Some of the B-17 crews were worried that their guns would melt from the constant firing. They stood ankle-deep in shells as the battle raged for more than half an hour, and they were still a hundred miles from the target. One airman said it looked like a parachute division because so many men had to bail out. Another said that he had flown sixty-nine missions and "none of them were this bad."[15]

In some cases, crews witnessed things so horrific that they literally could not believe their eyes. Only later, when their stories were corroborated by others, did they sink in. One crew saw the bomber next to it catch a direct hit and the cockpit fill with flames. "The co-pilot crawled out of his window, held on with one hand, reached back for his chute, buckled it on, let go, and was whisked back into the horizontal stabilizer," remembered the pilot in the next plane. "I believe the impact killed him. His chute never opened."[16]

It wasn't just the Americans who were unnerved by this battle. The sight of the vast U.S. armada also left the German pilots shaken. "We climbed and made perfect contact with the Boeings," recalled Lieutenant Alfred Grislawski. "There were so many of them that we were all shaken to the marrow."[17]

The day was not over. Those planes that made it through the battle, regardless of whether they had been hit and had wounded on board, still had to fly to Africa. Two of the Groups—the 94th and the 385th—ran into still more German fighters as they headed south over the Alps, and three more B-17s were lost. All the bombers were supposed to rally over the Brenner Pass, but because of the long wait in forming over England, they were already short on gas and had to fly to Africa immediately. By this time, they were free of the German fighters. When they reached the Mediterranean, they descended to a lower altitude to save fuel. They made it to Telergma at about 6:00 p.m., after an 18-mile course correction due to a navigational error. Their fuel tanks were empty.

There, they found the day's next surprise. All the mechanics, spare parts, fuel, and bombs that Lauris Norstad had promised just two weeks earlier were gone. When the final group of twelve planes, which had seen the worst of the fighting, reached Telergma, the leader, Colonel Beirne Lay, was surprised to hear LeMay grousing about the lack of mechanics. "Didn't he know what a beating his division had taken? The plain fact was he did not know. This mission, like all others, had been flown in radio silence."[18]

The majority of the planes were so badly damaged that they were no longer flyable. There were no mechanics or spare parts.

There was not even much food for the men, except for the provisions LeMay wisely told each man to bring for himself. They slept on the ground under the wings of their planes like the pilots in the old Army Air Corps that LeMay remembered from his college days. Parachutes were bunched up and used as pillows.

In World War II parlance, it was a "snafu."[19] Every war contends with them when incorrect information is passed along, assumptions are made, and nothing goes right, resulting in costly mistakes. But the most important element regarding these errors is how commanders deal with them. Ira Eaker had originally expected LeMay's planes to head back to the Continent the next day. Between the disastrous losses in both divisions over Schweinfurt and Regensburg, and the mess in Africa, that was clearly impossible. Eaker headed down to Telergma himself on August 19 to see if he could help. What he saw when he arrived left him dumbfounded.

LeMay had already set up his headquarters in a tent and was personally overseeing the maintenance work on the planes, which was being done by the crew members. The most damaged planes were cannibalized for spare parts to get the others flying. The men were not qualified mechanics, but LeMay knew every bolt in the B-17 and was able to guide each crew along. What amazed Eaker was that LeMay did not complain and showed no sign of discouragement. There he was, in the desert, moving quietly and efficiently from bomber to bomber in order to get the job done.

What followed next was one of the stranger arguments between LeMay and Eaker to occur in the war. Eaker wanted the division to merely return and avoid the continent altogether. LeMay wanted to proceed as planned with a bomb run on the way back. Though the mission back to England had to be delayed, he had every intention of going through with it. "No Curt," Eaker disagreed. "There'll be no mission. Your men will not be subjected to hostilities on the return to England. We'll see to it that you go across North Africa and over the Bay of Biscay at night."[20] But LeMay observed that the Germans already thought the Division was out of the war. They would be caught off guard if the same Division rematerialized and came back across France to bomb it in broad daylight. Besides, said LeMay, it would be bad for morale if they had to sneak back home.

LeMay's argument prevailed. In spite of the disaster in front of him, Eaker was comforted by the sight of the commander and all his men busily working on their planes despite having almost nothing to work with. Never had he seen the best of American tenacity and ingenuity so vividly demonstrated. Just one week later, on August 24, 1943, LeMay made the return trip to England, hitting Bordeaux on the way with bombs shipped in from bases near Telergma. Whatever planes could not be repaired were left in the African desert.

Once again the Allies did not understand the impact of the mission on the other side, as ball bearing production dropped by 38 percent after the raid. Albert Speer said that Germany "barely escaped a catastrophic blow" and that the Allies were right to take aim at the ball bearing plants. But their crucial mistake was spreading out their forces and not concentrating on Schweinfurt.[21] It was not just the Allies who did not understand the impact of these attacks. When Speer spoke to Hitler after the attack on Schweinfurt, the German leader was in great spirits because "the countryside was strewn with downed American bombers." Although true, every plant in Schweinfurt had been hit and was on fire. "But what really saved us was the fact that from this time on the enemy to our astonishment once again ceased his attacks on the ball-bearing industry," Speer later revealed.[22]

In spite of the losses in the Schweinfurt-Regensburg mission, Arnold and Eaker were certain that daylight, pinpoint raids would eventually work. They were not ready to accept the British concept of nighttime area bombing. LeMay was equally positive about the future of this strategy. "I think everybody is convinced now that four-engine bombers are here to stay, that they can't be stopped," LeMay told an interviewer. "We have never been turned back from a target and never will be turned back from a target."[23] But the day before that interview took place, the Eighth came close to being stopped over Stuttgart. Between bad weather and green crews, 45 B-17s out of 338 were lost in yet another very costly mission. The numbers of B-17s lost to German fighters was growing worse, not better. The arrival of new American planes and crews in faster numbers was the only source of optimism.

During that bloody autumn, there were times when both sides wondered who actually had the upper hand in the air war over Europe. The Eighth Air Force was suffering catastrophic losses. One unit, the 100th, arrived just four months earlier with 140 officers in its crews. By October, only three of them were left. Ralph Nutter was one of two surviving navigators out of an original contingent of thirty-five.

But even though the losses seemed unsustainable, LeMay remained focused, determined, and kept his eye on the larger picture. He knew that the German ability to wage war was slowly being whittled away. "It will swing back and forth," he told the men in a post-mission briefing. "The fighters are the last weapon the Germans have, but they will not stop us. From our intelligence reports we get from Germany from underground sources, we are accomplishing our mission—to destroy the German war industries. We are doing it! We are going to have to pay a price for it, but we are doing it . . . . They are using twin-engine (fighter) planes and accurate reports state they are using a lot of obsolete stuff."[24]

LeMay was correct. The Germans were losing the fight, but not because they were using obsolete planes. The German capacity for building fighters had not diminished. Under the brilliant supervision of Speer, the production of fighters, rockets, and even advanced jet planes would only increase in the coming year. Just before the end of the war, German industry produced an impressive 40,000 aircraft in 1944, in spite of constant bombing and delays in obtaining materials. But the United States produced 96,000 that year. Although German design was phenomenally creative, the Germans concentrated on craft and not mass production like the Americans. And although they had an abundance of slave labor, it could not match American labor, which was more motivated, better fed, and lived in freedom. Finally, the ultimate downfall for the Germans was the one commodity they could not replace: seasoned pilots. The most experienced pilots in the Luftwaffe were lost on every raid and they were replaced by inexperienced pilots.

When the war began, the Luftwaffe pilots were, by far, the best trained and most experienced pilots in the world. None of them came to combat units until they had 250 hours of flight training—far more than the Americans—creating a strong fraternity of fighting elites. Four years later, in 1943, pilots came into combat with as little as 100 hours of training. Conversely, by 1944 American pilots had much better training and would not go into combat until they had between 325 to 400 hours. In just one month in 1944, 20 percent of the veteran fighter pilots in the Luftwaffe were lost and replaced with pilots who had very limited understanding of the complexities of what they were facing.

That same autumn, Hap Arnold came to visit LeMay at his head-quarters in Elveden Hall on an inspection trip to the Eighth Air Force. It was their first time meeting. Arnold had heard a great deal about the young commander. Less than a month after the visit, LeMay was promoted to brigadier general on September 28, 1943, becoming the youngest general in the United States Army at the age of thirty-six. Instead of being pleased, however, LeMay was annoyed that he had not been promoted earlier, despite being the head of a Division and commanding people of higher rank for several months. It was an oversight. When people congratulated him on receiving his star, all he could mutter was, "It's about time."[25]

After the deadly mission to Stuttgart, the Eighth Air Force did not go back to Germany for three weeks. But when it resumed, the death toll was just as bad. On September 27, 1943, the bombers were unable to hit the port of Emden and had to make a return run five days later. On October 4, twelve B-17s went down over Aachen. On October 8, thirty went down over Bremen. But the following day, the bombers had such spectacular results hitting and knocking out the aircraft factories in Marienburg that an RAF chief called it "the best bombing we have seen in the war."[26] It did not come without a cost. Twenty-eight bombers were lost. And the next day, thirty bombers were destroyed on a mission to Munster. More than one thousand Americans were lost altogether.

Following the bombing mission to Munster on October 11, LeMay conducted a debriefing, and went down the list as each group leader stood up in the auditorium and recounted his group's results. But the auditorium suddenly grew quiet when he called on Robert Rosenthal, a young lieutenant from Brooklyn. Rosenthal was the leader of the 100th group, and the only pilot to stand up. All the others—twelve out of thirteen B-17s—had been lost. During a furious seven-minute battle with German fighters, Rosenthal's plane was riddled with bullets, and both his waist gunners were severely wounded. He still managed to hit his target, but then he had to fight his way back through the onslaught until he made it to the English Channel.

LeMay's face was contorted in anger as Rosenthal spoke, but his wrath was not directed at the young lieutenant. Instead, LeMay was furious with the commanding officer of Rosenthal's group, Colonel Chick Harding. Harding was a West Pointer, a charismatic and popular officer, but LeMay thought Harding was too lax with his crews. Harding did not push his groups to train enough, so they consistently produced terrible results. The 100th became known as a "hard luck" group. LeMay should have fired him, but, uncharacteristically, he hesitated because he liked him. He kept putting it off until he was relieved of the task when Harding returned to the States for health reasons. But years after the war, LeMay was still critical of the way he handled this episode, writing, "I knew I had to fire him but I just couldn't. I thought he'd snap out of it. That taught me a lesson."27

If it was bleak for the Americans, it was worse for the pilots in the Luftwaffe. But the Germans were about to add a new weapon to their arsenal.

On October 14, 291 B-17s flew on a second mission to Schweinfurt. Sixty planes were lost. The German fighters had developed the ability to fire air-to-air rockets at the bombers while they were out of range of the B-17 guns. When these rockets hit, they could cut an American bomber in half. Historian Donald Miller described the engagement as "a titanic struggle between two large and murderous air armies, one with 229 bombers and the other with over 300 fighters. The battle line extended for 800 miles and the action was continuous for three hours and fourteen minutes."[28]

LeMay was grounded for these missions. Eaker would not allow him to fly after the mission to Africa. LeMay protested, but to no avail. Arnold and Eaker could not afford to lose him. He seemed to talk less than ever, but those closest to him explained that he always had his men on his mind. In one incident, the 385th Group could not take off because the Luftwaffe had bombed its runways. The group commander, Colonel Elliott Vandevanter, tried to get instructions from his immediate superior. He was told by the officer's assistant that the group commander was asleep and was not to be disturbed. Vandevanter must have been annoyed, because he then called LeMay for advice, knowing full well what would happen next. LeMay told him exactly what to do. Then LeMay sent his chief of staff, August Kissner, to immediately wake up the Group commander and fire him.[29]

August Kissner had become LeMay's alter ego. A West Point graduate who had done his flight training a year after LeMay, Kissner had been assigned by Eaker when LeMay became the head of the Third Division. It may have seemed like an odd fit to an outside observer. Kissner had impeccable taste, perfect social grace, and was quite cultivated. Unlike LeMay, he was perfectly comfortable in social settings and knew how to comport himself. As LeMay's chief of staff, he focused on relieving him of the paperwork of command so he could concentrate on fighting the war. He would stay with him for many years to come.

"Augie was the most polite individual I ever encountered. Never used a bad word or picked up the wrong fork," LeMay remembered. "Helen would tell me about him coming around to talk to her (in postwar years) about the things I did which I shouldn't do. But he was a tower of strength. I had complete confidence in him."[30]

In almost every other case, Kissner would have been seen as LeMay's "hatchet man," but because he was such a gentleman, no one ever referred to him that way. For his part, Kissner thought LeMay's reputation of being surly and nasty was unfair and undeserved. "He was always intensely serious rather than tough," Kissner insisted. "His responsibility was so much on his mind every minute of the day that he wanted results from others in the earliest possible time. He never raised his voice, but by virtue of facial expression he could seem to be angered and adamant. He demanded results in a few words and [then] frequently walked away. To me he was never tough."[31]

LeMay did not allow himself much recreation. Occasionally he took a hunting trip to the nearby fields owned by the local lords who opened up their game reserves to the Americans. Even more rarely, he would play softball, wearing a beat-up orange baseball cap. He was a very strong hitter. But LeMay never went in much for physical exercise and, unlike other commanders in all the services, he did not push his men to do regular calisthenics. Ralph Nutter could not remember any exercise programs during his entire time serving under LeMay. He also did not push the men to attend religious services.

The devastating autumn of 1943 brought about a shuffle in leadership. Ira Eaker was replaced by Lieutenant General James Doolittle, the national hero who led and survived the carrier-based bombing raid over Tokyo just four months after Pearl Harbor. Eaker pleaded with his old friend Hap Arnold to reconsider, but Arnold would not. It was not an easy choice, but for Arnold, results were all that counted and Eaker was not getting them fast enough. Old friendships did not matter. Eaker was transferred to lead the effort in the Mediterranean and told it was a promotion, but he knew the truth. Carl Spaatz was also brought to London to help General Eisenhower with the air operations for D-Day.

Doolittle understood that the stalemate over Europe would end only when the Luftwaffe was defeated. On his first visit with the head of the Eighth Air Force Fighter unit, General William Kepner, he noticed a sign on the wall that read: "The first duty of the Eighth Air Force Fighters is to bring the bombers back alive." Doolittle told Kepner to take it down immediately and replace it with: "The first duty of the Eighth Air Force is to destroy German fighters!"[32] Kepner had been waiting for just this sort of directive.

Inversely, the head of the German Air Force, Hermann Goering, issued a change in tactics around the same time, which had a very negative effect on his pilots. According to Adolf Galland, the German fighter commander, the day the Luftwaffe lost the air war was the day Goering told his fighters to avoid the American fighters altogether. Galland called it Germany's "greatest tactical error" of the war, causing his pilots to lose their élan and develop a deep fear of the American fighter.[33]

In November 1943, LeMay was ordered to return to the States to offer a first-hand account of the air war at training bases around the country and speak at Bond Drives. "A Bond Show Bill" was what LeMay called his public speaking duties. He would have preferred to be in the lead plane facing a fighter attack than at a lectern in front of a large audience. But it would give him the chance to see Helen and Janie and, of course, it was an order. He was joined by Hubert "Hub" Zemke from the fighter force. At first they planned to fly back, but the November weather was forbidding—winter had come early to the North Atlantic. When they were told the *Queen Elizabeth* was sailing for New York that night, LeMay and Zemke were driven quickly to the harbor. Finding space on the ship was not a problem as the huge passenger ship had been converted to a troop carrier. It ferried soldiers to England but was almost empty on the return trip to America. The voyage took five days and offered Curtis LeMay the first chance since 1941 to relax and read without the pressures of command. Transatlantic crossings were still subject to U-boat attacks, but the *Queen Elizabeth*, although an enormous target, was also the fastest cruising ship in the world and could outrun a U-boat. Upon arrival in Manhattan, LeMay, Zemke, and a few other combat veterans in the group took the first train to Washington.

To LeMay's surprise, he was considered a hero in the halls of the Pentagon. He saw Arnold again, and they talked about the war in Europe. Arnold mentioned almost in passing that the new B-29 was running into more problems than anyone anticipated. But he said little more. LeMay was given a schedule of his tour and a copy of his speech, written by Sy Bartlett, a writer who was serving as a communications officer.[34] The speech told some personal stories about the air war to convey to the audience the nature of the difficulties the men faced, but although the stories were vivid, the true extent of the terror and death was left out. Helen met her husband in Washington, and the two of them went back to Cleveland together for a two-day leave.

LeMay had not seen his family in fifteen months. He was shocked when he saw Janie, who was now a very precocious five-year-old—hardly the small child he left in 1942. Janie and Helen had been living with Helen's parents in Cleveland the entire time. On the first night back, LeMay was amazed at the abundance of food, the abundance of central heat, the abundance of hot water, and just about everything else. Even with shortages and rationing, Americans had more than anyone else on earth.

When LeMay sat down in the living room in front of the fire with Janie, he did not understand why the little girl wanted him to come out on the front porch and sit in the swing with her. It was unusually cold for late November, and he tried to talk his daughter into staying inside the warm house next to the fire. No, she insisted on going out. Just when he was about to argue the point further, he noticed Helen motioning him to stop talking and go outside.

It was early evening and already dark. People were bustling by on their way home from work as his daughter swung with a father she barely remembered. Passersby nodded to the pair. Janie acknowledged the gesture with a large smile and a wave. That evening, after Janie had gone to sleep, Helen explained to her husband why it was so important for him to sit outside with his daughter. Some of the kids in the neighborhood, Helen said, had begun to doubt that Janie really had a father at all, since no one had ever seen him. Janie wanted everyone to see that he existed.

The speeches were concentrated, and the tour was intense. LeMay spoke at civilian halls, training bases, and the factories that produced the big bombers they flew. It did not make sense to LeMay that people could not grasp the importance of their work on their own. "In one way it seems strange that workers back in the United States had to be bopped in the face with such accounts, in order for them to offer a whole-souled devotion to the job which they were doing, in providing the mechanical equipment with which we warred. But there was that calculable difference between the initiated and the uninitiated—the person at the Front and the person at home—the soldier and the civilian," he later wrote.[35] He told the graphic stories as best he could—he thought the other speakers far superior to himself—and he was happy when the whole thing was over.

LeMay was in the States a little over a month and back in England before Christmas. It was not the happiest Christmas for the troops of the Eighth Air Force. After the bloody autumn, the odds of surviving to the magic 25th mission seemed close to impossible.[36] Americans were asked to stay off the railroad during the holiday to allow English servicemen and civilians the chance to get home, so London was off-limits. The Americans spent the holiday on their bases, and although the cooks did their best to spruce up the meals and there was some singing, it was remembered as one of the gloomier holidays. Most of the servicemen were just as happy when it passed, not realizing that the worst of the war was over.

•   •   •   •

FIGHTER SUPPORT

One of the costliest mistakes made by the Army Air Forces in World War II was not developing a fighter plane that could escort the bombers to the target and back. The high command in Washington reasoned the B-17s could defend themselves. They were wrong. And after the terrible casualties of the Schweinfurt-Regensburg mission, Washington could no longer ignore the problem. The day after that disastrous raid, September 7, 1943, 185 B-17s hit three locations in France and Belgium. However, this time they had American fighters with them on the entire trip. Not one Luftwaffe fighter got near a bomber. The answer was now obvious.

In early 1944, the air war in the skies over Europe took a dramatic turn when a small plane produced by the Americans years before but then ignored was brought into combat. The P-51 "Mustang" was a sleek, fast, highly agile single-engine fighter. It was a beautiful plane designed by a German-born engineer, Edgar Schmued, who emigrated to the United States after World War I. Schmued worked for North American Aviation, which built the plane for the Royal Air Force to use in 1941. But although the plane was tremendously flexible and in many ways superior to the German fighters, it had one serious flaw—it was vastly underpowered with a small engine and limited range. That changed when an American air attaché in England, Lieutenant Colonel Thomas Hitchcock, saw the Mustang fly and suggested that Washington switch its engine with the British-built Merlin by Rolls Royce. This, Hitchcock thought, could turn the plane into a high altitude fighter. A larger fuel tank was added as well. The experiment worked far better than anyone hoped.

Suddenly, the plane that Hap Arnold, Ira Eaker, and Carl Spaatz did not have on their priority list became the most sought after fighter in the American arsenal. Soon, additional drop tanks appeared under each wing, and within six months, the P-51s had the ability to fly all the way to Poland and back at remarkable speeds of over 400 miles an hour, reaching altitudes of 40,000 feet. In the first three months, the Mustangs scored up to three times more kills per sortie than the P-47 Thunderbolts.[37]

On a mission to Brunswick, Halberstadt, and Oschersleben in Central Germany, where most of the German fighter planes were built, the Luftwaffe was shocked when the Mustangs came up behind them over their own territory. It was still a costly day for the U.S. Army Air Forces. Because the weather grew worse over England, two of the three divisions were called back. But the First Division, being only an hour from its target, was told to go on alone. Sixty bombers went down over Germany that day, along with another 600 airmen. It was not a good opener for Spaatz or Doolittle. But there was a bright spot. The Mustangs had destroyed fifteen German fighters without one loss.

Shortly afterwards, the blunt and caustic head of Germany's fighter force, General Adolf Galland, discovered the limits of telling the truth to the higher command. *Riechsmarschall* Hermann Goering was furious at Galland for telling Hitler that an American fighter had been shot down over Aachen.

"What's the idea of telling the Fuehrer that American fighters have penetrated into the territory of the Reich?" Goering demanded over the phone.

"*Herr Reichsmarschall*," Galland calmly responded, "they will soon be flying even deeper."

"That's nonsense, Galland, what gives you such fantasies? That's pure bluff!"

"Those are the facts, Herr Reichsmarschall!" Galland stood his ground. "American fighters have been shot down over Aachen. There is no doubt about it!"

"That's simply not true, Galland. It's impossible."

"You might go and check it yourself, sir; the downed planes are there in Aachen."

"Come now, Galland, let me tell you something. I'm an experienced fighter pilot myself. I know what is possible. But I know what isn't too. Admit you made a mistake."

Galland refused.

"What must have happened is that they were shot down much farther to the west. I mean, if they were very high when they were shot down they could have glided quite a distance farther before they crashed."

"Glided to the east, sir? If my plane were shot up ..."

"Now then, Herr Galland, I officially assert that American fighter planes did not reach Aachen."

"But, sir, they were there!"

"I herewith give you an official order that they weren't there! Do you understand? The American fighters were not there! Get that! I intend to report that to the Fuehrer."

Galland, who would lose his command and be placed under house arrest because of his tongue, shrugged as he responded to Goering, "Orders are orders, sir."[38]

The Eighth Air Force was beginning to swell with more planes and crews. There were now fourteen groups in LeMay's Third Division alone—almost 500 bombers. The U.S. Army Air Forces would put many hundreds of B-17s in the sky at one time, along with hundreds of fighter escorts. In March of 1944, just six months after he was made a Brigadier General, Curtis LeMay was promoted to Major General. He was thirty-seven years old, now the youngest Major General in the U.S. military.

In spite of the greater numbers of bombers and the P-51 escorts, the Germans continued to inflict heavy casualties. There was another huge offensive in late February called "Big Week." Its purpose was to destroy the German aircraft industry once and for all. Waves of B-17s in the hundreds went after the plane manufacturing plants, beginning with Brunswick-Leipzig in central Germany. At the same time, hundreds of fighters went after the Luftwaffe squadrons that were also known as Wolf Packs. On the first day, the reports were better than expected. The Germans lost 153 fighter planes. But the air battles that filled the sky with long, white, crisscrossing streaks of contrails were the most intense battles of the war and the most horrific—226 bombers were shot down over Germany. As costly as the losses were—and they were terrible—something else was happening. The crews of the Eighth Air Force were now convinced they were winning this war. Morale, which had hit bottom just a few months earlier, was high. But LeMay would not let up on his men. He continued to push them. They finally understood why he was so relentless. He was now the commander men wanted to fly under.

At the end of Big Week, the Eighth Air Force targeted Germany's heart and Hitler's capital—Berlin—with all its fury. It was understood that the Luftwaffe would put everything it had in the air to defend its capital, but it did not matter; the knowledge alone that these bombs were falling near Hitler gave the bomber crews an extra lift. Tommy LaMore, a descendant of the Cherokee tribe, was a B-17 gunner. "This was Hitler's town," LaMore remembered. "Go ahead, send the Luftwaffe up, go ahead, shoot at us with everything you've got, but here we are, blowing up your houses in front of your master-race eyeballs. I cheered when the bombs left the racks. 'Hold on to your sauerkraut, Adolf!' I yelled."[39]

On an 800-plane mission to Berlin later in the spring of 1944, Lieutenant Colonel Bob David was a Squadron Commander of thirty-six B-17s in the Third Division under LeMay. As the large contingent of planes assembled over England, the weather began to take a bad turn. The planes were recalled when David's group was already over the Channel, but because of radio jamming by the Germans, David and another group of thirty-six bombers ahead of him never received the order. Instead of an 800-plane mission, it was now a 72-plane mission. When they reached Berlin they encountered extremely heavy anti-aircraft fire. David was able to drop his bombs on the target, and amazingly he did not lose one plane. But the group ahead could not find the target. At the rallying point for the return home, the first group commander wanted to take another run at Berlin and ordered David to come along. David refused, thinking it was a foolhardy idea. "It would be a waste of planes and good flight crews to go back with no bombs to drop," David said, and told the other commander he would wait for him at the rally point. When the commander returned from his second run over Berlin, he had only six planes left out of the original thirty-six. In the debrief after the mission, LeMay listened to the explanation as to why the groups did not hear the recall. Then, after David explained why he refused to go back over Berlin, LeMay, cigar in mouth, berated him in front of the entire group for not following an order. David thought he had done right, but he felt terrible getting chewed out "by the old man."

The next day, David was called into the office of his commanding officer. This time, he thought he might be disciplined more severely and even lose his rank. Instead, to his amazement, LeMay offered him a cup of coffee. LeMay explained that although he could not condone David disobeying an order, he said he had "done the right thing." LeMay told him he was sending the officer of the first group back to the States because "he had obviously been here too long." Then LeMay pinned David's second Distinguished Flying Cross on him. "That was it," remembers David. "That was the ceremony—but it was the one most moving for me."[40]

LeMay showed little emotion. Those who saw him for the first time were taken aback by his personality. One congressman visiting the Eighth Air Force from Washington early in the war misinterpreted LeMay's rough edge as inhuman and unfeeling towards his troops and complained to LeMay's commander, General Eaker at the time, suggesting he be replaced. Ira Eaker ignored the congressman. The indifference even came across in his writings. After the disastrous first Regensburg mission and his week-long stay in Africa, LeMay summed it all up this way:

> People who were burned up in the air or on the ground, were burned up; and people buried by the Germans when there was anything left to bury, were buried; and people who were alive were carted off to Stalag Luft-something-or-other. The ones who drowned in the ocean were drowned, and the ones who were picked up by Air-Sea Rescue were picked up. The crews who were in Switzerland sat and ate Swiss chocolate, far as I know. And the crews who were left B-17-less because of battle damage which could not be quickly repaired at Telergma—they went home by transport. The rest of us attacked the Bordeaux/Merignac airfield on Tuesday, August 24th (1943), just one week after Regensburg. Then we came home too (minus three more airplanes) and went to work on other targets.[41]

It was more than matter-of-fact. He sounded cavalier. And since most people barely knew him, it is understandable that their first conclusion was that he was inhuman, feeling nothing about the death that surrounded him. The fact is, he felt each loss quite deeply. But few people outside his small inner circle understood this. He let no one else in. Those few who understood picked it up by intuition, not by anything he ever said.

But to his wife he could explain the thoughts and feelings that plagued him. One of a commander's more difficult jobs was going through the personal effects of crewmen killed in combat before they were sent to the survivors. In one of his many nightly letters back home to Helen, LeMay included a portion of a letter that a young flyer wrote to his next of kin. LeMay had typed it out from the long-hand note. Opening himself up in a way he never would with any-one else, he wrote this note to Helen by way of introduction:

> This letter was left by one of my boys shot down over L'orient. I am constantly amazed at the heights these kids rise to, when the big test comes. I sometimes wonder what I have ever done to deserve the command of an outfit like this. You have always com-plained about my not being sentimental enough. I think some-times I'm too soft to properly fight a war. After raising these kids from pups and leading them against the best pursuit and anti-aircraft defenses in the world, and having them come through the way they have, it hurts like hell to lose them.[42]

In Washington, the head of the Air Force, Hap Arnold, over-looked any negatives in LeMay's style for one reason: he produced better results than any other commander. Arnold certainly wanted victory. But there was another motive behind his drive to prove the success of strategic bombing. Arnold knew that if bombing played the key role in that victory for the U.S., then the chance of the Air

Force breaking away from the Army and becoming its own separate branch of the service was more likely.

Losses were still high. In April 1944 alone, the Eighth Air Force lost 409 bombers, more than any month in the war. But that spring, American planes were decisively winning the brutal war of attrition in the skies over Europe. The United States military machine finally caught up with its lack of preparedness at the start of the war, just as Germany and Japan were turning in the other direction. Although the Germans would fight on, most already foresaw the outcome. "Every time I close the canopy before taking off," wrote a Luftwaffe pilot that spring, "I feel I am closing the lid on my own coffin."[43]

After the war, during the war crime tribunal, as Hermann Goering sat in a jail cell in Nuremberg, an army intelligence officer asked him when he realized that Germany would lose the war. "The first time your bombers came over Hanover, escorted by fighters, I began to be worried. When they came with fighter escorts over Berlin—I knew the jig was up."[44]

CHAPTER SEVEN

THE BIGGEST GAMBLE OF THE WAR

By the spring of 1944, Curtis LeMay had soared out of obscurity to become the most innovative problem solver in the United States Army Air Forces. Only four years earlier, LeMay was an unknown lieutenant in the one branch of the military that had yet to prove itself. He had a reputation for being a good navigator and hard worker, but little more. He was now the youngest two-star general in the entire U.S. Army, and he had achieved that rank by merit alone.

His achievement was astounding in light of his relative isolation from his fellow officers in a system that rewarded relational connections. He did not chat with them at night over drinks, being incapable of small talk as well as too busy to socialize. He was a social misfit and known for being blunt, sarcastic, and sitting in the mess hall in complete silence. His facetious nickname from flight school—the "Diplomat"—was used as much as ever. Yet LeMay breezed past West Pointers and more popular officers because of his constant innovations in the nascent science of strategic bombing and his style of command, which inspired his troops and achieved better results than any one else. Both his superiors and contemporaries watched him closely as they adopted his ideas.

"LeMay came *naturally* to the bomber business," according to Air Force historian Herman S. Wolk. "He was simply very good at it. He knew how to identify a problem, zero in on it, and solve it. [He had] an ability to convince the men he led that he knew his business—how to command and to protect his men when they were in the skies. Success leads to success. His men knew that he could accomplish the mission with the *lowest possible loss rate.* They liked to fly for him because they knew he was the best at what he did."[1] The men were also willing to follow a commander who, rather than simply order them into battle, led them—no matter what the odds.

LeMay's rapid trajectory was pulling him further up the chain and away from the other men around him. Just as things finally moved in favor of U.S. forces in the late spring of 1944, Curtis LeMay's "Big Week," as he called it, came to an abrupt end. He was suddenly pulled from the Eighth Air Force and ordered back to Washington for reassignment. "No one ever felt it essential to explain exactly what this switching . . . was all about,"[2] he recalled with annoyance.

Up until that moment LeMay's complete concentration was on the war in Europe. His instrument was the B-17. He knew every moving part of that plane. He had been working with it since 1936. He knew the targets, the lousy weather, and the personalities at Bomber Command—what to avoid and whom to trust. He learned how to get around anything that blocked his immediate goal. LeMay did not have time to follow events in the Pacific, except for reading occasional intelligence reports. The transfer, which began as a rumor, was finally confirmed when he ran into Ira Eaker who was in England from his post in the Mediterranean for meetings. "You're going to India," he bluntly informed him in the clipped manner LeMay used so often himself. "It's the B-29."

Brilliant, LeMay thought. He knew nothing about the B-29 beyond stories he had heard—none of them positive. Though Hap Arnold had briefly mentioned that there were *problems* with the program when he saw him in Washington the previous November, he had not suspected that Arnold was thinking of bringing him in to solve them. He also did not realize that the word "problems" was an understatement.

LeMay was packing to leave England in June 1944. He had been fighting the Nazis for almost two years, longer than almost any other American, but he had been killing Germans from a distance of 25,000 feet. He had never seen his enemy, never taken aim at a human being through the sight of a rifle, or watched an enemy soldier fall after being hit with a bullet. So shortly after the D-Day invasion and before leaving Europe, LeMay called Bill Kepner, an old friend and commander of the Eighth Fighter Command, and asked to borrow a plane to go over and "have a look" at the men on the ground. Kepner laughed and said he had been thinking of doing the same thing. Two temporary landing strips had just been constructed near Omaha Beach, so the generals set out for Normandy in P-47 fighters.

After landing, they headed directly toward the fighting. Yet neither Kepner nor LeMay had thought of bringing helmets or weapons. Even worse, the battle lines were not static; Germans and Americans were all over Normandy and there was an equal chance of running into either. "We felt like a couple of extremely unarmed and defenseless civilians," LeMay recalled with some honesty. "Course, the dogfaces looked at us as if they shared that opinion."[3]

As the two visiting Army Air Force officers pushed farther towards the German lines, they came upon a new Opel automobile that had been abandoned by its Nazi owners. Like two teenagers, they started to work on it, hoping to take it for a drive, completely oblivious to their environment. As LeMay later recalled, "This was a lot of fun for Bill and myself too, because neither of us had ever seen a new Opel sitting innocently like a waif in a battlefield."[4]

If that was not strange enough, when ten combat engineers suddenly emerged from the woods with their captain, the entire group, apparently infected by this boyish spirit, joined them in working on the car. Suddenly, LeMay heard a loud crash and thought one of the engineers had thrown dirt on everyone. He looked around, saw all the men on the ground, and realized they had been shelled. It was a completely different experience from being high above the earth. He quickly joined the others on the ground where they stayed for the next ten minutes as the Germans shelled them. When it ended, the group returned to working on the vehicle and eventually got it started.

It was an uncharacteristic experience for LeMay. Known for sober judgment and taking only calculated risks, this battlefield jaunt and reaction to enemy fire seemed to be at odds with the instinct of common sense that he typically employed.

While LeMay admitted that the quick trip hardly gave him a true understanding of what an infantryman faced, his reaction to the entire experience was oddly detached, "On the whole I felt disappointed; I'd expected to see more in the way of actual fighting. All I got to see: a few dead Germans, a few captured Germans, a few shells exploding without causing any fatalities."[5]

He and Kepner were lucky that Arnold never heard about their jaunt.

· · · ·

"THE BIGGEST PLANE WE'D EVER SEEN"

LeMay flew back to the States near the end of June, retracing the same route he took heading to England in the autumn of 1942. His first stop in the continental U.S. was the military base in Presque Isle, Maine, where he and his crew spent the night. LeMay treated the men to a steak dinner with "extras" they had not seen in a long time: fresh milk, butter, and ice cream for dessert. "After nearly two years in England," his aide-de-camp, Major Theodore Beckmeier, wrote in his diary, "this was the grandest tasting meal many of us could remember."[6]

The next morning they flew to Washington, where LeMay granted his staff a two-week leave while he headed to the Pentagon to meet with General Arnold. LeMay assumed Arnold would sit down with him and explain all the problems he had briefly mentioned earlier. Instead, Arnold, having neither combat experience in the war nor answers to the B-29's problems, did not waste LeMay's time. He simply hung another Distinguished Flying Cross on LeMay's uniform and ordered him to replace the commander in India—immediately.

Once again, Curtis LeMay faced an enormous puzzle alone, with no one offering the slightest assistance.

It was understood that LeMay had to turn the operation around or else he would be fired. LeMay also knew that when Arnold ordered someone to do something, he was supposed to do it immediately. But LeMay protested. "If I'm going to have command of a bunch of airplanes that are strange to me, I'm going to fly that airplane first."[7] Arnold perceived the wisdom in LeMay's point and quickly ordered a special training program to be set up for LeMay in Grand Island, Nebraska, the B-29's main training facility.

After the meeting, LeMay was finally able to head to Cleveland to see Helen and Janie. But after only three days, the impatient Arnold sent an Air Force plane to take him to Grand Island. Without asking, LeMay put Helen and Janie onboard and brought them along, not knowing when or if he would see them again after he headed to the Pacific. With little housing available in this Midwestern city, it was fortuitous when LeMay ran into Sy Bartlett, his speechwriter from the bond drive in November. Bartlett was serving as an intelligence officer in Grand Island and living alone in a small cottage on a lake not far from the base. He invited the three LeMays to join him, and they were happy to accept. Janie LeMay was six years old and would recall that summer as an idyllic time in her childhood, the only period during the entire war when she saw her father almost nightly. The peaceful period sandwiched between two fronts, so different as to almost be different wars, lasted less than two months.

LeMay understood what he was up against immediately. On his very first flight, he noticed the B-29 had an inclination to veer to the left. He could compensate for that, but the mechanical issues were another story. He immersed himself in the plane's technology. But rather than asking the ground crews incessant questions, he simply worked alongside them and seemed to just absorb what they knew.

After LeMay qualified as a B-29 pilot, he said goodbye to his wife and daughter one more time. They went back to Cleveland while LeMay flew to New York and on to Asia. Although LeMay now had a taste of the "problems" Arnold had talked about, he still did not know the full extent of them.

The B-29 was the largest and costliest program of the entire war. With a price tag of $3 billion, it was even more expensive than the Manhattan Project.[8] It was also turning out to be the great fiasco of the war. "Innocence built the B-29," admitted one of its creators. "We could not have done it if we had known what we were getting into."[9]

The bomber was the most advanced airplane of its time. It was supposed to destroy the enemy's war industry without the terrible cost of an infantry war, saving lives and ensuring victory. Instead, plagued by problems, it was turning into a political football that the Navy kicked at every opportunity.

Yet it was a marvel to behold. People who first saw the B-29 in flight simply stood in awe, gaping at the silver giant and astounded at the sound of its four huge engines. Later in the war, on a destroyer in the middle of the Pacific, the surprised crew looked up to see a formation of B-29s flying over their ship. "Are they ours?" one of them asked, awestruck. "Nobody else could build anything as big and pretty and make it work," came his shipmate's reply.[10] It had a wingspan of 141 feet, twenty feet *longer* than the Wright Brothers' entire first flight forty years earlier. Two B-29s could fill a football field. The plane weighed more than 135,000 pounds fully loaded, twice as much as the B-17, and carried almost three times the bomb load—20,000 pounds. It was the first pressurized, high-altitude bomber in history. Its crew of eleven could travel comfortably for eighteen hours at an altitude above 30,000 feet—not unlike today's passenger jets.

The B-29 had an amazing range—it could fly 3,700 miles without refueling and travel up to 350 miles an hour. Its futuristic design caught the imagination of everyone who saw it. The shiny aluminum exterior with contrasting blue and white Army Air Forces insignia on the side and under its wings became the modern symbol of American strength and engineering capabilities. In contrast, the olive drab B-17, with its open gun hatches and temperatures of fifty degrees below zero now seemed as out of date as the tin helmets worn by troops in World War I. The B-29 quickly became as iconic as the Hershey bar or a bottle of Coke. The B-29 was the future. The B-29 was the U.S.A.

"As we adjusted our eyes to the bright sunlight," wrote twenty-year-old pilot Daniel Miller, Jr. in his diary upon first laying eyes on the B-29, "there before us about 150 yards away was a brand new, bright silver plane, much bigger than anything we had ever seen or even dreamed of." Miller, along with five other volunteers, had been brought to Alamogordo, New Mexico, to train on the B-29 in early 1944. "The blunt nose and the huge props were totally different than anything we had ever flown. My God it looked huge."[11]

But Hap Arnold had rushed the plane into service before solving its massive mechanical problems. Six months before the first prototype left the ground, 250 of them had been ordered. After the first flight, 1,600 were already on order.[12] Test pilots in Grand Island, Nebraska, were the first to notice the long list of defects that LeMay encountered. "The engines of the B-29 developed a very mean tendency to swallow valves and catch fire," wrote General Haywood "Possum" Hansell, who would be the first to command a squadron of B-29s. "The magnesium crankcases burned with a fury that defied all efforts to put them out. In addition, gun sighting blisters were either blowing out at high altitude or frosting up so badly that it was impossible to see through them."[13]

Those huge engines burned with such intense heat that they would just peel right off the wing in flight. Oil seemed to leak from every possible valve. "There were scores of other defects," LeMay later remembered, "either readily apparent or—worse—appearing insidiously when an aircraft was actually at work and at altitude. If you ever saw a buggy airplane, this was it."[14]

The problem was two-fold: the plane was a very complicated design, and it had been pushed into service before all the kinks could be worked out. In the official history of the war for the Department of the Army, Irving Brinton Holley, Jr. wrote:

> The B-29 program was the most complex joint production undertaking of the war....There were, for example, 1,174 engineering changes introduced even before the first item was officially accepted by the Air Forces. Some 900 of these had to be rushed through at the last minute as a result of findings made during flight tests.[15]

And some of these problems were being worked out as the plane flew missions. Beyond the mechanical problems, the plane was too complicated for crews to learn it in the time they had. "It was so complex that the average individual simply couldn't operate it.

A gunner had to take care of three motions at once, which is extremely difficult for anybody, especially in combat," General Hansell observed. "It was one of those cases where technology really did outrun itself."[16]

The accident rate in the training program back in the States was much higher than that of any other plane during the war. In fact, it turned out to be statistically safer to fly the B-29 in raids over Japan than to train in one back in the states. An airman who returned from combat in England to train navigators in B-29s was told by experienced colleagues: "The name Superfortress is for public relations purposes only....The pressure system is a joke.... You'd have been safer if you'd stayed in England."[17]

When the first contingent of B-29s flew off to India in early 1944, almost every one of them encountered some sort of mechanical problem. Two planes were lost in Karachi. One just disappeared with its crew over the ocean. No one knew why.

During the entire war, more American airmen would be lost in B-29s due to mechanical failure than enemy fire. "There are something like 55,000 different parts in a B-29," LeMay once observed, "and frequently it seemed that maybe 50,000 of them were all going wrong at once. Fast as they got the bugs licked, new ones crawled out from under the cowling."[18]

The plane's design dated back to 1939, when war planners feared England and then Russia might fall to the Nazis, requiring U.S. planes to fly much farther to retaliate in the event of war with Germany. But Boeing engineers had already been tinkering with the design for a much larger and more powerful bomber as early as 1936. Eleven months before World War II began, in January 1939, Hap Arnold asked General W. G. Kilner, a trusted aide and brilliant engineer, to anticipate the future and tell him what exactly this very large bomber would look like. Kilner's report was ready by June 1939, two months before Germany invaded Poland. Shortly after the invasion, Arnold asked the War Department to authorize him to ask the American aircraft industry to begin submitting designs for the super bomber based on the Kilner Report. He got the green light just three weeks later.[19] Boeing put together a team of its best aeronautical engineers, who were breathtaking in their genius. They were led by 28-year-old chief engineer, Edward Curtis Wells. On May 11, 1940, the first design plans reached the Air Corps Material Command at Wright Field. General Oliver Echols looked at the design and designated it the XB-29, nicknaming it the "Superfortress."[20] Eventually, 3,970 would be produced.[21]

The B-29 made its first flight on September 21, 1942, at Boeing Field in Seattle. Its chief test pilot, Eddie Allen, flew the large plane around Seattle for just over an hour and was greeted by the engineering staff upon his return. "She flew" was Allen's response, anticipating all the questions he knew would be coming his way. Throughout that fall, Allen took the plane up for more tests. The plane continued to perform perfectly, but in December Allen started to notice problems with the engines. On December 28, two engines went out during the flight. They were replaced, but two days later Allen encountered more engine problems. One month later, another engine went out on a test flight, and in February the other test plane had a serious fuel leak. These ominous problems culminated in the fateful test flight on February 18, 1943.[22] Allen was at the controls with nine of Boeing's best engineers on board. Shortly after takeoff, the number one engine caught on fire. Allen decided to return to the field and radioed back, "Fire in number one engine. Coming in. Had fire in engine and used CO_2 bottle and think we have it under control."[23] As he banked the great plane around and headed back to Boeing Field, he requested fire equipment stand by. But he was losing altitude quickly. Then the men at the Boeing tower heard someone shout: "Allen! Better get this thing down in a hurry—the wing spar's burning badly."[24] People at lunch in downtown Seattle looked up in horror to see the great aircraft just over 1,000 feet overhead with one of its wings on fire. One engineer tried to bail out, but the plane was already too low and he struck a power line, killing himself and flickering the electrical power in southern Seattle. Another engineer followed him, but his chute did not have time to open and he hit the ground. Seconds later, the plane hit the five-story Frye meat packing plant, killing everyone still on board, an untold number of employees in the building, and eventually six firemen who died fighting the intense blaze.[25]

Many people nearby assumed it was a Japanese attack. The B-29 was still a secret project, and FBI agents quickly created a cover story that the plane was a B-17. The fire was so intense that there was almost nothing left of the wreckage for anyone to know the difference. Two months later, pictures of the doomed plane taken by a bus driver were printed in a professional bus driver's newspaper. FBI agents confiscated all 500 copies.

The entire incident was reminiscent of the first test flight of the B-17 that also crashed, killing its crew. But this time, the program went ahead at full speed. "Arnold had committed himself to the B-29 project," observed LeMay, "and it would go forward."[26]

By 1944, the huge bomber had become a messy political problem. With a total production cost heading into the billions, Hap Arnold knew all too well that the B-29 had to justify its expense.

So far, that was not even close to happening. Inter-service rivalry exacerbated the problem. The Navy played the dominant role in the Pacific Theater. With all service branches competing for funds and limited materials, the Navy openly questioned this strikingly expensive airplane that was getting top priority in factories, precious metal, and tens of thousands of workers, but had not dented one roof in Japan. It was a salient point, especially when the Navy's sailors and marines were dying by the thousands to secure bases for these great planes; in July 1944, marines captured Saipan in the Marianas for the sole purpose of providing runways for the B-29 at a cost of 3,426 Marines killed and over 16,000 wounded. And those numbers of American casualties would only rise on Iwo Jima (6,000 dead) and Okinawa (12,000 dead).

The public, egged on by the press, was getting impatient for the United States to bomb Tokyo. After more than three years of war and horrific casualties, no American planes had struck the Japanese mainland since the carrier-based Doolittle raid shortly after Pearl Harbor—and that was done solely to boost morale. The Doolittle planes had done no damage to Japan's war industry. The inability of the B-29s to perform delayed both the likelihood of hitting Japan as well as the Air Force ever becoming a separate, respected entity from the Army. With all the stress, Hap Arnold was hospitalized with a heart attack, his third.

By 1944, the looming worry in the Pentagon was not whether the U.S. would win the war. That had already been determined. The only question would be the extent of casualties that the nation would suffer in order to reach the final chapter, and whether the public could endure the devastating losses that planners were predicting for an invasion of the Japanese mainland. General George Marshall worried that the war effort could lose public support if the ominous casualty predictions were even close to accurate. The Japanese were also beginning to confront their reduced chances of winning and were hoping for better surrender terms if Americans lost heart. The Pentagon pinned its hopes on the B-29. But there was very little reason for hope.

So while LeMay was still in Europe, Hap Arnold turned to one of his most capable commanders to get the B-29 back on track. General Haywood "Possum" Hansell was a slight, handsome, and brilliant officer. Nicknamed "Possum" in his West Point days, he was only three years older than LeMay. Yet the two men could not have been more different. Hansell was a Southern gentleman from a refined family, and was as garrulous as LeMay was reserved. He had served on Arnold's staff in Washington and had been LeMay's commander at the Eighth Air Force in the early days in England. He was also part of the four-man team that came up with a brilliant war estimate for FDR, projecting back in 1940 what the Air Forces would need in men and material to win the war—an estimate that would prove to be uncannily on target.

Hansell would lead the main B-29 operation in the Pacific, the Twenty-First Air Forces (XXI). It would be based in the Marianas, a small group of islands in the South Pacific that included Saipan, Guam, and Tinian. Even before the Marines had finished clearing the islands of Japanese troops, an army of construction workers came ashore and started transforming these South Pacific islands into gigantic modern airports, along with roads, barracks, mess halls, and hospitals—essentially building medium-sized American cities within weeks.

Hansell worked quietly and shied away from publicity. In a brief appearance in a War Department film produced to promote the

Erving and Arizona LeMay with their growing family, around 1916.
Curtis is standing next to his mother.

LeMay's Model-T Ford—a handyman's special he kept as an undergraduate at
Ohio State.

The graduating air cadet class, 1929. LeMay is third from left.

LeMay with Amelia Earhart at Wheeler Field in Hawaii in 1935. Two years later, she would disappear over the Pacific.

Second Lieutenant Curtis LeMay, wearing a parachute, after his graduation from cadet school.

LeMay with his daughter, Janie, 1939.

A rare moment during the war: LeMay relaxing with his bomber crews.

Major General LeMay greets Lieutenant Colonel Robert McNamara, an Army Air Forces statistician. Twenty years later, their roles were reversed when McNamara became LeMay's boss at the Pentagon.

Lieutenant Ralph Nutter in England, 1943.

"Possum" Hansell (left) and LeMay listen to a pilot named Ashcroft as he recounts a particularly harrowing mission over Europe, 1943.

Plane counting in England. Curtis LeMay would watch the skies until there was no chance of any more bombers returning from a mission.

Curtis and Helen LeMay with Janie in Cleveland on one of his rare visits home during the war.

Surviving B-17s head over the Alps on their way to Africa after the double strike mission at Schweinfurt and Regensburg.

One of the lucky B-17s in Africa after the disastrous Schweinfurt–Regensburg mission, 1943.

LeMay at the controls of a B-17 during the war.

LeMay briefing officers in England on operations surrounding D-Day, June 1944.

Standing on Japanese soil for the first time (keeping his gun handy in case of an ambush). LeMay in Yokohama, prior to the surrender ceremony on the USS *Missouri*, September 2, 1945.

Tokyo—March 10, 1945.

Dancing with Janie at a social function in Omaha, around 1952.

In the White House Rose Garden with President John F. Kennedy greeting foreign air force officers, 1962.

President Lyndon Johnson with Air Force Chief Curtis LeMay at the LBJ ranch in December 1963, just one month after Johnson assumed office.

February 1, 1965. Following the retirement ceremony at the White House with President Johnson, LeMay watches a fly-by in his honor at Andrews Air Force Base, ending thirty-seven years of active duty.

Major General Curtis LeMay, 1944.

first B-29's arrival in the Marianas (narrated by Captain Ronald Reagan), Hansell looked like he had been pushed in front of the camera and microphone. His comments were self-effacing and hardly boastful: "Well, the first element of the 21st Bomber Command has arrived," Hansell said, standing next to the bomber. "When we've done some more fighting, we'll do some more talking."[27] The officer in charge of public relations looked at him, hoping there would be more. But that was it.

As the huge planes and their crews began arriving from the States, the small islands of Guam and Tinian quickly became the busiest airports in the world. The islands were periodic targets of Japanese fighters based exactly halfway between the Marianas and Tokyo on Iwo Jima. These fighters could be deadly, destroying B-29s on the ground. Only after Iwo Jima was captured could the maintenance crews finally use lights to work on the planes at night.

Hansell did everything by the book. He immediately began training his new crews in formation flying, just as LeMay had done in England two years earlier. The tech personnel worked day and night to solve the many mechanical problems. Two Navy ships were commandeered to ferry spare parts between the Boeing plant in Seattle and the Marianas without stopping in Hawaii. Engineers and construction crews continued their work of transforming the island. But as hard as Hansell and his men worked, the problems multiplied.

• • • •

A VERY BAD IDEA

To make matters worse, the Marianas were not the Air Force's biggest B-29 headache. There was a second B-29 effort in the Pacific,

2,000 miles to the west, which was essentially too ill-conceived to work. The Twentieth (XX) Air Forces operation had been spread across a huge expanse known as the China-India-Burma Theater. It was commanded by General Kenneth Wolfe with headquarters in Kharagpur, India, and forward bases around Chengtu, China. It was the result of a political agenda trumping a military solution. Franklin Roosevelt felt he had to placate Chiang Kai-shek in order to persuade the reluctant Chinese leader to put a greater effort into his fight with the Japanese. Additionally, early in the war, with the Marianas invasions planned for two years after the B-29s would be ready, FDR and his military commanders saw China as the only available land base within striking distance of Japan.[28] To make matters worse, FDR had fallen under the persuasive influence of the flamboyant and charismatic commander of the American fighter squadrons in the Pacific, Major General Claire Chennault, who had close personal ties to Chiang Kai-shek. Chennault boldly stated that he could defeat Japan with 105 fighters, 30 medium bombers, and 12 heavy bombers, an estimate that he would have to revise—and revise again. Chiang Kai-shek instinctively understood that the Americans would pick up the slack, so he could save his army and the vast arsenal of U.S.-made weapons for what he believed to be the real fight ahead with Mao Zedong.

The China-Burma-India (CBI) theater was a logistical nightmare—something LeMay said could only have been dreamed up in Washington. "The B-29s themselves could be flown into such bases, but the problem was that the bases would have to be flown in as well."[29]

Because the entire operation was landlocked and essentially behind enemy lines, the most efficient method of supply—by ship—was not possible. Here, everything had to be flown in: the fuel, the bombs, the spare parts, the food—everything. For every gallon of gas used in combat, more than seven were burned up to deliver it. C-47 transport planes (the military version of the small passenger DC-3) had to fly it all across the Himalayas, "over the hump." Flying these planes over the tallest mountain ranges in the world through some of the worst weather on the planet was a very dangerous assignment. "It was a grueling hell, climbing the big bombers over the rugged Himalayas—the roof of the world," LeMay wrote. "It was 1,200 miles of the worst flying imaginable. The mountains were a veritable smorgasbord of meteorological treachery—violent downdrafts, high winds, and sudden snowstorms—all served up in temperatures 20 degrees below zero. As if they needed any reminding, the crews could frequently glimpse the 29,028 foot peak of Mt. Everest thrusting up through the clouds just 150 miles from their flight path."[30]

In many areas when planes crashed, air and sea rescue was impossible. In the forbidding wasteland of the Himalayas, when a plane encountered problems, the crew knew they would have to walk out, if they even survived. Few were heard from again.

The Japanese defenses were almost a secondary problem in comparison. In Wolfe's first mission on June 15, 1944, sixty-eight B-29s flew from Chengtu to bomb the steel plants around Yawata. Because of the cloud cover, only one bomb hit the target. One plane was downed by Japanese fire. Six more were lost to mechanical problems and the weather. The Navy's criticism of the B-29 program certainly appeared to be warranted—seventy-seven

American airmen killed, seven multi-million-dollar planes destroyed—and all to drop one bomb. Looking back on the entire operation, LeMay pointed out sarcastically that even the code name for China-India-Burma, "Matterhorn," was poorly thought out: "Might as well have called our D-Day landing in France by the code name of 'Normandy'... it wouldn't have taken an excessively smart Japanese to figure out the whole thing."[31]

But as dismal as this first performance was from the American perspective, the Japanese took a very different view. Americans are impatient by nature. After all the effort put into the program, some seemed to think that the first B-29 raid on Yawata should have destroyed the Imperial Iron & Steel works, if not the entire city. However, what the Japanese saw and heard on the ground was startlingly different, and it frightened them. A Japanese journalist wrote:

Now all the city is black. Suddenly in the north we heard the sound of plane engines. The orders were flashed everywhere and all the sounds on the street still. The propeller noise of the enemy planes spread over the whole sky. Minute by minute the noise approached. At this moment there was a shot, like a sky-rocket, into the air. Several tons of shots. I could see clearly the figures of the enemy planes. At once antiaircraft began to shoot. The guns shouted like lightning. But the hateful enemy planes flew on. Suddenly fire dropped from them—one, two, three. These were the flares. The whole city could be clearly seen in reddish light. Then came big black things from the white bodies of the planes. Bombs! And boom! Boom! Boom! The devils, the beasts! Again boom! Boom! Boom![32]

• • • •

THE C-B-I

It was a sign of things to come that the B-29 Curtis LeMay was supposed to fly to India encountered mechanical problems before he took off. After waiting for two days at LaGuardia airport in New York, LeMay commandeered an available C-54 transport plane and took off in the late afternoon of August 25, 1944. He arrived at Harmon Field with his crew in Stevensville, Newfoundland, for breakfast on the morning of August 26 and flew on to the Azores where they had dinner. From there, they flew to Casablanca, arriving on August 27, taking just enough time to eat breakfast, shower, and gas up the plane. Next they flew to Tripoli, then to Cairo, and on to Aboden, Iran, on August 28, where LeMay recorded the temperature at 130 degrees. They were greatly relieved when they were finally able to cool off at several thousand feet. But heat blasted them again at their next stops, first Karachi and then New Delhi, where they spent the night. They finally arrived at Kharagpur, their new home, on August 29, almost five days after they left New York. In 1944, this was very good time.

LeMay had been to South America, North Africa, and more recently, England. But he felt profound culture shock in India. "Kharagpur was like nothing I'd ever seen before,"[33] LeMay remembered. The heat, smells, and the density of people made a lasting impression. His headquarters was based in a former prison. His personal quarters, complete with servants, had been the grand home of the warden. But after one look at the operation, the stupidity of the entire plan became immediately clear to LeMay: "It didn't work and no one could have made it work. It was founded on an utterly absurd logistic basis," LeMay remembered. "The scheme of operations had been dreamed up like something out of the *Wizard of Oz*."[34] He had faced big problems before, but this one seemed impossible. "The first few nights I went to bed with my ears buzzing from what I had heard and my eyes aching from what I had seen."[35]

This is what happens, he thought, when political decisions overtake common sense during a war. There was a strong pro-China lobby in the United States, led by the powerful Henry Luce, the publisher of *Time* and *Life* magazines (who was born in China to missionary parents). Madame Chiang was a frequent guest in the White House. FDR had given up one of his most brilliant generals, "Vinegar Joe" Stilwell, who spent nearly the entire war trying to encourage Chiang to be more aggressive against the Japanese.

The hard-working Chinese themselves left a lasting impression on any American who served in this theater of war. Chiang Kai-shek promised Roosevelt that he would build the bases and he did—but in a way that dumbfounded the Americans. Over 100,000 Chinese workers built four bases by hand—without any mechanical equipment. The Air Force men watched as hundreds of Chinese in long lines pulled large cement rollers over the runways. "Sometimes, one of them would fall under the roller," remembered Paul Carlton, "they would stop for a moment... they'd laugh... and then keep right on going. We couldn't believe what we were seeing."[36]

When LeMay arrived to take over command from General Wolfe, he found a new order waiting for him. He was no longer allowed to fly in combat. It was an integral part of his command philosophy—always lead your men into combat, never send them out ahead of you. But there was a practical side to this as well:

LeMay knew he could better understand the situation and solve problems when he saw and experienced them himself. But Hap Arnold would not relent. Infuriated, LeMay tried a new tack that was alien to him—diplomacy. "I should fly missions regularly," he reasoned, "but right now I must fly at least one, at the start. I won't know what's going on until I do."[37]

Arnold was a very tough individual. In spite of a genial smile, there was very little joy to his personality. Once, early in the war, he screamed at a subordinate in front of his staff with such fury that the man had a heart attack and died in front of them. In response, Arnold suggested everyone go home for the day. Instead, they all retreated to their offices and continued their work. In an unusual demonstration of just how much Arnold needed LeMay and wanted to please him, the four star general did something he almost never did: he backed down, but only slightly. One mission. That was it. Arnold crossed his fingers and hoped he had not done something he would regret. He could not afford to lose LeMay. The fact that Arnold compromised at all shows just how forceful LeMay could be—a trait that Arnold ultimately liked.

LeMay wasted no time. His first and only combat mission in Asia took place ten days after he arrived. Looking over the target list carefully, he selected the Anshan coke ovens in Manchuria. He chose Anshen because it reportedly had the best Japanese fighter defense. This way, LeMay reasoned, he would have the best chance to determine just how good the Japanese pilots were. On September 8, 1944, with LeMay in the lead B-29, cigar clenched between his teeth, he went into battle against this new enemy in a new airplane. As he approached the target, LeMay saw the Japanese fighters already in the air waiting in squadrons at a lower altitude.

"Now we'll see what they can do," he murmured. But it ended with LeMay hardly impressed. "Hell, they never mounted a decent attack. I think only one airplane got in close enough to fire," he later commented, sounding disappointed.[38]

The Japanese had misjudged the speed of the B-29s and by the time they corrected, it was too late. They never came close. As LeMay flew right over the target, his plane was hit by flak. Two of the crewmen started yelling over the intercom that they had been wounded. LeMay still wanted to observe any possible Japanese counter-measures. "Hope you're not too badly hit," he told them. "Wait until the fighters have come in. Then I'll crawl back there and help you."[39] In order to get from the forward section of a B-29 to the rear, a crewman had to crawl through a long aluminum tube that resembled a large pipe. When things finally settled down, LeMay handed the controls over to his co-pilot, picked up a first aid pouch, and—despite not being a svelte individual—unceremoniously crawled through the length of the long plane on his stomach.

It turned out that the radio operator's body armor had stopped a large piece of flak, just knocking him to the deck. A second chunk of metal hit the grips of one of the gun mountings and only slightly wounded the fire control officer's knuckle. "So that was his wound," LeMay remarked dismissively. The crewman had regained his composure and looked embarrassed, facing his commander with such a minor injury. "'Course I was just as glad that I didn't have to put on any tourniquets or stick in any needles,"[40] LeMay observed. Now his only worry was whether the plane would maintain its pressurization, which it did.

LeMay quickly deduced that the Japanese anti-aircraft capability was not nearly as dangerous as the Germans'. But he still had to overcome mechanical problems, the lousy weather, and a logistical nightmare. Even with these problems, LeMay managed to double the number of combat flights over his predecessor. But his greatest success in China-Burma-India would be persuading Washington to abandon the entire operation.

Adding to the many problems vexing any commander in the China-Burma-India Theater, there was the internal struggle between the Chinese Nationalists led by Chiang Kai-shek and the Communists led by Mao Tse-tung. Both men had been fighting each other since 1925, but called a temporary truce while they both fought off the Japanese, who controlled large sections of China and had installed puppet governors. Chiang was aligned with the U.S., and it was unclear how Mao would deal with the Americans, especially B-29 crews who might have to land in Communist controlled areas. On his own initiative, LeMay sent one of his officers to talk with the Communists, and one of the stranger episodes of the war ensued.

The Air Force officer flew to Yenan, the Communist stronghold, in a C-47 transport. He brought radio equipment to leave with Mao. That way, if Mao was willing to assist the Americans, he could notify the Twentieth Air Force if they had any downed crews. Even though Mao knew the Americans were helping Chiang with weapons and supplies, he agreed to help any American crews. LeMay responded almost immediately by sending another C-47 to Mao loaded with medical supplies. "I should not pretend that this was all sweetness and light on my part," LeMay later remembered, "and that I was making so free with our U.S. taxpayers' sulfanilamide that I need to furnish it to any Communists, Chinese or otherwise. But I wanted to be damn sure that there were medical supplies in those areas when my own people came in, busted up or wounded."[41]

The Chinese Communists lived under the most desperate conditions in the mountains of Yenan. They had never even seen this type of medical equipment before. According to the Air Force crews that delivered it, many of the Chinese doctors were in tears. "They stayed up the entire night, looking over the material we had sent, and Ooh-ing and Ah-ing over the contents of each case or crate," LeMay reported. He then sent back doctors who explained how all the medicines worked. On that return trip, Mao sent gifts back to LeMay—a Japanese Samurai sword and some woodcuts made by the Chinese. LeMay reciprocated with a pair of binoculars. They corresponded with letters after that. Before the war's end, Mao's troops performed admirably. In one case, they fought a battle with the Japanese over a B-29 crew, and then fought a second battle over the plane. One crew had to come thousands of miles back to American lines, but was escorted every step of the way by dozens of Chinese Communist soldiers, sometimes fighting their way through Japanese territory.

The great irony is that LeMay, who was a staunch anti-Communist, respected Mao and greatly appreciated what he had done for his crews. But it went beyond irony. It was part of LeMay's indifference to his enemies that seemed at odds with his outward personality. He led great formations of bombers against the Germans and would send out vast armadas against the Japanese, yet he bore no personal grudge against either. There was a simple calculus behind his perseverance—these people had threatened his country. His duty as an officer in the military was to defend the United States. It was never personal. It was business.

. . . .

THE U.S. JUGGERNAUT

Until 1944, with the exception of one Doolittle raid in 1942, the Japanese mainland remained untouched. Its citizens believed what they had been told, that their homeland and especially Tokyo, the home of their Emperor, was divinely invulnerable to the enemy. Except for severe rationing and the fact that Japanese soldiers and sailors were fighting and dying throughout Asia, life in Japan carried on, to the point that civilians had grown complacent after three years of war against the United States.

There was no reason for them to feel otherwise. The Doolittle raid did what it was intended to do, lifting the spirits of Americans stunned by the disaster at Pearl Harbor. There were banner headlines throughout the U.S., newsreels inciting thunderous applause in theaters, and two movies that came out of Hollywood about it—*Thirty Seconds Over Tokyo* starring Spencer Tracy and *The Purple Heart* with Dana Andrews—both hugely popular films. But for all the publicity it provoked back in the United States, the Japanese scoffed at it. And they had reason to mock. The damage was negligible, and afterwards no more American planes followed. Japan relaxed.

The point of origin for the huge enterprise that would turn things around began in the heart of America, when newly trained crews picked up their B-29s at the factories either in Nebraska or Kansas. That is where 20-year-old Dan Miller, Jr. and his crew began their odyssey across the ocean. Miller's journey, recorded in his diary, is one of the few detailed records of a special journey traveled by thousands of young Americans between 1944 and 1945.

Miller's crew picked up their shiny new B-29 in Topeka right off the assembly line. They were ordered to fly to Sacramento, but were given no further instructions. They would be told the rest along the way. At each stop the plane would be serviced; mail and machinery would be off-loaded, and new items would be loaded on. The crew would sleep—sometimes in barracks, sometimes in tents, and in one case, under the wing of the plane in the sand.

From their first stop in Sacramento after a two-day layover where they phoned home for the last time, the planes departed after midnight for security. The tower's final instructions: "Make a left turn out of traffic and goodnight, sir."

They headed out over the solid blackness of the Pacific. "We were told to open up our sealed envelope of flight instructions when we were two-hundred miles offshore." Their next stop: Honolulu, where the plane was again serviced, the crew slept for a few hours, gear was taken off, new gear put on, and they were off to their next stop: the Kwajalein Atoll.

"A tiny island that had the hell blown out of it." The crew marveled that there was not a single tree or bush left standing anywhere on the island. "It was hot as hell," remembered Miller. They slept under the plane and were fed from a portable kitchen.

When they left the next day and opened their flight instructions, their individual boxes contained a .45 caliber pistol, a holster and ammunition, and various emergency items. They were now in a combat zone. The next leg of the journey took them over 1,000 miles of the South Pacific to Guam, luckily with the sun behind them. "As we touched down and continued our forward roll, I climbed back and up to open the overhead hatch and allow the fresh air to circulate throughout the plane. I stood with the upper half of my body outside and could clearly smell vegetation and hear the amazing shrill calls of hundreds of cockatoos and other parrot-like birds. That moment will always stay with me."

Two engines were loaded in the bomb bay for the next and final leg of the trip along with more mailbags. It was a short hop of a hundred miles to Tinian. Miller and his crew were taken to a reception area where they registered. From there a truck ferried them to a nine-man tent filled with army cots. This would be home until the war was over. "Our crew was just glad to be there and so thankful that we had a brand new plane delivered without a scratch and no problems," he wrote in his journal.[42] Three days later, Miller and the crew flew their first mission.

In the Marianas, the Marines and Seabees (naval construction engineers) paused at their work to look at the huge B-29s as they arrived, not by the dozens, but by the hundreds. As soon as the construction trucks built another parking area for the long line of bombers, the spot was filled. With every factory humming, and military barracks turning millions of American teenagers into soldiers, sailors, marines, and airmen, the United States no longer resembled the struggling nation of early 1942. It had become the most powerful country on earth. But up until now the Japanese had seen almost none of this. They could not possibly know what was coming their way.

CHAPTER EIGHT

THE EMPIRE BURNING

JAPAN'S COMPLACENCY ENDED ON A SPECTACULARLY BEAUTIFUL autumn day. On October 13, 1944, an ominous sound drew the eyes of the Japanese towards the heavens from Nagasaki all the way to Tokyo. It was the first B-29 to fly over Japan, and it was riding high in the troposphere. Robert Guillain, a French journalist living in Japan throughout the war, recorded the reaction in Tokyo: "The city waited. Millions of lives were suspended in the silence of the radiant autumn afternoon. For a moment, antiaircraft fire shook the horizon with a noise of doors slamming in the sky. Then—nothing: the all clear was sounded without sight of the plane."[1]

Radios throughout the country anxiously reported the event but sought to calm the population by explaining that it had only been a single airplane, and no bombs had been dropped.[2] The Japanese, however, understood this was a sign. There would be more to come. Yet even the most realistic among them could never imagine just how many.

The Japanese would come to call the giant planes "B-san" or "Bikko." The bomber produced that mesmerizing sound, "an odd, rhythmic buzzing... [a] deep, powerful pulsation [that] made my whole house vibrate," wrote Guillain.[3] From that moment on, no matter what these gleaming monsters brought or how vulnerable these planes made them feel, the Japanese on the ground could not help looking up in awe. Even the wife of Emperor Hirohito, Empress Nagako, was not immune. Less than a year after that first flight, she would write in a private letter: "Every day from morning to night, B-29s, naval bombers and fighters freely fly over the palace making an enormous noise. As I sit at my desk writing and look up at the sky, countless numbers are passing over.... Unfortunately, the B-29 is a splendid plane."[4]

The radio reports from the Japanese War Ministry were correct that day. The lone airplane dropped not a single bomb, but it would turn out to be one of the most crucial flights in the entire war. "A lot of things that happen in wartime are attributable to luck," LeMay wrote later, sounding philosophical, but referring directly to this flight. One can plan everything down to the last detail but "good planning can be destroyed by bad fortune, then another experience... [can be] exactly the opposite."[5]

The pathetic fact was that while the massive B-29 legion was arriving on Guam and Saipan and Tinian, the U.S. had almost no information on where these planes should drop their bombs. There was almost no target information. "We really didn't know anything about Japan," LeMay observed, "because the Japanese had kept the place pretty well closed before the war. We didn't have any secret agents creeping around in Japan sending us information."[6]

For the United States, World War II began with an appalling intelligence failure at Pearl Harbor, and the intelligence problems continued almost to the end. Altogether, the information on Japan was extremely poor in spite of the fact that the U.S. broke the Japanese code early on and listened to their messages throughout the war. The U.S. Army Air Forces only had a vague idea of where some factories were located.

"They had an 'intelligence' division in the State Department before the war," LeMay would bitingly recall, "but members of the division didn't do anything but balance teacups."[7]

Hap Arnold corroborated the dire situation with a vivid recollection: "When we were talking in the Joint and Combined Chiefs of Staff meetings about possible landings on the island of Hokkaido, in Japan, the only information I could get from the G-2 [intelligence] section of the Army and the ONI [Office of Naval Intelligence] Section of the Navy, was a book dated 1858!"[8]

On the day the plane flew over Japan, more brand new B-29s had arrived on the runway of Saipan having completed their trip from Kansas. But one of these bombers, the *Tokyo Rose*, was different from all the rest. It was modified as a photo-reconnaissance airplane. Captain Ralph Steakley and his specially trained crew had just made the long, grueling flight across the Pacific. Without wanting to waste a moment, Steakley immediately reported to General Hansell and told him he was ready to take a crack at Japan to see if he could get any pictures with his new equipment. Hansell suggested that he get squared away and give his crew a rest after the long flight. No, Steakley replied, they were good to go. "Okay," Hansell reluctantly told him, "go ahead."[9]

Hansell was a thoughtful and kind officer, who was always thinking of his men. But had Steakley followed his advice that day,

the U.S. would have lost a golden opportunity. It turned out that
Steakley's flight on the same day he arrived from Kansas fell on the
one and only crystal clear day for the next two years. The *Tokyo
Rose* captured detailed pictures of almost every urban area, dock,
factory, and transportation hub in Japan, and spent thirty-five minutes over Tokyo itself. The plane flew so high that the anti-aircraft
fire was harmless. Steakley and his exhausted crew returned to Tinian fifteen hours later. But they came back with thousands of price-
less photographs that would be used in every mission to follow.
The B-29s finally had their targets.[10] "There wasn't really another
chance like that for the rest of the war. Those photographs were a
godsend," LeMay would remember.[11]

However, the reconnaissance flight was not what ultimately
changed the course of the air war in the Pacific. It was a chain reaction of events that began with General Hansell's failure to produce
any significant results in the Marianas. Hansell methodically
trained his pilots to fly in great formations through the autumn of
1944. They practiced target bombing and fighter defense, but the
general resisted any attempt at area bombing. He believed the
B-29s would ultimately succeed at pin-point targeting. He just
needed time to figure out how to make the big planes work.
Hansell wanted to avoid unnecessary Japanese casualties on the
ground. It would become the classic argument over strategic
bombing that would continue long after the war ended: avoiding
civilian deaths versus quickly defeating the enemy and conclu-
sively ending the war.

Finally, on November 24, 1944, one month after the solo reconnaissance flight which was flown in abnormally balmy weather,
Hansell sent 128 B-29s on their first mission against the Mushashi

aircraft engine factory just ten miles north of the Imperial Palace in Tokyo. It was here that the B-29s encountered a phenomenon that no one had even heard of because no plane had ever flown that high over Japan on a normal day. The B-29s discovered the jet stream, ferocious winds from 150 to over 200 miles an hour that were almost constant in the skies high above Japan. To make matters worse, the planes consumed much more fuel than anticipated. The high winds strained the already trouble-prone engines and made bombing accuracy impossible. "If we were going with the jet stream," one B-29 pilot remembered, "our bombs were going long over the target. And if we were going against it, the bombs would fall short."[12] No one knew how to compensate for this.

The problems did not end there. The cloud cover—also nearly constant over Japan—further destroyed any hope of accuracy. It was a disappointing performance. Seventeen planes were forced back with mechanical problems. Only twenty-four out of 111 planes dropped their bombs even close to the target. Damage to the aircraft plant was limited. The only good news that day was that Japanese ground fire did not bring down one Superfortress. It was a very different experience from bombing Germany. The only loss came when a Japanese fighter plane deliberately crashed into a B-29, killing all aboard in one of the earliest suicide attacks. The following month, in December, Hansell could only mount two raids because of bad weather, again causing only limited damage, but this time losing eight Superfortresses and eighty-eight crewmen.

Even with the enormous logistical problems he faced in India, LeMay astounded everyone by actually outperforming Hansell. In fact, LeMay had a higher performance record than any other heavy bomber operation, with the exception of the Mediterranean.

In numbers of hours flown, accidents, and lives lost, LeMay even came close to outperforming the stateside B-29 training operation that had no enemy opposition and a maintenance force three times larger.[13]

At that point, Hap Arnold had no alternative. There was enormous pressure on him from the White House, the Navy, and the War Department—the Joint Chiefs were already planning the invasion of the mainland. The costs of the B-29 program were continuing to skyrocket. "He couldn't wait for Hansell to defeat the Japanese with his theories of civilized precision bombing," according to Ralph Nutter.[14]

Everyone from the president down to the store clerk on Main Street was growing weary and impatient of the rising casualties. The Battle of the Bulge in Europe had just caught the Allies off guard, occurring after the top generals believed the Germans were already defeated and proving to be one of the costliest battles of the entire war with more than 19,000 Americans dead and over 10,000 captured. Iwo Jima and Okinawa were still months away. The Joint Chiefs were concerned that they would lose public support of the war if the casualties of an invasion of Japan were as great as predicted. "Hansell seemed oblivious to the change in tempo of the war," observed Nutter, who served under him in England.[15]

The pressure on Arnold trickled down the chain of command. In their meetings, the Joint Chiefs constantly asked Arnold when the B-29s were going to start doing some damage in Japan. The strain was making him physically sick; he would have four heart attacks before the end of the war. Arnold had to replace Hansell as the commander of the main B-29 thrust in the Pacific and put in

LeMay. But as tough as Arnold was, he did not want to fire his former deputy himself. Instead, the normally fierce commander fal-
tered and sent his second-in-command, General Lauris Norstad, to
deliver the news to Hansell in person.

Surprisingly, Arnold failed to think of an alternative assignment
for Hansell. The offer he presented was the worst possible suggestion. He told Norris that Hansell could remain on Guam as LeMay's
second-in-command. This was a shocking proposal, demonstrating the pressure Arnold was under. When a commander is relieved
of duty, the best thing for all concerned is to remove him from his
former command. The new commander cannot afford to have old
loyalties to the former commander undermine him, or to be
second-guessed in front of his troops. It was a terrible idea.

The meeting was awkward. Norstad made the flight out to
Guam and was greeted by Hansell as he landed. Hansell had no
inkling of what was coming—he assumed they were going to go
over plans for future operations. To make matters worse, the two
men were personal friends as well as colleagues. They had worked
together for over a year in Washington, and their families had
become close. In a further complication, Hansell had been LeMay's
superior in Europe, even though LeMay now outranked him by
one star. All three men—Norstad, Hansell, and LeMay—were
among the youngest generals in the Army, but LeMay was the
youngest of all. But as far as Norstad was concerned, none of this
mattered. Hansell had simply been unable to achieve results.

When Norstad told Hansell the news, he was genuinely
shocked. Norstad was cold blooded about it and said things he
later regretted. "He told Hansell that perhaps he was too civilized
to fight a war the way it had to be fought,"[16] remembers Ralph

Nutter. Hansell later told Nutter, "Norstad was probably correct in saying that I didn't have the killer instinct."[17] Nutter observed that Hansell tried to avoid confrontations with his subordinates, and Hansell himself knew he was not aggressive by nature, while "LeMay accepted confrontation with group commanders as part of the territory."[18] The answer was obvious to everyone and, ultimately, to Hansell as well.

LeMay did not give a damn what people around him thought. And he was even less concerned with what the history books would say, with one exception—that he was a failure. This tremendous lack of concern for his own reputation, demonstrated by his refusal to extend himself in social situations, bordered on being pathological. But he was also extremely ambitious, which created an odd mix. He worked at cultivating a personality that appeared inhuman because he understood this persona worked best with command. He also did this to cover what he felt was a soft side. Although there was definitely a part of him that understood and even felt sympathy for the bombing victims on the ground, as revealed in later writings, he drove those feelings so far below the surface that no one suspected he could possibly possess them. If he felt any concern for the human life he was extinguishing far below the contrails of his bombers, he did not articulate it to anyone around him.

Though LeMay rarely opened up, accounting for his relative silence about his views of the means of warfare, those moments did occur. Years later, he was unusually introspective during a television interview when he conceded that with any form of bombing, nothing was certain. "You just could not avoid doing collateral damage and I'm sure we burned down a lot of Japanese buildings that had nothing to do with the war industry at all. This, of course, is one of the sad things of war that just can't be helped." It is significant that LeMay mentioned "buildings" that had nothing to do with the war effort, clearly avoiding the obvious impact on the human beings inside. Later in that same interview, LeMay explained that, in his mind, the ends justified the means, saying, "It was a long drawn out war. You began to get casualties from the side effects—the exhaustion, deprivation, disease and things of that sort. So getting it over with as quickly as possible is the moral responsibility of everyone concerned."[19]

Hansell saw things differently. He told Norstad he felt that "even if the Japanese acted like beasts, Americans shouldn't do the same. Killing innocent civilians was a matter of moral and ethical consideration. The Hague International Convention made it clear that international law prohibited terror attacks on innocent civilians."[20]

LeMay had the rare quality of being able to concentrate on the smallest details, while not micro-managing the people under him. Bombing was now his job, and he had taken every job seriously since he was a child. He approached it as if it were any other mechanical issue—here's the problem, what's the solution? "He analyzed every combat problem as an engineer," Ralph Nutter later reflected. "He considered every combat mission as if it were an engine with component parts, which had to mesh and interact perfectly. LeMay not only analyzed the performance of our crewmembers, the aircraft, and engines, but he studied the bombsights, armament, bomb trajectories, and bomb characteristics. He attempted to balance the cost and calculate the price of each mission. Those of us who flew with him knew that his rigid discipline and rigorous training program saved many lives."[21]

"LeMay is an operator," Norstad told Hansell bluntly as he relieved him of command. "All the rest of us are planners. That's all there is to it."[22] Old friendships did not matter.

All of this came together in this first week of January 1945, when, after three years of total war, Washington demanded a complete reversal of the U.S. policy of strategic bombing. Patience was exhausted. Targeted attacks had not worked. Hap Arnold was now placing the one commander whom he believed and hoped could do the job in charge of the effort against Japan.

After Ralph Nutter had completed twenty-seven[23] missions in Europe, he returned to the States in 1944. On the troop ship that brought him home, he finally had the chance to relax and reflect on what he had just gone through. Nutter reflected on how his experience would have a great impact on the rest of his life. "Almost all of my comrades who flew with our group across the North Atlantic were either dead, wounded or prisoners of war." He never gave himself the opportunity to think these thoughts while he was in combat. As he later explained, "Now I wondered how and why I had survived and if some of the losses of my friends could have reasonably been prevented."[24]

Nutter could have remained in the States for the rest of the war and taught navigation to the new waves of recruits entering the Air Force. But in the spring of 1944, he ran into his former commander, Possum Hansell, at the Great Bend B-29 training base in Kansas. Hansell told Nutter he was going to the Pacific and asked him to come with him to the Marianas. In thinking it over, Nutter felt a duty to impart whatever information he had learned to hopefully prevent more crew losses in the Pacific. Yet, as he recalled, "Later, when I was being strafed by kamikazes on Saipan, washing

my clothes in a helmet, fighting off the flies, and taking cold show-
ers with seawater, I had second thoughts about my decision."[25]
When the change of command took place in January, Nutter found
himself back with his original boss, General LeMay.

From the moment LeMay took command, it was clear a new man
was in charge. At his very first meeting with his senior staff, LeMay
made it apparent he would not tolerate any whining. He stressed
discipline and training, which would save lives in the end. "Some
of you may conclude that I'm a tough SOB," he told them at the end
of his talk. "I'll accept that. I am not a Boy Scout leader, but you will
find that I will be tougher on myself than any of you."[26] Nutter
liked and respected Hansell. He was in awe of LeMay.

When Norstad relieved Hansell of command, he was equally
blunt with LeMay, who had also been summoned for a meeting on
Guam without knowing why. LeMay assumed they would discuss
ending the beleaguered operation in India and folding it into one
main effort in the Marianas. He showed no emotion when he was
told he would replace Hansell. But wittingly or unwittingly, Norstad
drove home his point. "You go ahead and get results with the B-29,"
Norstad told him. "If you don't, you'll be fired." Then Norstad reinforced the edict with a second point that dovetailed his two messages with LeMay's two greatest personal anxieties: "If you don't get
results, it will mean eventually a mass amphibious invasion of
Japan, to cost probably half a million more American lives."[27]

In the strange mathematics of war, and with the hindsight of
more than half a century, it turns out that the planners in
Washington were correct. The more humane tactics of Hansell—
trying to hit only military targets—may not have been all that
humane in the end, and probably would have prolonged the

conflict. That would have led to the invasion beginning in November 1945 with a second wave to back it up in March 1946. The Japanese military leaders were beginning the massive training of the civilian population for total war known as "Ketsu-Go." The plan called for every able-bodied Japanese citizen—women and youngsters included—to form suicide squads and swarm the Americans.[28] By ending the conflict without an invasion of Japan, not only would a vast number of American lives be saved, but many more Japanese lives would be spared as well.

Years later, Robert McNamara summed up LeMay's focus. "He cared about only two things," McNamara remembered, "hitting the target and saving the lives of his men."[29]

"Here's another great big bear for you," LeMay wrote about this reassignment as head of the Twenty-First Air Force in the Marianas. "Come and grab it by the tail."[30] Again he was handed an impossible task with a high risk of failure and losing more young American lives and was expected to accomplish it with a trouble-prone airplane that had yet to perform.

Hansell wisely declined Arnold's offer to stay in the Marianas: "Not because of any friction with General LeMay," Hansell wrote later, "but I knew him well enough to know he did not need any 'assistant commander' and I knew myself well enough to know that I would not be content to stay completely in the background. It is not a good thing to leave an ex-commander in the same outfit that he commanded."[31]

LeMay agreed. Hansell took the news like the gentleman he was. He said his goodbyes and quickly packed and left for the States, where he had an extended leave with his family after years apart and then faded into military obscurity, spending the rest of his career in research and teaching, but always staying in touch with

LeMay. The two men had handled an uncomfortable situation with great dignity. Years later, when LeMay was asked why he thought Arnold replaced Hansell with him, he seemed to go out of his way to avoid any criticism of Hansell whatsoever, saying it probably was because they were folding the India operation into the Marianas, and he simply outranked Hansell.[32] LeMay never openly criticized a fellow officer.

LeMay was greatly relieved on one score. The fiasco in India would die a quiet death. "Someone had finally tumbled to the fact that there was no profit in trying to supply the Chengtu Valley with gasoline for attacks on Japan."[33] He wasted no time, and immediately flew back to India. As Wolfe had done for him, LeMay would brief his replacement, Roger Ramey, whose chief job was to wind down the entire operation and move it to the Marianas. Within two weeks, LeMay was back on Guam and in charge.

•   •   •   •

THE GENERAL AND THE NEW YORKER

It was on Guam that LeMay met St. Clair McKelway and struck up an unlikely friendship only possible in the unusual circumstances of war. A distinguished writer for the *New Yorker* magazine before he volunteered for the service, McKelway was serving as the chief public affairs officer for the Air Force on Guam. He had left the refined world of Manhattan and its literary salons for life in a tent, twenty-hour work days, swarms of mosquitoes, and lousy food—all for a severe cut in pay. It was that kind of war. McKelway was in charge of briefing reporters—who worked almost exclusively for newspapers. He and his staff then censored each story to make sure no vital information could fall into enemy hands.

McKelway had lived in the tent next to Hansell and become close to the Southern gentleman who was his commander. The two men would often sit together late at night, talking over bourbon. They were cut from the same cloth. Like many of the men, McKelway resented the manner in which the likable Hansell was summarily fired. "Holy God, Possum," he told Hansell when he first learned of the change, "they can't do this to you."[34]

Everyone on the island had heard about LeMay, and most of what they heard was not positive. Their first impressions of their new commander only cemented those opinions. "His looks," McKelway wrote several months later in a *New Yorker* profile, "had not helped us take a jolly view of the future." LeMay went around the base, unsmiling and saying nothing in those first days. LeMay's lack of communication made everyone feel uncomfortable, especially after Hansell's geniality. He was obviously very different. "He apparently couldn't make himself heard even in a small room except when you bent all your ears in his direction," McKelway wrote. "And when you did, he appeared to evade your attempt to hear him. He did this by interposing a cigar or pipe among the words which were trying to escape through teeth that had obviously been pried open only with effort, an effort with which the speaker had no real sympathy and to which he was unwilling to lend more than half-hearted assistance."[35] LeMay, McKelway observed, would be considered rude by civilian standards.

McKelway's negative feelings towards LeMay took a sudden turn during the change of command ceremony. After the speeches and the parade, McKelway, as press officer, suggested a picture be taken of the two generals shaking hands. LeMay had been trying to stay off to the side, hugging the background.

When he reluctantly came forward for the required picture, McKelway thought LeMay seemed surprised that somebody even wanted him in a photo. As he stood there, his awkward attempts to hide his lit pipe to the point of trying to put it in his pocket made him seem both human and vulnerable to McKelway. Trying to help, McKelway suggested he hold the pipe for LeMay while the picture was taken.

McKelway was, by profession, an astute observer of human beings. He would look at the world around him, see parts of it that most people might not notice, and then describe them masterfully in a prose that would be typeset in one of the world's outstanding literary journals. Rarely was McKelway caught off guard. But here, in the middle of the Pacific in an ordinary military ceremony, McKelway saw something in LeMay that made him realize this silent, occassionally rude and somewhat fumbling man might actually have those very rare human qualities of brains and heroism. Oddly, he found this very disturbing. After all the long, sleepless nights and losses and the hard lessons he had learned in his three years in the Army Air Forces, McKelway was physically bone tired and mentally exhausted. "My God, I think I was saying soundlessly to myself, if this LeMay turns out to be another great young Air Forces general, I will desert. Couldn't I have a lousy, easygoing mediocre general just for a few weeks, a few days? I want to relax! I've got to relax! Dear God, don't tell me this LeMay is as good as he looked just now."

Right after the picture was taken, LeMay came back to McKelway, who had been up the entire night before, and interrupted his thoughts. "Better get some sleep," LeMay told him in a voice that was barely audible. "Thanks for holding my pipe."[36]

What soon became apparent to everyone on the base was not just that this new commander was different from anyone else they had served under previously; he brought an indefinable air that motivated them to work a little harder and strive a little further than they had in the past. But it was impossible to explain it in words. McKelway found that a lot of the men walked away from LeMay scratching their heads and simply saying in the parlance of the day, "That guy's a pistol. A real pistol."[37]

"That was hardly an articulate explanation of LeMay's apparently profound effect upon the man," wrote biographer Thomas Coffey, "nor does [it explain] LeMay's ability to get men to break their necks for him." Coffey explained that this innate part of LeMay's character was even difficult for great writers like McKelway to describe.

LeMay exuded some powerful kind of masculine, straight, demanding but honest, clear and simple aura to which other men responded almost hypnotically. When he talked to someone, he spent more time seeking information than giving it. And after he had digested this information, he spent very few words discussing it. Until he made up his mind about something, he was inclined to listen and say nothing. After he made up his mind, he remained silent long enough to figure out how he could announce it in the fewest possible words. One or two sentences was his idea of a speech. Perhaps this paucity of words was by itself a factor in riveting the men around him. He had a way of sounding as if he had considered all the options, then chosen the only possible one. And by saying so in so few words, he seemed to convince everyone that, however surprising his decision might be, it was probably the right one.[38]

The semblance of shyness that McKelway thought he saw ceased to exist when it came to command. LeMay took over the Twenty-first like a force of nature hitting the tiny South Pacific Island. The first thing that caught LeMay's eye was the Navy's construction schedule for Guam, which aroused his substantial anger. Because the Navy was in charge of bringing in all the supplies, including the Army Air Force's bombs and fuel, it also supervised all engineering and construction on the island. Given the high cost in American lives to secure these islands (almost exclusively Navy and Marines), LeMay was outraged to see that tennis courts had been built before barracks for his air crews.

LeMay managed to get hold of a construction priority list and found it was not until page five that plans dealt with building anything for fighting. "Thousands and thousands of young Americans died on those islands in order to give us a base of operations against the Japanese homeland," he observed with dismay. "And here people were, piddling around with all this other stuff, and not giving us anything to fly from or fight with." When the head of one of his Wings arrived with his complement of B-29s, the crews had to sleep under the planes on the runways.

LeMay also discovered what he considered a completely foolish formality in protocol on Guam. Upon his arrival, he had quickly received an invitation to dine with the theater commander who "had built himself a splendid house, way up on the very highest peak," complete with Filipino houseboys. The next invitation came from the island commander who had "built himself another nice house." The third invitation came from the submarine commander who was living on the Vanderbilt yacht, which had been requisitioned for wartime service, again with fine linens and houseboys.

LeMay never excelled in these social situations, and with everything on his mind, these nightly visits struck him as an obscene waste of time and money. But he got this point across in his own unique style. After dining with each commander, he extended reciprocal invitations to all three commanders to join him in his tent where they ate canned rations like all the rest of his crews. "I did promote a bottle of liquor, but I had to wheedle that from a Neptune (Navy) type." The point was made, "and eventually they came up with the facilities we needed. And they built fine quarters for us."[39] LeMay eventually acknowledged that no one could have built things fast enough for him. But he was still steamed every time he saw those tennis courts.

Throughout the first month, LeMay's performance was as poor as Hansell's. In his first mission on January 23, LeMay sent seventy-three B-29s against the aircraft-engine plant in Nagoya. One B-29 crashed on takeoff. One was downed by Japanese fighters. Only twenty-three Superfortresses managed to bomb the plant through the thick cloud cover, and of those, only four bombs and a few incendiaries hit the target.

LeMay found the constant bad weather over Japan particularly vexing. Had the Soviets been willing to pass on any reports from Siberia—where Japan's weather originates—it would have helped. But "they were reluctant and suspicious by nature," LeMay noticed, which added to his growing distrust of the Russians. In order to glean crucial weather data, the Americans resorted to trying, unsuccessfully, to break some of the Russian codes in order to obtain the information. The cloud cover broke long enough to allow only three or four bombing runs per month at best. LeMay was more than aware of his own poor performance. "I realized that we had not accomplished very much during those six or seven weeks. We were still going in too high, still running into those big jet stream winds upstairs. Weather was almost always bad." He was up again at night going over everything in his mind. Intelligence, photos, and all available statistics were spread out on a table in the headquarters office where he sat and studied them for hours. It was not unlike his early days in the mess hall at Chelveston, except the problems and the environment were completely different.

In Europe, LeMay had faced a horrific defense from the Germans in fighter planes and flak. Here in the Pacific, the Japanese defenses were nowhere near as destructive. But because of high winds, bad weather, and technical problems, he still could not get this new plane with three times the bomb load to drop bombs on the target. In Europe, he solved the puzzle by flying in tighter formations and just grinding the Germans down. How could he compensate for this very different set of variables?

·   ·   ·   ·

THE INCENDIARY

LeMay found no answers to the problem of failing to strike the Japanese in front of him except for using an alternative weapon. Though LeMay preferred high explosive ordnance, in India General Chennault pressured him into trying the recently introduced incendiary bombs. LeMay sent almost 100 B-29s against the large Japanese supply base in Hankow, loaded with 500 tons of incendiaries.

What became clear soon afterwards was that the massive fires created by the new bombs knocked out Hankow as a base of operations for the Japanese. He realized he had been wrong. The attack left an impression on LeMay.

The incendiary—or napalm—was a jelly-like substance produced by DuPont and Standard Oil and developed by a team of Harvard chemists led by Louis Fieser. The scientists found that when they mixed two chemicals, *naph*thalene and *palm*itate, with gasoline, the mixture turned from a liquid to a jelly. When ignited, the new substance burned at extremely high temperatures. In testing out the new substance, the War Department employed art historians, architects, and set designers from RKO studios to build replicas of Berlin and Tokyo at the Dugway Proving Grounds in Utah. They then "attacked" the mock capitals using incendiaries to evaluate how to use the weapon to its maximum advantage. LeMay remembered reading in *National Geographic* magazine as a boy that most Japanese cities were constructed of wood and paper—98 percent of Tokyo's factory district, as it turned out.

On February 13–15, 1945, British and American bombers using incendiary bombs created a firestorm in the center of Dresden, Germany, gutting over thirteen square miles of the city. Estimates of civilian dead range from 24,000 to 40,000. Earlier in the war, on July 24, 1943, British bombers dropped incendiaries on Hamburg, Germany, killing as many as 40,000 people. In both cases, the Allies claimed the cities were legitimate military targets. Hamburg was a crucial industrial center with important harbor facilities. Dresden was considered a communications hub and transit center. But the debate over military legitimacy and outright terror bombing has intensified in the years since. Considered an Allied atrocity by some today, the public reaction at the time was largely supportive. It was considered a legitimate option by LeMay.

Late at night, as he studied all available reports of the British and American raid on Dresden, the idea started to come together. What if he abandoned the concept of target bombing altogether? Instead of daylight raids, what if he went in at night, just as Bomber Harris in England had been advocating all along? It made sense to pursue target bombing in Germany, but this situation called for something else.

The radical change did not stop there as he considered the complicated problem from all angles and expanded the concept. The B-29 had been created to fly higher than any other plane. But that technique had produced no results. As he considered abandoning the entire reason the B-29 had been developed in the first place, other possibilities began to emerge. If he used Thomas Power's idea[40] (his friend and strict commander of the 314th Wing) and flew his planes in very low—at, say, 5,000 or 6,000 feet, instead of 30,000 feet where the jet stream was so fierce, the planes would burn up far less fuel. Though the large planes would be perfectly visible then, even at night, the Japanese would be caught off guard. They would never expect them that low. He took out his slide rule and began to calculate the change in weight from the enormous savings in fuel, which would allow the planes to carry more bombs. Everything started to click, and he extended his calculations into another unprecedented thought.

He determined from intelligence reports and his own personal experiences in China that the Japanese had almost no night fighter capability. If that were the case, the B-29s would not need their defense guns and their ammunition and their gunners, saving even more weight. That meant room for even more bombs. Now the slide rule was working at double time. The calculations poured onto the paper, and each one reinforced his conclusions. He knew the men would howl about it all, but he thought he could persuade them with this reasoning: the Japanese anti-aircraft guns—set at higher altitudes—would be ineffective at 5,000 to 7,000 feet. The planes should be safe. The Japanese would quickly compensate for this, but he thought he could get in a few missions before they figured it out. And in the short span of time, he hoped to be able to knock them so hard and so fast that they might just consider surrendering.

Although LeMay thought the raid would succeed without huge losses to Japanese flak, the rest on his team were not convinced. His intelligence officers, familiar with the low-level mission to the Ploesti oil fields in Romania that resulted in B-24s being torn to shreds by German flak "almost to a man" predicted B-29 losses in the appalling range of 70 percent. They were all worried about "light flak"—smaller weapons that would be able to hit planes at such low altitudes. But proving it would fail was impossible without at least trying out his theory.

LeMay was most troubled by the potential for a massive loss of his own crewmen, not Japanese civilians. In his memoirs, LeMay makes more than one reference to a letter that continually weighed on him.

Dear General: This is the anniversary of my son Nicky being killed over Hamburg/Berlin/Tokyo. You killed him General. I just wanted to remind you of it. I'm going to send you a letter each year on the same date, the anniversary of his death, to remind you.

LeMay's only way to stop these types of letters from coming was to end the war. He rationalized the potentially significant loss of Japanese life on the ground with the following logic: Marines were suffering horrendous casualties on Iwo Jima in slow, agonizing fighting, evidence that the Japanese were becoming even more ferocious the closer Americans came to the home islands. And unlike the U.S. or German industry, which was factory centered, Japanese manufacturing was greatly decentralized—individual parts for airplanes, tanks, and bombs were produced in homes and in backyards. "No matter how you slice it, you're going to kill an awful lot of civilians. Thousands and thousands. But if you don't destroy Japan's capacity to wage war, we're going to have to invade Japan. And how many Americans will be killed in an invasion of Japan? Five hundred thousand seems to be the lowest estimate. Some say a million. We're at war with Japan. We were attacked by Japan," LeMay later wrote. For LeMay, the debate over civilian deaths came down to one blunt question: "Do you want to kill Japanese or would you rather have Americans killed?" His logic left little room for nuance.[41]

How to successfully bomb Japan with the B-29 was the question that tormented him as he lay on his cot throughout those muggy nights on Guam during late February. The worry of not producing results and having Americans killed in an invasion overrode any other concerns, especially killing Japanese civilians. He decided using the incendiary was worth a try.

LeMay did have to take into account the impact on Washington of a tremendous loss of Japanese civilian life and property. He understood the military chain-of-command, and he knew how to get around any issue that could stop his plan. On March 1, 1945, Lauris Norstad paid another visit to Guam. The alleged purpose of the visit was to check up on the B-29 operation. The real reason was to push LeMay to get the job done. So LeMay asked Norstad about his incendiary idea without really asking him. All he said was: "You know General Arnold. I don't know him. Does he ever go for a gamble? What do you think?"[42]

Norstad's answer was as vague as LeMay's question. He told LeMay that he thought General Arnold was "all for going in and getting the war won."[43] By asking Norstad such an oblique question, LeMay protected both Arnold and Norstad while putting his own career on the line. If it were an utter failure, only LeMay would answer for it. Everyone else was evasive. There was never a direct reference to an incendiary attack on one of the world's most populated cities. According to historian Richard Rhodes, LeMay's predecessor, Possum Hansell, was relieved of command because he would not rise to the bait that the Pentagon offered. "Billy Mitchell, the Air Force's earliest strategic champion, had pointed out the vulnerability of Japanese cities to fire as long ago as 1924. [Hansell's refusal to use incendiaries] doomed his command."[44]

Although LeMay had good reason to believe that he would get the green light for this mission, he never asked anyone above him directly for permission, but it was there in a variety of circumstantial ways. The ordnance dumps on Guam and Tinian were already filled with thousands of tons of incendiaries. They had to be there for a reason. It was almost as if Arnold was waiting for a commander to go ahead with the raid without actually suggesting it himself. But successful mission or catastrophic failure, LeMay would present it as a fait accompli. As Air Force historian Michael Sherry wrote, LeMay's "command genius lay in his decision to avoid introducing these methods piecemeal, to take the parts and throw them together at once, producing a whole dwarfing the sum of the parts."[45]

His decision made, LeMay worked on the problem with Tom Power who would lead such a mission. From that point on, it became a matter of engineering and mathematics. Together they came up with a plan to go in at lower altitudes in a series of massive lightning raids that would occur on consecutive nights, catching the Japanese off guard. They decided to abandon formation flying altogether. Each plane would fly individually, in three staggered lines between 5,000 and 7,000 feet. The first planes to take off would fly at slower speeds in order for the later planes to catch up. It would be unlike anything seen yet in the War: three long lines of bombers coming in at a very low altitude. The bombardier's job would be greatly simplified, because a small group of planes coming from a different direction would drop incendiaries in the front and back of the target zone before the lines of bombers arrived, similar to lighting up both ends of a football field at night. The planes coming after them from another direction would see the fires that the lead bombers had set and then bomb the area in between. The plan was brilliant in its simplicity. The human cost would be determined later.

The two men, along with their armaments officer and chief engineer, worked out the ordnance questions. LeMay decided to drop E-46 clusters that would explode at 2,000 feet above the ground. Each cluster would release thirty-eight incendiary bombs of napalm and phosphorus, creating a rain of fire over the city. In all, 8,519 clusters would be dropped, releasing 496,000 individual cylinders weighing 6.2 pounds each, resulting in 1,665 tons of incendiaries to be dropped on Tokyo that night.

A senior staff meeting was held with Norstad, Power, the commanders of the various wings that would participate in the mission, and the intelligence and ordnance officers. Ralph Nutter was there, as well as the command navigator. LeMay began by admitting the B-29 operations had been a failure up until then, and that there was no hope of waiting for better weather and lower winds—that just was not going to happen. Then he presented his plan for the night incendiary attack in detail. According to Nutter, "LeMay looked around the room, letting his gaze fall on each one of us. [Then he said,] 'I haven't heard anyone say that a low-altitude night mission is an unreasonable risk to our crews.'"[46] No one challenged LeMay's plan.

Near the end of the briefing, an intelligence officer asked the question that was on everyone's mind: "Aren't firebomb attacks on cities the type of terror bombing used by the RAF that our air force has been trying to avoid?"

"I know there may be some who call it uncivilized warfare," replied LeMay. "But you simply can't fight a war without some civilian casualties. General Norstad tells me that the press has been howling about the civilian casualties caused in Dresden. We didn't start this war, but the quicker we finish it, the more lives we will save—and not just American. We want to avoid killing civilians if possible, but keep in mind that the Japanese workers who manufacture weapons are part and parcel of their military machine. My first duty is to protect and save as many of our crews as possible."[47]

Nutter was perceptive enough to realize that Norstad did not say much throughout the briefing. He neither questioned what LeMay was saying nor second guessed him. But Nutter also understood that if the mission failed, it would not be Arnold or Norstad who would be hung out to dry.

There was one part of the operation LeMay was not looking forward to. When the crews came into the main hall, Tom Power, who gave the briefing as mission commander, explained that no defensive guns and gunners would be flying on this mission. Only the rear gunner would fly, and he would be there only to observe. There were some murmurs, and some of the officers protested the idea of breaking up the crews. Power told them that they had given this a great deal of thought and explained the reasons they thought it would be okay. One person said "5,000 feet, you've got to be kidding." And another voice called it a suicide mission. LeMay was there and said nothing. But Power answered these men, saying he would not lead the mission if he thought that was the case, and General LeMay, who had the most bomber experience in the whole Air Force against the Germans and the Japanese, would not send them on a mission he did not think would work.[48]

At the end of the briefing, Power said this was the most important mission yet in the entire war, and if it was successful, it could prevent an invasion. Then he turned to LeMay and asked, "Would you like to make any comments, sir?" LeMay shook his head and responded, "No, you said it all much better than I could."[49]

The men appeared to have faith that their commander had truly calculated the risks with an eye toward their well being. Colonel Glen W. Martin, who commanded the 504th Bomb Group, was in the briefing room. He described the strange scene that occurred after the usual announcements concerning procedural matters and the target—Tokyo. "The tension and the interest on the part of those hundreds of people in that briefing room were truly remarkable. There was visible excitement and interest and eagerness."[50]

There was one dynamic at play that LeMay had not predicted—the men were also frustrated with their poor performance up to that point. They wanted results as much as he did. And they trusted him. They were not upset about the gunners because they thought they needed the protection. If LeMay said they did not, they believed him. They were uncomfortable because each crew worked as a team, and that team had now been broken up. In spite of the danger, many of the gunners were not happy to have to stay behind.

The first planes took off on March 9, 1945, starting at 4:36 in the afternoon, with the final bombers lifting off the runway three hours later. 325 B-29s in total took off from three separate groups. In bomb tonnage, it was equivalent to over 1,000 B-17s. LeMay watched each plane take off at the flight line. He stayed down at the field until the last one was gone. He was frustrated that he was not flying this one. But beyond the strict prohibition from Washington, there was an additional reason that kept LeMay grounded.

Shortly after he took command of the Twenty-First Air Forces in January, an Army engineer officer came to see him. LeMay knew something was unusual because it was listed as a meeting of extreme importance, but the officer was only a captain. In his office on Guam, the captain told him about the Manhattan Project and the status of the nuclear bomb. "Generally speaking, I could understand what the Army man was talking about. We had a very powerful weapon. But it was late in the war and I was busy."[51] LeMay was at first dismissive of the atomic bomb. He was more amazed that the Army was able to keep a project of that size secret. But once he was briefed on the Manhattan project, any consideration of flying missions again was out of the question. No one with that information could risk falling into Japanese hands. His flying days in the war were over for good.

LeMay would not hear anything from the planes until sometime after midnight (March 10) Guam time when the bombs were released. He spent those hours with Lieutenant Colonel McKelway. Out of nervousness, LeMay opened up in an uncharacteristic fashion. Without being asked, LeMay offered some insight into a surprising piece of his personality—his lack of confidence. "I never think anything is going to work," he told McKelway, "until I've seen the pictures after the raid. But if this one works, we will shorten this damned war out here."[52]

Several hours later, in an effort to kill time, LeMay said, "We won't get a bombs away for another half hour. Would you like a Coca-Cola? I can sneak in my quarters without waking up the other guys and get two Coca-Colas and we can drink them in my car. That'll kill most of the half hour." Norstad was sacked out on a guest cot in LeMay's hut. It was a strange juxtaposition—like a Hollywood moment out of an Andy Hardy film. As this massive force of bombers headed towards Tokyo with more destructive power than any armada in the history of man, the architect of the raid sat in a Chevrolet, drank a Coke, and chatted about his observations during his last assignment. "The way all those people are in India gets you down. It makes you feel rotten," he told McKelway. If he sensed the irony of that statement on this particular night, he did not expand on it.

·   ·   ·   ·

THE CATASTROPHE

Over a thousand miles to the north, all the elements to create a monumental disaster unprecedented in human history were falling into place. Before the planes arrived, winds started gusting at over forty miles an hour. It was a cold, dry wind, typical of early spring in that region. As midnight approached, the coastal watchers were the first to hear the long hums of the B-29s. But because there was no formation, there was some confusion and the alarms were not sounded until 12:15, a full seven minutes after the bombs began to fall. It would not have mattered anyway. In their hubris, Japanese officials had never built adequate shelters for the civilian population. They did not believe the Americans were capable of bombing from these great distances.

Across Tokyo, residents looked up in amazement. They had never seen the "B-sans" so low, nor had they ever seen so many at once. But more than the numbers and the strange, long line of planes, it was the unusual flowers of light that fell from the night sky that mesmerized an entire population. The fire falling from the sky reminded a German Catholic priest, Father Gustav Bitter, of the tinsel hung on a Christmas tree back home, "and where these silver streamers would touch the earth, red fires would spring up."[53] Father Bitter also recorded, in an almost poetic fashion, the effect of the light and shadows on the planes above: "The red and yellow flames reflected from below on the silvery undersides [of the planes] so that they were like giant dragon flies with jeweled wings against the upper darkness."[54]

Then, in a sudden fury, everything changed as the incendiaries hit home. People ran in panic. Not just rooftops and houses caught on fire, but the clothes and hair of the people running were also ignited. People who ran to a nearby river for relief found that the water was boiling. One young woman described a school where people sought refuge:

The entire building had become a huge oven three stories high. Every human being inside the school was literally baked or boiled alive in the heat. Dead bodies were everywhere in grisly heaps. None of them appeared to be badly charred. They looked like mannequins, some of them with a pinkish complexion.[55]

French journalist Robert Guillain wrote: "A B-29 flew by with an odd rhythmic buzzing that filled the night."[56] A Danish diplomat, Lars Tillitse, described how searchlights illuminated the huge undersides of the B-29s, which quickly became targets. But the planes flew on seemingly immune to the ground fire. Finally, a cheer went up from a panicked crowd as one B-29 was hit. "The whole body glowed red, but the plane continued its flight until, like lightning, white flames burst from the sides. Enveloped in fire, the Superfortress plummeted to the ground."

The greatest problem the Americans encountered had not been foreseen. Because of the heat, huge updrafts suddenly yanked the planes thousands of feet higher, some as high as 15,000 feet. One B-29 was flipped upside down and crashed. One story, never confirmed, tells how a Japanese newspaper that sailed upwards and entered one of the B-29s was not discovered until the plane landed back in Guam. The crews in the planes near the back of the line felt the immense heat and had to put on their oxygen masks. Some claimed they could smell burning flesh. Since Tom Power was the commander of the mission, his plane was the first in and last one out. He circled the area and recorded his observations and radioed back his reports to Guam.

On the ground, something extraordinary was happening. The incendiaries had created tornadoes of fire, sucking the oxygen from the entire area. A majority of the victims died of asphyxiation. Estimates put the number of people who died in Tokyo that night at 100,000, but the actual number can never be known. Over sixteen square miles of Tokyo—among the most densely populated sixteen square miles in the world—were destroyed. More than a million people were left homeless. Another two million people left Tokyo, not to return until after the war. The Air Force history of the war records that "the physical destruction and loss of life at Tokyo exceeded that at Rome...or that of any of the great conflagrations of the western world—London, 1666...Moscow, 1812...Chicago, 1871...San Francisco, 1906. No other air attack of the war, either in Japan or Europe, was so destructive of life and property."[57]

The U.S. Strategic Bombing Survey was more direct: "Probably more persons lost their lives by fire at Tokyo in a 6-hour period than at any [equivalent period of] time in the history of man."[58]

Masuko Harino ran from the factory where she worked. "People's clothes were on fire...some people were writhing about in torment and no one had time to help them. Intense heat was coming from the firestorm. My eyes seemed about to pop out...we ran. We saw fleeing shapes, but little else."[59] As people tried to flee, the flames seemed to outrun them as they abandoned the possessions they carried along the roads. The entire raid over the target lasted two hours and forty minutes.

"They came in majesty," wrote Father Bitter, giving the B-29s almost human, even divine power, "like kings of the earth. The flak from the ground poured up toward them, but they held their course, proud and regal and haughty, as if they said 'I am too great for any man to do me harm.' I watched them as if I were in a trance."[60]

Shortly after midnight LeMay was in the command center when word came back of a conflagration. "The staff cheered when we received the first optimistic radio reports from Power," wrote Nutter, who was also waiting there. "LeMay told us to be quiet. He wanted to know the extent of our losses before we did any celebrating."[61] When he heard that losses were, so far, light, he began to relax a bit. Closer to morning, LeMay went down to the field to wait for the planes to return. It was already after dawn on March 10 when Power emerged from his aircraft. He looked tired, but shouted to LeMay: "It was a hell of a good mission." Twelve planes out of 346 were lost. Many more were damaged. Out of 3,307 crewmen, 96 were killed or missing, and 6 more were wounded. The loss rate of 5 percent was much lower than the average mission in Europe.

In Washington, there were debates over the morality of mass civilian casualties. But these debates were held in private rooms behind closed doors. There is no record that Franklin Roosevelt ever opposed the bombing campaigns in Japan or Europe. The only person to question the incendiary campaign was Secretary of War Henry Stimson. But he accepted Hap Arnold's explanation that it was necessary because of the dispersion of Japanese industry. According to historian Richard B. Frank, the Allied leaders were firm in their resolve to destroy fascism and "massive urban bombing complemented the aim of unconditional surrender. It was not just a handful of men in rogue governments who flaunted vile ideologies; whole populations imbibed these beliefs and acted as willing acolytes. Unconditional surrender and vast physical destruction would sear the price of aggression into the minds of the German and Japanese peoples."[62]

General George Marshall, who led the military of the United States, had to weigh two contrasting public viewpoints: Americans wanted to see the war through . . . but unlike the War in Europe where, after the Battle of the Bulge, the German army began to crumble near the end, the Japanese fought even harder the closer Americans came to the home islands. The losses on both sides were getting worse, not better. The brutality was spinning out of control, and the Japanese showed no signs of giving up. On Tarawa, 99.7 percent of the Japanese defenders chose death rather than surrender. In the Marshall Islands it was 98.5 percent. Then on Saipan, where 97 percent of the Japanese soldiers chose death, the Marines, who were by now used to death and destruction, witnessed something that unnerved even battle-hardened veterans of previous campaigns. Of the 20,000 civilians who lived on the island, half of them, 10,000 women and children, chose death by suicide rather than surrender. The Americans were dealing with something unique in their experience: a death culture. Marshall knew an invasion would be far more costly than anything seen yet, and he was not sure just how long a democracy would accept the unbelievably high rate of loss before they turned against the war.

The Japanese, as well, calculated that though they could no longer win the war, Americans might grow weary and allow the Japanese to exact better terms if the price of victory was costly enough. As historian Edward Drea aptly phrased it, "Undergirding all Japanese strategy was a dismissive view that Americans [were] products of liberalism and individualism and incapable of fighting a protracted war."[63] The War Journal of the Japanese Imperial Headquarters backed this up in July 1944: "We can no longer direct the war with any hope of success. The only course left is for Japan's one hundred million people (the real count was closer to 72 million) to sacrifice their lives by charging the enemy to make them lose the will to fight."[64]

Something else was occurring at the time of which most Americans were unaware. In any given month in the first half of 1945, upwards of 250,000 Asians were dying at the hands of the Japanese—a quarter of a million lives every thirty days. In all, more than 15 million Chinese, Koreans, and Filipinos died in a lesser-known holocaust of World War II. That slaughter only came to a halt when the Japanese were forced to surrender and the Imperial Army came home.[65]

LeMay's reaction to the raid was certainly in character. He went to the PX and treated himself to an expensive cigar. Then, even though he had been up for close to forty-eight hours, he did not go to bed. Wasting no time, he ordered the ground crews to turn the planes right around and push their advantage. LeMay knew the Japanese would adapt themselves to this new form of warfare, and he wanted to strike again before they could figure out a counter defense. He wanted to fly out that night, but the crews were unable to regroup. Everyone around him argued against it, and he stood down. However, just twenty-four hours later, on March 11, the planes were ready again, and this time they flew to Nagoya. Then, on March 13, 301 B-29s firebombed Osaka. On March 16, they firebombed Kobe. And on March 19, another 290 B-29s went back to hit Nagoya for a second time.

Then they were forced to stop. The Navy, which was in charge of transporting all the ordnance used by the Air Force, never believed LeMay could possibly use up all the incendiaries they had stockpiled. They were wrong. LeMay had to stop because he ran out.

CHAPTER NINE

"BRUTAL LEMAY"

SURVIVORS DESCRIBED TOKYO AS A MOONSCAPE OF TWISTED reddish-black iron, roasted sheet metal and rubble scattered across sixteen square miles of what two days earlier was one of the most densely populated areas in the world. Not a single man-made structure still stood within the fire zone. Perhaps the worst part was what Captain Funato Kazuyo described as

[the] forest of corpses packed so tightly they could have been touching as they died: the entire river surface was black as far as the eye could see, black with burned corpses, logs and who knew what else, but uniformly black from the immense heat that had seared its way through the area as the fire dragon passed. It was impossible to tell the bodies from the logs at a distance. The bodies were all nude, the clothes had been burned away, and there was a dreadful sameness about them, no telling men from

women or even children. All that remained were pieces of charred meat. Bodies and parts of bodies were carbonized and absolutely black.[1]

The dead were the lucky ones. Those who survived walked around like ghosts saying nothing; those who could not walk and were in great pain were just left to die. There was no medicine or food or even drinking water for them. In truth, no amount of preparedness would have been adequate for the scope of devastation caused by the firebombing. Many of the bodies just crumbled when they were lifted, like the remnants of a charcoal fire. On the riverbanks, the tide became the villain, disgorging masses of bodies onto the shore as it pushed forward and then receded.[2] The grisly retrieval of bodies took weeks.

Before this raid, slightly fewer than 1,300 people total had died in air raids on Tokyo. Now, in one night, nearly a hundred times that number were killed—many lying in piles at the end of every block. The actual numbers varied. Just as the Japanese were incapable of a concerted rescue effort, their statistical data was ineffective for an accurate counting of the dead. Ultimately, a number of 100,000 has been considered closest to correct, but because it was impossible to identify the bodies, and because entire families and neighborhoods were wiped out, the real number will never be known. At least 70,000 people were buried in mass pits.[3]

Against the advice of his counselors, Emperor Hirohito drove through the stricken area on March 18. Automobiles were an unusual sight at that point in the war because of the extreme shortage of gasoline. A military aide recalled the event: "The victims, who had been digging through the rubble with empty expressions on their faces, watched the imperial motorcade pass by with reproachful expressions. Were they grudgeful to the emperor because they had lost relatives, their houses and belongings? Or were they in a state of utter exhaustion and bewilderment?"[4]

The Japanese now had a special name for the man who caused this catastrophe: "Brutal LeMay." Radio Tokyo called him a "blood-thirsty maniac" and "wanton killer." One Japanese broadcaster described him this way: "Only a lieutenant in the United States Air Forces in 1938, he was promoted to major-general and was placed in command of the United States heavy bombers attacking Germany. It was none other than LeMay who reduced Hamburg to ashes." LeMay's response when he heard this: "Guess that would be news to the RAF!"[5]

When the planes returned from the mission on March 10, 1945, the greatest upset LeMay had to field had nothing to do with the casualties on the ground. Robert McNamara was one of the officers who debriefed the crews that day, and he was present at the main debriefing session in the large auditorium, watching as one angry pilot stood up in the crowded auditorium and directly confronted LeMay. "God Dammit!" the pilot shouted, looking right at LeMay, "who was the son-of-a-bitch who took this airplane down to 5,000 feet? I lost my wingman." The pilot already knew the answer to his question. He was furious. He thought LeMay had been reckless, not in the firebombing, but in lowering the altitude of the attack, which made the Air Force more vulnerable.

"LeMay was legendary for being monosyllabic," remembered McNamara. "I never heard him use more than two words in sequence. It was basically yes, no, yup. But this time, LeMay looked at the pilot who had shouted at him and, uncharacteristically, tried

to reason with him, 'Why are we here?' LeMay asked, almost plead-
ing, not just to the pilot, but to everyone else sitting in the large,
silent room. 'Why are we here? Yes, you lost your wingman and it
hurts me as much as it does you. I was the one who sent him there.
And I've been there. I know what this is. But we lost one wingman
and we destroyed Tokyo.'"[6] LeMay understood that sacrifice was
necessary in the short term for the greater goal of winning the war
and ending the massive killing—on all sides. That included U.S.
airmen as well as Japanese civilian casualties.

The very fact that a pilot could stand up and talk like this to his
commanding officer, a general, no less, was another revolutionary
concept LeMay initiated. The "closed-door briefing" that followed
every mission broke all military tradition. Here, a man of any rank
could call his commander a stupid son-of-a-bitch if he thought his
boss had done something foolish. The accuser would never be reprimanded for it. LeMay's reasoning was as simple as it was necessary: it was another opportunity for him to learn more. "You have
to stay at least two steps ahead of the enemy," he would say. He
needed to learn everything faster than his opponent, and this could
only happen if crews felt they could speak freely, without recrimi-
nation. The last thing LeMay wanted was to be surrounded by yes-
men, and he never once reprimanded anyone for speaking his
mind during a debriefing.

Although there was criticism after the Dresden fire bombings in
February, the Air Force sought to limit any negative response to
the Tokyo raid. Norstad sent a memo to LeMay suggesting he
emphasize this was the only way to target dispersed industries.[7] It
seemed to work, since there were no public protests over the massive number of deaths. General Arnold, recuperating from his

fourth major heart attack in a Florida hospital, gave no indication that there was any debate over civilian casualties. "Congratulations," he cabled LeMay, giving him the green light to proceed. "This mission shows your crews have the guts for anything." Ten days later, he wrote a longer, even more complimentary letter to LeMay reminding him that by July 1, 1945, he would have 1,000 B-29s under his command, which "leads one to conclusions which are impressive even to old hands at bombardment operations. Under reasonably favorable conditions you should then have the ability to destroy whole industrial cities, should that be required."[8] It was Arnold who had gambled with a $3 billion project that had not worked up until March 9, 1945. If he felt anything, it was probably relief.

Newspapers trumpeted the firebombing. Press reports were uniformly supportive. The *New York Times* reported the mission on its front page the morning of March 10, 1945:

RECORD AIR ATTACK: B-29S POUR OVER
1,000 TONS OF INCENDIARIES ON JAPANESE CAPITAL
BOMBS RAIN 1 HOUR
TREMENDOUS FIRES LEAP
UP IN THICKLY POPULATED CENTER OF BIG CITY
ENEMY IS SURPRISED.[9]

All the information, which went through McKelway on Guam, gave accurate accounts of the details, the numbers of B-29s, and the estimated damage. (McKelway himself would write a three-part account of the B-29 effort, the firebombing, and a glowing profile of LeMay for the *New Yorker* three months later.) Front page headlines would run for ten days straight on the raid and aftermath as the incendiary campaign burned more and more Japanese cities. On March 11, the *New York Times* ran another boldface headline: "City's Heart Gone, Not A Building Is Left Intact In 15 Square Miles Photos Show." Perhaps more revealing were two *Times* editorials that ran, first on March 12, entitled "Tokyo in Flames," and then the following day entitled "Japan's Target Cities." In the first, the *Times* editorial writers focused on the dispersal of industry (as directed by Norstad); as it conceded that the area of Tokyo was among the most densely populated on earth, it pointed out that "the people, factories and small establishments all contributed to Japan's war effort." The second editorial ended with a warning to Japan of what was to come as it drove home the reality of what the war in the Pacific had become: "These great cities may become no more than holes in the ground. But so far in this war the Japanese have done their deadliest fighting from holes in the ground."[10]

The press only reflected the mood of the public where little or no debate over the morality of killing civilians took place. Almost every family had a child, husband, or father in the service. The public was watching the horrific fighting on Iwo Jima, which had still not ended. Battle hardened divisions in Europe, which had survived some of the most brutal combat against the Germans, were being rotated back to the States. Soldiers were given a thirty-day leave, and then ordered to report to their units on the West Coast for eventual redeployment to the Pacific. Preparations for the invasion of the Japanese mainland were gathering steam. On Tinian, besides the long runways and the quarters for the B-29 crews that were being built, the Seabees and engineers were also building large hospital facilities that would accommodate some of the tens of thousands of wounded soldiers that were expected.

The Tokyo raid had an electric effect on U.S. troops throughout the theater. Jim Pattillo was a B-29 pilot in China. He had lost his brother two months after Pearl Harbor and had trained for four years to drop bombs on the enemy. Like everyone else in the China-Burma-India Theater, he was mightily frustrated. "After a year of losing people and equipment with little to show for it, on the night of March 9–10, 1945, it was the first thing of strategic importance accomplished by the B-29 airplane. And we in India were spectators!" But Pattillo recalls the impact that the fire raid had on everyone around him. "You could have heard us cheering from India if you had just gone outside and listened. What the 73rd had accomplished raised not only their morale, but ours too."[11]

The debate over killing civilians in World War II has increased in the sixty-plus years since the war ended. Three generations later, the Allied victory over Japan may seem like a preordained conclusion, but the facts at the time do not bear this up. A few turns of fortune could have produced a very different outcome altogether. As in all wars, there were certain crucial moments that turned events in the favor of the Allies. The bombing of Tokyo was one of those moments.

Many Americans in the twenty-first century are shocked by the B-29s' destruction of Japan and view it in very negative terms, which is understandable given the horrific numbers of dead civilians. But there was no debate in America on March 10, 1945. There was pride, relief, and even gladness. Part of this came from residual anger over Pearl Harbor and the news reports about the Japanese treatment of practically any non-Japanese they encountered.

And part came from a wish to end the war and the bloodletting as quickly as possible. After the war, Ralph Nutter became a respected judge in California, and his legally trained mind found an explanation for the firebombing of Japan in an obscure opinion written by Supreme Court Justice Felix Frankfurter, who wrote, "The language of the picket line is very different from the language of the drawing room."

"I would say the problems facing a combat commander are very different from those of scholars and philosophers in the comfort of a library," Nutter explains. "[The firebombing] was a good faith decision on LeMay's part when faced with one million American casualties."[12]

The invasion of Japan itself was scheduled to come in two waves. The first wave, code named "Olympic," would consist of a large amphibious assault on the southernmost island of Kyushu on November 1, 1945. The second wave, operation "Coronet," would land near Tokyo Bay on March 1, 1946. The landing zones were named after cars, like Beach Buick and Beach Chevrolet. But there were so many landing zones that there were not enough automobiles to fill them all, and planners had to resort to the different parts of cars such as Beach Chassis and Beach Axle. The draft callup of fresh 18-year-olds and men previously exempt increased in the first months of 1945 because the Pentagon was worried that it might not have enough men in uniform for a prolonged and bloody battle in Japan. There was good reason to worry. Intercepted messages showed that Japan anticipated exactly where the invasion would take place, and instead of the three divisions that Americans expected to face, six to eight divisions were lying in wait by the summer. There was also a real concern (later proved correct) that the Japanese had kept thousands of aircraft hidden, to be used as suicide bombs aimed at the invasion fleet.

One American who had lived in Japan before the war was imprisoned in the Philippines and watched as the Japanese prepared to die to the last man. "American fighting men back from the front have been trying to tell America this is a war of extermination. They have seen it from foxholes and barren strips of bullet-strafed sand. I have seen it from behind enemy lines. Our picture coincides. This is a war of extermination. The Japanese militarists have made it that way."[13]

Following the Tokyo raid, Curtis LeMay was given the green light to expand his bombing campaign throughout all of Japan. At first, the Navy did not believe LeMay when he first increased his order for incendiaries. When LeMay predicted he would fly the B-29s 120 hours a month, they thought he was boasting because the best the Army Air Force could fly in England was thirty hours a month with a much more dependable airplane. But LeMay accomplished this logarithmic increase by creating a new and improved maintenance system for the B-29s, and the low level incendiary attacks caused less stress on the plane's troubled engines. After the second Nagoya mission on March 19, 1945, the Navy finally realized it would have to speed up deliveries, but the soonest LeMay could continue was not until April. After this adjustment, however, there was no let up in the supply, like the steady stream of B-29s and crews that arrived from the States daily.

Two days after Tokyo, LeMay had to deal with an unusual protest from the crews. The gunners who sat out the Tokyo raid were upset that they were left behind, and the crews demanded to be reunited. Although LeMay hated to give up the weight to carry fewer bombs, he also realized that each crew had become a team. Besides, he worried that the Japanese might adapt a new defense to the low-level attacks, so he acquiesced and had the guns and the gunners put back on the planes.

On the mission following Tokyo, LeMay made a rare engineering mistake. Because the fire in the first raid had been so intense, he thought he could spread out the field to hit a wider area. He was wrong. The fires in Nagoya were too far apart and unable to produce the same conflagration they had seen in Tokyo. Only two square miles of the city were destroyed. LeMay realized his mistake, and it did not happen again. The March 16 raid against Kobe destroyed three square miles. The bombers had to return to Nagoya because of LeMay's earlier miscalculation, but this time they laid waste to another three square miles of the city. Altogether, in those ten days in March 1945, thirty-three square miles of Japan's four most important industrial centers were gutted.[14]

Just as LeMay began charting the destruction of the mainland, he was pulled away for another operation. The Navy had figured out how to lay mines in the waters around Japan's harbors, but it would need the B-29s to accomplish the huge task. The B-29s were the only planes big enough to drop the one-ton mines by parachute into the waters around the Shimonoseki Strait. This entrance to Japan's Inland Sea was the vital link between the different islands that make up Japan that were central to the flow of raw material for its war production. The idea came from the planners on Admiral Nimitz's staff, and it may have been as important in ending the war as the incendiary raids and the atomic bombs. According to historian Richard B. Frank, "It is doubtful that any effort in World War II returned such a dramatic strategic effect for such a relatively trivial investment of resources as did the aerial mine laying campaign against Japan."[15]

Japan needed ten million tons of raw materials per year to maintain its economy, but could only produce six million on its own. All the rest came from the lands it had captured at the start of the war. Eighty-eight percent of the iron ore Japan needed to produce its steel came from China and Korea, along with 20 percent of its food and almost a quarter of its coal. Japan produced 250,000 tons of oil each year, but it needed more than six million tons for the war. No tanker reached Japan after March 1945.[16]

The mines were large, heavy, and ugly. Their genius was in the different ways they worked. When dropped, they immediately sank to rest on the ocean floor. One type of mine was triggered by the magnetic field created from the steel hulls of the ships. Another mine was triggered by the noises that emanated from a ship's propellers. And a third type was detonated by the pressure change when a ship passed overhead.[17] They were devastating in their effectiveness.

LeMay argued against the mining operation at first, echoing his boss, Hap Arnold, who did not want to cede any part of the Air Force to Admiral Nimitz as the head of the Navy. But the Air Force was overruled by the Joint Chiefs in March 1945. Washington ordered LeMay to provide Nimitz and the Navy with whatever they would need for the operation, and he did just that. Soon enough, LeMay saw the results and realized that he had been wrong. All told, the Air Force dropped over 12,000 mines and brought Japan's shipping down to one-tenth of what it had been before the mining. The Japanese failed to anticipate this type of warfare, and did not have the means to prevent it or to sweep the mines from the harbors. The success of the mission would later lead to a cata-strophic shortage of food for the population. Between the bomb-ing campaign, the mining, and the U.S. naval operations—especially with its submarine fleet—Japan should have realized the futility of the continuation of the war by that spring. Instead, its leaders continued to set up a devastating response to the coming invasion. In a clear sign of things to come, Japan sent out waves of kamikaze planes against the United States naval forces off Okinawa. Japan's all-out war continued.

The battle for Okinawa began at the end of March and would be the bloodiest of the war in the Pacific. Twelve thousand Americans died there, a greater number than on D-Day, and more than twice the number on Iwo Jima. LeMay was again asked to assist the Navy in whatever they needed, and this time he agreed. "An amphibious operation is the toughest military chore you can dream up," he admitted. "And it's up to everybody to turn to and get the dough-boys ashore. So we had a string of good weather and in seven days we had every airfield plastered."[18] The Navy was losing ships and sailors to the waves of kamikazes coming in from bases on the main island of Kyushu. Although LeMay pounded every Japanese base he could find, the Japanese went out afterwards with men and women using baskets of dirt to fill in the holes. The planes did not need to land again. They only had to take off, and they were able to accomplish this. When LeMay asked to go back to pounding the cities, he was ordered to continue the effort for Okinawa.

By April, LeMay had the incendiaries he needed and a massive fleet of B-29s, as more and more planes and crews were arriving from India and the States every day. To add to those growing num-bers, B-17 crews from Europe, where the war was coming to an end, were being retrained on the B-29s and began showing up in Guam and Tinian as well. With the added crews, the Twenty-first Air Force in the Marianas would now be known as the Twentieth Air Force.

LeMay sent his growing arsenal of bombers back to Tokyo on April 13, 1945, and destroyed over eleven square miles north of the Imperial Palace; two days later, on April 15, another six square miles were gutted. After another interlude to help again with the effort on Okinawa, LeMay focused exclusively on his bombing campaign through mid-May.

On April 12, 1945, Franklin Roosevelt, who had led the nation first through the depression and then the war, died suddenly. From LeMay's perspective, FDR had been his commander-in-chief since his early days at Selfridge in pursuit aircraft. He could barely even remember another president. The new president, Harry Truman, was unknown except for his Senate committee hearings that looked at waste in war production, in which the B-29 program was investigated. Truman quickly put the military at ease when he reassured the Pentagon that he had every intention of pursuing the same unconditional surrender policy as his predecessor. Less than three weeks later, Adolf Hitler shot himself in his bunker, bringing the war in Europe to an end on May 7, 1945, with the unconditional surrender of Germany. Now the entire focus of the U.S. military was directed to the Pacific.

With a *World Almanac* in hand, LeMay went down the list of Japanese cities one by one by population. On May 14, 1945, LeMay sent 529 B-29s in a daylight incendiary raid over Nagoya, destroying the Mitsubishi engine plant and 3.6 square miles of the city around it. Two days later, 457 bombers went back to Nagoya and destroyed another 3.8 square miles. On May 23 and 25, there were two more raids against Tokyo, destroying 5.3 and then 16.8 square miles. On May 29, it was 6.9 square miles of Yokohama, and on June 1, Osaka lost 3.1 miles of its industrial base. On June 5, 4.3 square miles of Kobe went up in flames.

Although the air war was certainly controlled by the Americans, the skies were still far from safe. On the May 23 raid, the bombers began to sustain much greater losses. Seventeen B-29s were lost, and in the following raid against Tokyo another twenty bombers went down. Almost all the losses were due to fighters, not flak. On the June 1 raid against Osaka, a squadron of P-51 escorts out of Iwo Jima ran into an unexpected typhoon over the Pacific, and twenty-seven were lost. The planes went on bombing with an almost monotonous regularity, but the dangers were still quite real.

The possibility of becoming a prisoner of war of the Japanese was greatly feared by all airmen. It was a very different threat from fighting the Germans. Although the conditions in various stalag prison camps throughout Germany were extremely rough, the prisoners were, for the most part, treated along the lines of the Geneva Convention. This cannot be said about Japan, which treated prisoners abominably from the very start of the war. Of the 140,000 Caucasian prisoners of war captured in Bataan, a third of them died in captivity. The rest were subjected to such barbarous treatment that, in many cases, death was preferable. According to Richard B. Frank,

> The record Japan created in her treatment of prisoners of war and civilian internees still appalls. Prisoners were starved and brutalized systematically. They were murdered by deadly purpose

or on momentary whim. They were beaten to death, beheaded, buried alive, burned to death, crucified, marched to death, shot, stabbed, strangled, and simply abandoned to die. Among U.S. Army personnel alone, the Japanese captured 24,992 of whom 8,634 (35 percent) died in captivity. By contrast, only 833 of 93,653 Army personnel held by Germany died in captivity, a rate of 0.9 percent.

The Japanese saved their greatest venom for the B-29 crews that parachuted from stricken planes. "Captured B-29 Airmen were shot, bayoneted, decapitated, burned alive or killed as boiling water was poured over them. Other aircrew members were beaten to death by civilians and shot with bows and arrows then decapitated." Perhaps the most appalling episode, according to historian Richard Frank, took place when

> the Western Japan military command gave some medical professors at Kyushu Imperial University eight B-29 crewmen. The professor cut them up alive, in a dirty room with a tin table where students dissected corpses. They drained blood and replaced it with sea water. They cut out lungs, livers, and stomachs. They stopped blood flow in an artery near the heart, to see how long death took. They dug holes in a skull and stuck a knife into the living brains to see what would happen.[19]

There was a real fear that the Japanese would execute all prisoners if it looked like they were going to be liberated. To a man, Allied POWs believed the Japanese would kill them if the Homeland was invaded, and surviving written documentation supports this belief.[20]

In mid-June, Hap Arnold left Washington for the long trip to Guam. He was finally well enough to see the operation firsthand and tell the commanders on the ground about some changes that were about to take place. There was another reason for his trip. After his fourth major heart attack, he wanted to get out of Washington. Even a trip around the globe and into a war zone was a tonic after being restricted to the Pentagon. When he arrived, he was able to watch the long line of hundreds of B-29s leave on the June 15 mission to Osaka. After the long and difficult problems he had to endure with the program, it strengthened his ailing heart to know that he was not wrong in pushing for the big bombers. They were now destroying Japan the way he had envisioned. Arnold met with LeMay, Lieutenant General Barney Giles, Commander of the Pacific Ocean Area Air Force under Admiral Nimitz, and Wing Commander Emmett "Rosie" O'Donnell Jr., a native New Yorker with a thick Brooklyn accent.

Arnold told them he was bringing in Tooey Spaatz, Nathan Twining, and Jimmy Doolittle to take over operations in the Marianas. LeMay did not seem perturbed in the slightest at this change in command structure. In LeMay's view, Arnold was bringing in "his winning team" from Europe. He got along well with Spaatz, and he knew Spaatz would leave him alone. LeMay also knew and liked Twining and Doolittle. And of course, he knew it would not matter if he liked the decision or not. In a letter home to Helen after he learned about the switch, he said he did not expect the war to last more than a few months longer anyway, and of course he wanted to see it through to the end, but "I won't be disappointed if I come home [and] if we can get a house and live normally again."[21]

Just before LeMay wrote that letter, Arnold asked him when he thought the war would end. LeMay had been so busy with daily operations that he really had not calculated that question. But he took Arnold's query seriously and told him he would have an answer in the morning. LeMay sat down that night with his top aides. They looked at the damage they had inflicted on Japan thus far and measured it against the targets that still needed to be hit. "And we couldn't find any targets that were going to be in existence after about the first of September."[22] One observer suggested that after a few months, any bomb raids would only bounce the rubble.

To play it safe, LeMay told Arnold October 1, after he cleaned up another thirty industrial targets. Arnold made note of this in his diary: "So far on my trip across the Pacific, no one had hazarded the time for the defeat of Japan, except LeMay. Neither Admiral Nimitz nor General Richardson, nor their staffs talked about when the war would be over."[23]

When Arnold landed on Guam, there was a message waiting, informing him that President Truman was going to meet with the Joint Chiefs three days from then, on June 18, to go over the plans for the November 1 invasion of Japan. The quick turn-around would have been too grueling for Arnold's health, so he ordered LeMay to go to Washington before the meeting and brief the Joint Chiefs that an invasion might not be necessary. With a small group of his top people from operations, logistics, and intelligence, LeMay left Guam almost immediately. They flew from there to Hawaii—a distance of 3,780 miles—in fifteen hours and forty-three minutes. Then, after refueling, they flew the next leg non-stop from Hawaii to Washington in twenty hours and fifteen minutes, with LeMay at the controls. They covered the 4,640 miles in a new record, arriving in Washington at 11:43 p.m. on June 16. Immediately upon arriving, LeMay called Helen in Cleveland and told her to come to Washington. She left early the next morning by train.

The weather in Washington was as hot and steamy as the Pacific Islands when they went to the Pentagon the next morning. LeMay brought out his rudimentary charts, which in some ways resembled an elementary school exposition, since all they had available in the Marianas was large brown butcher's paper by the roll. LeMay showed General George Marshall, Admiral William D. Leahy, and Admiral Ernest J. King the cities that had been bombed, what was left to bomb, the results of laying the mines, and the intelligence estimates on what the Japanese Army, Navy, and Air Force had left. Added to this was Japan's inability to produce war material. On the whole, LeMay concluded, an invasion on November 1 would not be necessary since the war would probably end by October 1, perhaps even sooner.

As LeMay spoke he could see he was not getting his message across. As the final insult, LeMay watched as General Marshall started to doze off in the middle of the talk. "I didn't blame the old boy for sleeping through a dull briefing," LeMay said later. "Here were these dumb kids coming in, saying they were going to end the war for him."[24] The entire endeavor was less than successful. The top military commanders continued heading full steam towards an invasion with the president's approval. To some extent, they had no choice. If LeMay was wrong, or if the atomic bomb did not work, or if it did and the Japanese still refused to give up—which was completely plausible—an invasion on this scale still had to be planned in great detail in advance.

LeMay's gruff bluntness and even his physical demeanor coming right out of combat were probably an ill fit for the Pentagon, even during war time. But one of those present at the meeting on June 18 was Major James Gould Cozzens, who wrote speeches and confidential reports. It was Cozzens who cast a novelist's eye on this stocky commander and saw something many did not. He recorded it in his diary on June 18, 1945.

> He had a dead cigar in his mouth when he came in, and he never moved it for three quarters of an hour, though talking around it well enough when occasion arose. The superficial first impression was that he was dumb or gross; but he has one of those faces that grow on you—real intelligence and even a kind of sweetness—as though he would not do anything mean, or even think anything mean, though he is well known to be a hard man, and you can see that too—becoming more apparent the longer you look at him. Around the motionless cigar he spoke sensibly.[25]

LeMay had one more meeting at the Pentagon with Major General Leslie R. Groves, the army general who oversaw the Manhattan Project. Groves explained the workings of the two different bombs that were expected in Tinian sometime in the summer. He told LeMay how the enriched uranium bomb differed from the plutonium bomb, and the power they were expected to generate. This was almost one month before the first test that would take place in New Mexico on July 16, so it was still all just theory. Groves and LeMay talked about the requirements of the crews and the B-29s that were going to drop the bombs. Groves explained that the bombs would arrive within weeks of each other, and it was expected that they would be used unless Japan surrendered. They discussed the best way to deliver the bomb. LeMay said that rather than put a fleet of B-29s around the delivery vehicle, he thought that one lone bomber by itself would be safer, since there were constantly single weather planes and photo observers flying unchallenged over Japan. LeMay thought his second meeting was more successful than the first.

For his part, Groves recorded in his diary: "This was my first meeting with LeMay and I was highly impressed with him. It was very evident that he was a man of outstanding ability. Our discussion lasted about an hour, and we parted with everything understood."[26] LeMay's background in nuclear physics was limited. As he put it, "I knew this would be a big bang, but I didn't know how big."[27]

LeMay was only peripherally involved with the dropping of the atomic bombs. In May 1945, a target selection committee led by J. Robert Oppenheimer, the scientific director of the Manhattan Project in Los Alamos, chose a list of cities and presented it to LeMay for his approval because of his knowledge of the area. The month before that, in April, LeMay was asked to find the proper site on Tinian to build the structures necessary for the 509th Composite Group which would deliver the fatal load. The 509th, led by Colonel Paul Tibbets, had been practicing its mission in Wendover, Utah with a group of B-29s. LeMay personally flew Colonel Elmer Kirkpatrick of the Manhattan Project to Tinian on April 3, 1945, where the two scouted out a location that would be secure and off-limits to everyone else on the island. The Seabees would build what was on the construction list—five warehouses, an administration building, roads, parking areas, generator buildings, a compressor shed, and air-conditioned buildings where the bombs would be assembled. Amazingly, all of this was accomplished by July 1. Because the bombs were so big, a pit with an elevator lift was designed to get it onboard the plane. The doors of the bomb bay on the B-29s had to be redesigned to make them larger. The aircraft itself had been modified from the earlier models to make sure the mechanical problems that plagued the B-29s would not occur in these planes. The finest maintenance engineers had been assigned to service the planes. The first of the combat crews of the 509th began arriving on Tinian on June 10. In all, 1,100 men were there by July.

Tinian was a marvel set in the middle of the Pacific. One year earlier, there was almost nothing on the island. But twelve months after the Marines landed, a medium-size American city was functioning with one purpose—to destroy as much of Japan as possible. It was a marvel that only the United States was capable of producing at that time. Everything had to be built, and every single form of building material had to be brought there. First, giant earth movers grated down the hills. The roads, runways, and buildings were constructed with a regimented focus. Because it was shaped like the island of Manhattan, the engineers who first started the building program gave the island New York City street names. The 509th would be located at 125th and Eighth Avenue, near Riverside Drive.

A barter economy soon came into existence. The Navy and the Marines seemed to have the best food. The Air Force did not. "It got to the point that I just didn't eat," remembers Ralph Nutter. "The food was just so lousy, I was down to 125 pounds." Often, the airmen made friends with the Marines and just ate with them. "The Seabees had everything," recalls Seymour Tabacoff, a B-29 navigator, "but they didn't have a whiskey allotment and we did. So you could trade with them. Somehow, they even managed to have fresh milk and eggs . . . I'm not sure how."[28]

Morton Camac, a twenty-two-year-old genius, was spotted by the head of the physics department at the University of Chicago, given a scholarship at the start of the war, and finished his degree in one year. After working first at the University of Chicago and then Los Alamos, he was sent to Tinian. Camac's job was to assemble the second bomb that would be dropped on Nagasaki. "We put the plutonium into Fat Man, that was the second bomb," remembers Camac. "The entire process took about ten minutes. It fit perfectly. So the rest of the time, we fished, we went swimming. I took a lot of pictures."[29]

Life was much more stressful for the crews who flew out nightly on combat missions. "When we weren't flying, we were drinking," remembered Seymour Tabacoff. The Brooklyn native enlisted when he was nineteen and served first with the Twentieth Air Force in China. His unit eventually came to Tinian, where he flew sixteen night missions. "We lived in Quonset huts. The missions were from 15 to 17 hours."[30] Just as in England, many airmen tried to forget about their jobs when they were back at their base. Once again, whiskey was the preferred escape. Unlike England, there were no friendly British girls on the other side of the fence. Instead, there were only endless miles of blue water.

Work on Tinian would often come to a halt when the long line of bombers took off for a raid. If men were off-duty, they would go down to an area near the beach where they could watch the mighty armada of hundreds of planes lifting off the ground one after the other every fifteen seconds. This would continue for an hour and a half. Too often, a plane would experience a mechanical failure and crash just after the runway, setting off its huge load of bombs. It was a sound felt throughout the island. Although there were rescue crews waiting at the end of the runway, there was usually little they could do to save the lives of the crews in these accidents.

Curtis LeMay was in charge of this great mass of technology and manpower. And he had seen it transform from sheets of paper in the early 1940s to masses of giant silver airplanes on islands that were barren just months before. But there is nothing recorded of his being overwhelmed by any of what he saw. He was always focused on getting it all working in a coordinated fashion and did not spend time on reflection. The closest he came to this was in his letters to Helen and even then, it was limited.

"We had 600 ships over Japan last night without a single loss and we told them what towns we would burn down," he wrote home to Helen on July 30, 1945, but he quickly moved on in the very next line saying, "Well, I'll have to go and dress for dinner. Love, Curt."[31] He did, of course, understand the formidable might that had been created, but he did not revel in it.

While the 509th, the special unit designated to drop the atomic bombs, was setting up its program and running practice missions to Iwo Jima to drop what they called "pumpkins"—large practice bombs—Curtis LeMay was not letting up on Japan. He had created a sort of race, not only to see if he could bomb Japan into surrendering before the November invasion, but even before an atomic bomb could be used. General Spaatz, who had taken over command of the Twentieth, had made LeMay his Chief of Staff. But essentially, nothing had changed. Spaatz was there to help LeMay, to relieve him of some of the administrative chores, and essentially, to let LeMay do what he was best at doing. Spaatz was smart enough to know not to fix something that was not broken.

On July 16, President Truman was riding through Berlin in an open convertible, looking every bit the triumphant victor. He and his Secretary of State, Jimmy Byrne, were on their way to the Potsdam conference where Churchill and Stalin were waiting to go over the details of post-War Europe, and to discuss the Soviet entry into the war with Japan. 5,500 miles to the west, the scientists based in the Sangre de Cristo Mountains of Northern New Mexico at Los Alamos traveled down to the southern part of the state near the remote desert town of Alamogordo where they constructed a tower that held the first atomic bomb test. At 05:29:45 Mountain War Time, the device exploded with the power of 19 kilotons of TNT. The shockwave was felt 100 miles away. The coded message that went out to Truman: "Operated on this morning. Diagnosis not yet complete but results seem satisfactory and already exceed expectations."

Four days after the atomic test in New Mexico, the Psychological Warfare Branch under Nimitz requested that the B-29s under LeMay drop leaflets on the cities before they were bombed (which LeMay referenced in his July 30 letter to Helen). There was a debate over notifying the enemy of their intentions and telling them the destination of the planes. Understandably, this made some of the crews nervous. On the other hand, one American report observed that the very act of leafleting would have its own psychological impact: "Naming one's targets or objective in the face of opposition was a grand gesture and displayed great strength and self-confidence."[32] The leaflets were written by language and psychological experts.

But even here, LeMay, ever the tinkerer, changed the copy of the messages that were to be dropped. What he first saw from the

Navy, he described as the "same old propaganda stuff." He sat down with his staff in a hurry, because it had to go back to Hawaii to be translated and printed. The final outcome read as follows: "Civilians! Evacuate at once!" in large red and black letters. Then on the reverse side it read:

These leaflets are being dropped to notify you that your city has been listed for destruction by our powerful air force. The bombing will begin within 72 hours.

This advance notice will give your military authorities ample time to take necessary defensive measures to protect you from our inevitable attack. Watch and see how powerless they are to protect you.

Systematic destruction of city after city will continue as long as you blindly follow your military leaders whose blunders have placed you on the very brink of oblivion. It is your responsibility to overthrow the military government now and save what is left of your beautiful country.

In the meanwhile, we urge all civilians to evacuate at once.[33]

On July 26, six B-29s dropped 660,000 of these leaflets. "At first, they thought we were bluffing apparently," wrote LeMay. "There wasn't any mass exodus until we knocked the hell out of the first three towns on the list. Then the rest were practically depopulated in nothing flat."[34]

LeMay's letters home to Helen concerned mundane events— which old friends he ran into, how tired he was, and if he was fighting off a cold. He rarely mentioned details of what he was doing, except that he was always very busy, apologizing for not writing more. An exception to this rule was on July 10, 1945, when he wrote, "We are certainly giving the Japs a going over... in the last two missions we have burned down 8 towns of over 100,000 each without losing a man. Over 1200 sorties without a loss. If they don't give up soon they are dumber than I think they are. Love, Curt."[35]

According to historian Richard B. Frank:

The series of attacks on August 1, posted a horrifying record. The 58th Wing reduced 80 percent of the city of Hachioji, a major rail terminus twenty-three miles west of Tokyo, to ashes. Super-fortresses of the 313th Wing burned out 65.5 percent of the rail center of Nagaoka (population 67,000). Sixty miles northeast of Tokyo, the 314th Wing destroyed 65 percent of Mito, another rail center. Toyama, the "third largest city on the west coast of Honshu," drew attention for its ball-bearing and machine-tool industries, and the largest aluminum company in Japan. The attack by 182 Superfortresses of the 73rd Wing set an appalling mark for the entire strategic-bombing campaign. The 1,466 tons of bombs and incendiaries dropped in the raid destroyed an astounding 99.5 percent of the city. Of the 127,860 citizens of Toyama, 2,149 died— undoubtedly severe in absolute numbers, but remarkably low for the near-total annihilation of an urban area. On the Allied side, one 58th Wing crew of twelve men went missing.[36]

On August 5, 1945, the day before the Hiroshima mission, fif-teen B-29 groups headed for Nishinomiya-Mikage, Saga on Kyushu, Maebashi, and Imabari on Shikoku. Just under 2,000 Japanese died in these raids. But only one American airman was injured.

The next day, August 6, 1945, only one bomber left on a mission: the *Enola Gay*. Piloted by its commander, Paul Tibbets, the B-29 dropped the enriched uranium bomb called "Little Boy" on the city of Hiroshima. Eighty thousand people were killed instantly (fewer than the Tokyo raid on March 9, 1945), and an estimated 60,000 died later of radiation poisoning. Sixty-eight percent of the city's buildings were destroyed. Twenty years later, LeMay wrote: "I did not and do not decry the use of the bomb. Anything which will achieve the desired results should be employed. If those bombs shortened the war only by days, they rendered an inestimable service, and so did the men who were responsible for their construction and delivery."[37]

Although LeMay was surprised by the extent of the blast, he still thought that his B-29s would have brought about the surrender before the proposed November 1 invasion. The following day, August 7, 1945, the Soviets declared war on Japan.

Back in the States, the latest issue of *Time* magazine—August 13, 1945—displayed the grouchy face of Curtis Emerson LeMay on its cover, cigar in mouth, as the contrails of B-29s filled the sky above him. Underneath the picture, the caption read: "LeMay of the B-29s" with the subheading: "Can Japan stand twice the bombing that Germany got?" America was introduced to the tough, pragmatic, and demanding general who ran perhaps the most powerful military force in the history of man. Forgotten was the fact that only seven months earlier, the B-29 program had been an ineffective and costly failure.

Still there was no response from the directives sent to Tokyo. LeMay kept up the B-29 firebombing as the second atomic device was made ready. On August 8, the day before Nagasaki, B-29 bombers attacked Yawata, destroying 21 percent of the town, and another wing gutted almost 75 percent of Fukyama. Nagasaki was bombed on August 9 with the second atomic bomb. An estimated 39,000 people died in the initial blast, with another 34,000 killed afterwards from radiation disease. The next several days saw a flurry of communication between Washington and Tokyo, all through intermediaries, but still the surrender terms were not accepted. On August 14, the B-29s loaded up the bomb racks and flew to Kumagaya, where 45 percent of the town was destroyed, and Isezaki, where 17 percent of the city was burned. This would be the last bombing raid of the war. When the crews returned to the Marianas from the Isezaki raid, they were told that Japan had surrendered.[38]

LeMay had worked late that night. He was sitting on the screened porch of his headquarters—a Quonset hut—where he would relax in the evenings, usually with his staff. Sometimes, they would even watch a movie. On this particular night, they had just finished dinner when an announcement that the war had ended was made over the island's public address system. There were some shouts and some running around that lasted about five minutes. Then the lights around the base went out one by one, and the island was quiet. The air crews had been flying 120 hours a month. The ground crews were working around the clock to keep the big bombers flying. Everyone was living under stress, and this promised to be the first good night of sleep in a long while. Nobody was about to miss the opportunity. "They were too tired to celebrate,"[39] LeMay later commented.

The next day, the mission had changed. All logistical support went into finding and rescuing the POWs in camps throughout Japan. LeMay sent out the photo reconnaissance planes, followed by airlifts to drop food and medical supplies for the men. "It was very emotional," recalled Seymour Tabacoff, who flew on that first mission. "Probably the most emotional mission of the war. You saw the guys waving at you and you thought there but for the grace of God go I." Just days before, B-29s were obliterating cities. Now food, water, medicine, and clean, new uniforms were falling from their bomb bays. "It gave you a great feeling, helping these guys."[40]

General MacArthur, who up until that moment had been designated the commander of the November 1 invasion, was now put in charge of the surrender and occupation of Japan. MacArthur spoke to the Japanese first by radio to set up the rules and parameters of what was to come next. A Japanese delegation was to fly to Manila in an airplane painted white. There they would be instructed on the complete arrangements for the surrender. The first U.S. planes were to land at a field south of Yokohama. The Japanese were to furnish quarters and transportation for the first delegation. The official surrender would take place on September 2 onboard the battleship *Missouri* in Tokyo Harbor.

LeMay was on that first flight into Yokohama. "On landing up there, we observed that the enemy had complied faithfully in every detail, insofar as he was able. But the equipment was poor."[41] The cars kept breaking down as they drove down to Tokyo. LeMay and the others kept looking for Yokohama for a long time, "but finally we came to the city itself. There were only a couple of streets left along the waterfront where any masonry construction was still standing. The rest of Yokohama was gone. That's why it had taken us so long to go through the outskirts. There just weren't any inskirts. And at the beginning of the war that had been a city of 866,200. It had turned into an unpopulated wilderness."[42] One of the most striking visions that stayed with

LeMay was the sea of charred drill presses, all that was left throughout whole neighborhoods—a testament to the dispersal of Japanese industry, and one of LeMay's strongest reasons for his campaign of area bombing in Japan.

Shortly after that, General Joseph Stilwell stopped by the Marianas specifically to see LeMay. The two men knew each other from India and China. Stilwell was the commander in charge of all U.S. Forces in the China-Burma-India theater. When they met in 1944, LeMay tried to explain what he hoped to accomplish with the B-29. It was clear at the time that Stilwell did not get it. Now, after the surrender, he made the trip to see LeMay because he wanted to tell him something. "When I was a young officer," he told LeMay, "I went to Yokohama as a language student. I know what Yokohama was like; I was completely familiar with the place. On September 2 I saw what you B-29 people had done to Yokohama. Indeed it was the same thing you'd done to all the strategic cities of Japan. You had done what you set out to do. I recognize now the terrible military virtues of strategic bombardment."[43] Stilwell had gone out of his way to see LeMay to tell him this, something that always impressed LeMay.

Standing on the deck of the *Missouri* in line with the other senior officers, 38-year-old Curtis LeMay joined the ranks of the top generals who led the war in the Pacific. He fought two wars in the span of four and a half years. From those early days racing around the country with thirty-five crews and three B-17s, to the hellish days over Germany and then over Japan with the mighty and monstrous B-29, LeMay had experienced more of the war than many of the senior officers standing with him. But he had experienced the fight from a great distance. None of it was personal.

Perhaps because of that, or because of his own detachment, he felt no special sense of revenge that some of the others felt. Stilwell, for example, fought the Japanese in China and experienced their cruelty firsthand and was stinging in his appraisal: "buck-toothed bastards,"[44] he wrote in his diary of the once-arrogant soldiers now standing on the deck of the *Missouri*. Stilwell was also pleased that MacArthur purposely delayed his arrival on the deck, making the Japanese officials wait for a full ten minutes with the Allied officers just staring at them. "It must have seemed ten years to them." To Stilwell, they were "hard cruel hateful faces under excruciating humiliation as we stared at them."[45]

It was not that way at all for LeMay. "I wish I could recall exactly what went through my mind while standing on the open deck of the *Missouri*." He was aware that he was incapable of raising his personal feelings to the level that this momentous event warranted. Instead of feeling some sense of accomplishment for helping to bring this day about, he slid back to blaming himself. "I did think of the young men who died to bring about this moment of triumph and, as always, wondered just what I'd done wrong in losing as many as we did. Seemed to me that if I had done a better job we might have saved a few more crews."[46]

As the proceedings came to an end under the stern direction of MacArthur, a sound, at first barely audible, began to grow in crescendo, drawing everyone's attention from the wooden table where the Japanese had just signed the documents. There above them, the entire sky suddenly filled from one end to another with 462 B-29s. The huge bombers came from every wing and every group and every squadron of the Twentieth Air Force and flew in perfect formation over Tokyo Bay.

Now, for the first time in almost five years of nonstop work and extraordinary stress that he would acknowledge only to his wife, LeMay had one overpowering feeling.

"Like many other folks, probably, I stood there and felt pretty tired."[47]

CHAPTER TEN

HOME

THE AMERICA THAT MILLIONS OF SERVICEMEN AND WOMEN CAME back to in 1945 was a remarkably different country from the one they had left. But its physical appearance remained unchanged, making the transformation all the more deceptive. To begin with, the isolationism that limited America's view of itself was gone, as was the economic depression of the 1930s. In strategic terms, the United States now possessed the largest and strongest military and economy in the world. Its old rivals lay in ruin. Its dollar was not just the leading currency, but in many far-off lands the *only* currency accepted. Its Army, Navy, and Air Force had the most modern equipment in such vast numbers that few could even comprehend the total. And, of course, the United States was the only country that possessed the atomic bomb.

Americans as a whole had been transformed as well. People who rarely left their home states or even hometowns had traveled widely for the first time, across the country and overseas. This was the catalyst for a great post war migration. Black Americans moved north by the tens-of-thousands. Millions of Americans would move to California and other western states. Congress gave an entire generation the chance to be educated in college. In international terms, huge commitments came along with the powerful new status. Americans were now responsible for maintaining the peace that had eluded Europe and Asia over the past half century.

Despite their new platform and responsibilities, Americans wanted nothing more than to pare down the vast numbers of men and expenditures needed by the military in war time. Within five months of the surrender, General Eisenhower was besieged in his office by wives and mothers demanding their husbands return home faster, and G.I.s in the Army of Occupation even marched down the Champs Elysees in Paris and in Germany shouting, "We want to go home!"[1] Never in the history of the world had one country held such a strategic advantage over every other nation on earth, and yet been so reluctant to use it.

For the United States Army Air Forces, the change was remarkable as well. The Air Force had gone from a theory on paper to a powerful and deadly new reality. Hap Arnold's next goal, a completely independent Air Force on par with the Army and Navy, was in sight. In his mind, the Air Force had more than proven itself in this war. The great victory had not come solely from his mighty fleets of bombers, but they were definitely one of the deciding factors.

In its first demonstration of postwar power, the Air Force concocted a highly publicized return flight for three of its conquering heroes. The nation was in the mood for celebration, and here was

one that the papers would love. Within days of the Japanese surrender, LeMay, Rosie O'Donnell, and Barney Giles were ordered to
fly three B-29s back to the States. They would fly nonstop from
Japan to Washington in another demonstration of the power and
reach of the United States.

It was not as easy as the planners thought. One week after the
surrender, there were few airports in Japan with runways long
enough to accommodate a fully fueled B-29. Most of Japan's runways had been demolished by American bombers over the past
eight months. The only possibility was in the far north on the
island of Hokkaido, where the Japanese Naval Academy was
located. But there were no U.S. troops that far north yet, and would
not be for weeks. The U.S. had been planning an invasion of Japan
just days before and was not quite prepared for occupation duty
this quickly. LeMay sent one of his staff to scout out Hokkaido, and
he was told the Japanese appeared willing to help. In an abrupt
turnaround that demonstrated how quickly events were overtak-
ing and changing viewpoints, feelings, and mission, LeMay spent
the night before the flight in a barracks with 3,000 Japanese naval
cadets. The world was changing. Everyone would have to adapt.

"A queer situation," was how he described it to Helen. "About
200 of us and right in the midst of thousands of Jap sailors, etc.
However they seem most docile and helpful so I think we will get
off without any trouble."[2]

The three planes took off on September 18, 1945, arcing over
Alaska. But because of unusual headwinds and poor weather in
Washington, the B-29s were forced to stop in Chicago to gas up.
Hap Arnold himself was waiting to greet them at the D.C. airport
on the short hop from Chicago to D.C.—another measure of

LeMay's new stature in the Air Force. With his record of extraordinary success, his fame that went beyond the Air Force, and with his recent national exposure on the cover of *Time* magazine, even LeMay could not help being optimistic. In Japan, the *Nippon Times* listed the March 10 Tokyo raid as the most significant event of 1945 ahead of Hiroshima (#2), the Emperor's radio address to the nation (#4), and the surrender on the *Missouri* (#6).

In an odd diversion, the possibility of a political career suddenly arose. President Truman had just appointed Senator Harold Burton, an Ohio Republican, to fill a vacancy on the Supreme Court, so the Governor of Ohio, Frank Lausche, contacted LeMay to see if he wanted to fill the remainder of Burton's term. LeMay, although committed to the Air Force, was also personally very ambitious and began to do the calculations. If the Air Force granted him a leave of absence, he thought he could serve out the Senator's term and then return to the service. It would give him the opportunity to talk on the Senate floor about three things he held dear—the rapid demobilization of the military (he was squarely against it), his strong views against Communism and regarding the Soviet Union, and the need for a stronger and independent Air Force. He was all set to go ahead with his plan until the new Secretary of War, Robert Patterson, stopped it dead in its tracks. Patterson told LeMay to go home and read the Constitution. Although a commissioned officer could hold a seat in the House, the Senate was not allowed. LeMay had not been willing to give up his commission in the Depression for a lucrative job with Ford; he would not do it now either.[3] In retrospect, given the contrasting qualities of the Senate and LeMay—it being the nation's highest deliberative body, noted for congeniality and deal making among political

adversaries, and LeMay, world famous for his lack of diplomacy—
it can be surmised that all sides were better off with the decision.

After only one week's leave to see Helen and Janie, LeMay
reported back to Washington for reassignment. He returned to
chaos, reminiscent of what he saw at Westover after the Pearl Harbor attack. The military had figured out how to function perfectly
during hostilities, but because the war ended so suddenly, no one
was prepared for the immediate change of mission. Islands like
Tinian, which were in the process of being built up quickly, now
had to be taken apart. Defense contracts were halted immediately
as well—the plants producing the B-29s stopped cold. And the
troops, who were preparing for the largest invasion in history, were
now handed a police detail.

.   .   .   .

RAND

What followed over the next few months was, for LeMay, the
perfect bookend to the beginning of the war—orders, counter-orders,
followed by counter-counter-orders. Arnold and his second-in-
command, Carl Spaatz, disagreed on which position LeMay should
fill. Spaatz wanted LeMay to head up Research and Development (R
& D) for the Air Force. Arnold did not want Spaatz telling him what
to do, so he gave LeMay another new position—air-comptroller. He
would be in charge of all expenditures. But Spaatz was correct—
LeMay had demonstrated technological brilliance during the war. R
& D was the logical place for him, not accounting.

LeMay realized this himself, and never being one to sit by and let
the fates determine his future, he came up with a plan of his own.
LeMay suggested splitting the R & D operation with Rosie O'Donnell,

who would stay in Washington while he and Helen would head back to Wright Field in Ohio, where the more technical research into missiles was taking place. That was their home and he would prefer anywhere to Washington. O'Donnell would be the liaison with the government. The plan was approved and LeMay moved his family to Dayton, Ohio. This lasted less than a month.

LeMay did not have the aeronautical engineering skills needed for the job at Wright. "There were better people to do it," he quickly concluded. "It took about ten days to realize that." But in an odd twist, Arnold then placed LeMay where Spaatz wanted him in the first place—as the head of all R & D in Washington. Biographer Thomas Coffey speculates that while it did not make sense to put LeMay at the head of the program if he lacked the necessary skills, Arnold saw something in LeMay that he thought was vital in this new phase of the Air Force. LeMay had the ability to simplify complex problems for everyone so they could be understood and solved. This would be necessary as the Air Force was now headed into a new complex mosaic made of jets, rockets, missiles, satellites, and manned space flight in the very near future. Four years earlier, these were topics dealt with only in Flash Gordon movies.

There was another reason Arnold wanted LeMay in charge of Research and Development. "It was because he would focus powerful energy on the task and imbue it with the importance Arnold knew it deserved,"[4] wrote Air Force historian Walter Boyne.

Adding immediacy to the task, engineering teams combing Germany's technology and weapons productions had found the Third Reich shockingly ahead of the U.S. in aerospace. The Germans did not possess the big bombers or the industrial capacity of the

United States, but they had already developed working jet planes and long-range ballistic rockets that had devastated England. As a new threat in the form of the Soviets quickly developed, it was discovered that many of Germany's scientists had already been taken East, and not all voluntarily.

LeMay and the Air Force ran into problems inherent in a democracy. The military needed vast sums of money and creative minds immediately to develop this new wave of technology, but Congress and the entire country was in a demilitarizing mood. Americans felt they had done their part, especially the men who had served. In their minds they had already given up years of their lives. It was over, they thought. We won. We have done without cars and homes and refrigerators long enough. This was not isolationist, and no one could call it selfish, since Americans had done more than their share to bring about the victory against fascism and imperialism. But it presented a huge challenge to people like LeMay.

In a speech to the Ohio Society on November 19, 1945, LeMay tried to make citizens of his home state aware of what he felt was at stake. He articulated his vision of the course the United States should follow. One can detect in this speech the motto that he was already working on in this new world:

It is beyond my powers of description to picture to you the difference between the bomb-blackened ruins and the desolation of our enemy's cities and the peaceful Ohio cities and landscape, untouched and unmarred by war. I can only say to you, if you love America, do everything you can do to make sure that what happened to Germany and Japan will never happen to our country. Our preparedness for war should be the measure of our

desire for peace. The last war was started by air power and finished by [airpower.] America, if attacked, must be able to take
the initiative immediately. It must attack in turn.[5]

"Peace Through Strength" would eventually become the expression most closely linked to LeMay in the postwar years, its roots
based firmly in those years leading up to World War II, when
LeMay had anticipated approaching danger but was not given the
weapons to prepare to defend the country. The slogan would be
used in everything from advertisements to presidential campaigns.
At the beginning, though, it was used to alert a content nation to
the challenges of the Cold War.

To get around his immediate problem of securing funds to build
the space age technology that the Air Force needed, a private company was created with $10 million that were extracted from the
Army Air Force's annual budget. This "company" would be located
far away from Washington, in Santa Monica, California, near the
heart of the aerospace companies that had produced many of the
planes during the war. It was called the Research and Development
Corporation, but it soon became known as RAND. "It was a gimmick," admitted LeMay, "to get the project started within the legal
parameters we had to work with."[6]

LeMay understood that although there was some talent within
the Air Force, the great minds were outside. The "gimmick" was
simply a vehicle to get brilliant civilian scientists and academics at
competitive salaries. It would also provide a professional home for
the German scientists they hoped to bring out of Europe.

Once again, LeMay was given no guidance. As in Europe in
1942 or with the B-29, or even as far back as running the CCC in

the Michigan woods in 1934, he had to figure out things on his own. He began the only way he knew how, by listening to the "scientific types," as he called them. "We spent a lot of time sitting around, talking about what we ought to be doing."[7] Talking was never his favorite pastime, but because LeMay grasped the need for advanced technology if the Air Force was to stay ahead, he forced himself to sit through meeting after meeting so he could focus on the problem.

LeMay created a very broad charter for RAND in order to allow as much latitude as the scientists and engineers might need. When employees came to him and said: "OK, boss, what do you want to do now?" LeMay told them in his inimitable style, "Read your charter!"[8] subtly encouraging initiative and creativity that would keep the Air Force on the cutting edge of technology. LeMay also realized that a lot of people in the service had been interrupted in pursuing their educations by the war. Since it was in the interest of all branches of the military to have educated personnel, LeMay figured out a way for servicemen to go to the best schools, but again under certain parameters. The Air Force would pay for their education, but they had to remain in the service for a certain length of time. And they had to concentrate on studies that were pertinent to the Air Force. "Kept a lot of that liberal arts stuff for other people," he reminisced.[9]

Some idiosyncratic American geniuses, like Henry Ford, dismissed the value of higher education. LeMay was not one of them. Even when he was working his way through Ohio State back in the 1920s, he believed in the importance of college, and he was always grateful to the Air Force for allowing him to finish his degree at Ohio State. LeMay's education program was a huge success, and the Air Force eventually ran out of undergraduates. Although he also tried to include advanced degrees at the best schools in the country, he ran into bureaucratic problems that even he could not solve.

In 1946, the RAND corporation was already focusing on missiles. "I'm known as this big bomber guy, but I started the missile program,"[10] he shared with the Air Force oral history project. It was true—the pace of technological advancement at that stage was staggering. Four years earlier, LeMay had been struggling to teach squadrons of fliers how to pilot four engine propeller planes with little guidance, no radar, and navigational equipment that consisted of a compass and celestial readings. Now they were dealing with rockets, satellites, and the early stages of computers and smart bombs.

During this period, LeMay worked out of the Pentagon. It was not his favorite place, nor was Washington his favorite city, but he found the work challenging and interesting. He and Helen lived in a home in Arlington, Virginia; Janie was seven and attended the local elementary school. LeMay tried to stay out of the Washington social circuit, but he did not always succeed. On these occasions his reputation solidified for being an unusual implant on the Capitol scene. Helen did her best to fill in the gaps, but they could be wide.

"It's not quite true that he didn't talk," remembers Janie LeMay. "If you found a topic that he was interested in, he could talk quite a bit."[11] But small talk, of the variety that was popular at Washington parties, was something he aggressively failed at. Dr. James Lodge, who became LeMay's son-in-law, witnessed an odd phenomenon years later. "Because he made younger officers uncomfortable in this regard," explains Lodge, "they would overcompensate and talk too much to fill in the silence. He actually could learn quite a bit in these situations."[12]

He had an impact on Washington in other ways as well. On January 3, 1946, LeMay testified before the War Department Equipment Board. The topic: how the United States could defend itself from an atomic attack. LeMay offered one of the first visions of MAD—Mutually Assured Destruction—the policy the U.S. and the Soviet Union would follow through the entire Cold War. LeMay told the Board that an attack was impossible to stop. "Our only defense," he said, "is a striking-power-in-being of such size that it is capable of delivering a stronger blow than any of our potential enemies."[13]

LeMay was not completely satisfied with the job he did in R & D, but he set up a framework for technological advance that extended into the future with tremendous success. RAND became one of the great incubators for America's most brilliant defense scientists and theorists.

.   .   .   .

GERMANY

On July 26, 1947, President Truman signed the National Defense Act which, among other things, created the United States Air Force. Just over twenty years after the architect of a powerful, independent air force had his career destroyed for advocating exactly that, this branch of the military was now on equal par with the Army and Navy. There was great satisfaction within the hierarchy that had been pushing for this independence. Each branch would have its own secretary who reported to the Secretary of Defense. Hap Arnold had retired, so Tooey Spaatz became the first Chief of Staff of the United States Air Force.

In one way, however, it was a hollow victory. Two years after the war, the Air Force was a shadow of its former self. There were 2,400,000 individuals in the Air Force at its height in World War II and over 70,000 planes. By 1947, there were just 303,000 men and women, and most of those planes had been sold to other governments or scrapped. On August 15, 1945, the day the Japanese surrendered, there were 218 combat groups in the Air Force that were ready to fly. Just one year later, it was down to fifty-two and of those, only two were combat ready.[14] 90 percent of the 350,000 mechanics who worked during the war were gone. LeMay complained bitterly as he watched his magnificent Air Force just thrown away, "We'd think back . . . actually it was only a matter of three or four years since we had been down on our knees, crying for just such equipment. Now look what was happening to it."[15]

On October 1, 1947, Helen pinned a third star on his shoulder. At forty-one, he was now a Lieutenant General, and once again the youngest in the Air Force at his level. And he was about to leave Washington for Europe again. This time, it was not England but Germany where he would be Commander of the U.S. Air Forces in Europe. Ironically, for all the time he spent over Germany, he had never been on the ground. But just three years after his missions over Germany, LeMay turned his focus to a different enemy: the Soviet Union.

LeMay did not trust the Russians. It went back to his appeal for weather information when he was on Guam. Even though they were supposed to be allies, they had given him nothing. Plus, when damaged B-29s landed in Russian territory, which was supposedly allied territory, the crews disappeared, were confined, and in one case, were not returned for over a year. The planes never came back. Mao Zedong and the Chinese Communists were much more helpful. LeMay had been a strong anti-Communist starting in college where he heard some of the theories and dismissed them as naive and childish at best, and at worst, as bad as any other type of totalitarian government oppression. Now, he faced a Soviet military of great strength. While the United States went full throttle in its rapid demobilization, the Soviets were moving in the opposite direction. The Red Army that poured out of Russia and raised its flag over the Reichstag was stronger than ever.

There was a stark difference in his return to Europe with his new rank, evident in a change in accommodations. Now LeMay, Helen, and Janie were living in a 102-room mansion taken from the Germans—exactly 100 more rooms than their quarters in Hawaii—complete with a staff of 38 servants. Although the LeMays were granted an expense account, they could not afford all those servants—or the lifestyle they suddenly encountered. "When we got there, the upstairs maid was pregnant," remembered Helen. "The housekeeper had been one of Goebbels's people. She was very friendly with one of the [previous American] officers and her ten-year-old son was living in the house as well. I said, 'I'm not going to have this. We have an eight-year-old daughter and I'm not having any of this.'"[16] The LeMays pared down the staff.

That meant that the lion's share of the workload fell on Helen's shoulders, since the steady stream of visiting military men, congressmen, assistant secretaries, and anyone else would be staying with them. "We had to keep thirteen suites made up at all times," said Helen. Because of the stature of many of the guests, they had to be formally entertained, unhappily for LeMay: "Three or four times a week we had formal dinner parties. I budgeted very carefully."[17]

Helen was, in essence, running a hotel, which had its share of intrigue, despite her best efforts. In one instance, the downstairs maid became pregnant by a local policeman who already had a family. "We had everybody's family problems as well as our own. A crisis every day," LeMay remembered. [18]

LeMay's assessment of Germany just two years after the war was no different than what most Americans encountered: shock at the trance-like nature of the people. "They looked like zombies, like the walking dead. They went unheeding and aloof across the streets. An automobile would be coming . . . they didn't care, didn't look, didn't even turn their head when the screech of brakes exploded behind them. There was an eternal nothingness about the place."[19] Cigarettes were one of the chief currencies still used in 1947—a carton of cigarettes could be worth over $300. Many of the reichsmarks were counterfeit, printed by the Russians. The black market ran the economy, and many of the briefings LeMay attended involved Germany's struggling economy.

•   •   •   •

THE AIRLIFT

LeMay arrived in Germany during one of the most tumultuous periods of the Cold War. Relations between the West and the Soviets were deteriorating. As the United States, England, and France struggled to right the German economy, the Russians tried to thwart every effort. The U.S. needed Germany back on its feet as the financial backbone of a stable Europe. Washington especially did not want to repeat the extreme punishment that followed World War I and led to World War II. The Soviets, on the other hand, were in an expansionist phase and certainly not in a forgiving mood. After the deaths of 20 million Russian citizens, the Soviets wanted Germany to remain crushed.

As talks grew more acrimonious, an ominous article appeared in the Soviet's Red Army newspaper on January 11, 1948. While protesting the economic plan, the paper reminded its readers that Berlin was located in the Russian zone. Berlin was supposed to be controlled by all four powers—that was the agreement when the Allies carved up Germany—and the Russians were to allow three different open access roads through their sector to the German capital. On March 6, 1948, at a conference in London, the three Western powers united their three sectors and made that part of Germany the focal point of the redevelopment project known as the Marshall Plan.

Just over three months later, on June 24, 1948, close to the seven-year anniversary of the Nazi invasion of the Soviet Union (June 22, 1941), the Russians blocked the three main access roads, as well as all rail lines to Berlin from the other three sectors. This prevented all supplies from reaching the free sector of Berlin, leaving it completely isolated and in danger of falling to the Soviets. General Lucius Clay, the military governor of the U.S. zone, suggested sending an armor column across the border and through to Berlin. LeMay and the Air Force pushed for an airlift. Truman found Clay's proposal too provocative since the Soviets had 400,000 troops nearby. The United States had 60,000 troops, of which 10,000 were combat ready. Truman turned to the Air Force, which relied on LeMay to pull off the most historic air operation of the Cold War: the Berlin Airlift.

It began with an innocuous phone call.

Clay: "Could you haul some coal up to Berlin?"

LeMay: "Sure. We can haul anything. How much coal do you want us to haul?"

Clay: "All you can haul."[20]

LeMay had 102 C-47 transports, similar to the old DC-3s, the same planes that hauled all the supplies over the "Hump" to the China-Burma-India theater during the war. LeMay called it a pretty modest beginning. But when Clay kept increasing his requests, LeMay realized he had to "get some help from home." Transports flew over from the States, and LeMay put them to work immediately.

"Then, when it looked like we were going into a long-term aspect—that we were really going to have to haul gigantic tonnages in a max effort—we were compelled to build an even larger and more defined organization,"[21] LeMay recalled. In order to keep the planes flying, LeMay hired local German mechanics. Just four years earlier, these mechanics were working on the Luftwaffe fighters that destroyed so many American B-17s. The irony was not lost on LeMay. "Now—I won't say that we made Christians out of them, but we did make good C-54 and C-74 mechanics out of some of them."[22]

LeMay's ego never got in the way of his work. When it became apparent that the Soviets were not backing down, LeMay called for Lieutenant General William H. Tunner, the head of the Military Air Transportation Service (MATS), who had a genius for coordinating a massive airlift of this size. Tunner took over the operation on July 28, 1948, and continued running it into 1949. At the height of the Berlin Airlift, planes were landing every sixty seconds, unloading, and then returning. There were over 1000 flights every day. In all, the operation hauled over 1,700,000 tons of food and supplies. Whatever bad feelings the Germans had left over from the war towards American planes were somewhat mitigated by the effort the United States made to keep Berlin alive. More importantly, it was the first time since the Cold War began that the U.S. stood up to Soviet aggression, only to witness an interesting phenomenon: the Soviets backed down.

The Soviets quietly lifted the blockade at midnight on May 11, 1949, but the flights continued until the following September 30 in order to build up a surplus of supplies in case the Soviets changed their minds. The lesson LeMay took away from the experience was that the United States had to stand up to the Soviet Union with resolve, and when it did, "they didn't bother us very much."[23]

LeMay had some final thoughts on his stay in Germany, which he wrote in his memoirs in 1965. They are intriguing to this day, not just because of the insight into LeMay's understanding of events he witnessed, but also because of LeMay's prescience:

> I should not wish to have it pointed out to me by some Whiz Kid, at this late stage of the game, that World War II was a colossal mistake, an international misunderstanding for which the United States was proportionately responsible. World War II was nothing of the kind. It was an event wherein the military giants of those several Axis states decided that they could get away with an incredible land grab, a nation grab, a super-Napoleonic concept of defacement of a world-sized map. They did this with the enthusiasm of their nationals behind them. In minor dissension may have sounded the voices of a few ardent patriots

and heroic philosophers; but those were not the majority. An horrific chorus shouted, *"Duce!"* or *"Banzai!"* or *"Heil Hitler!"* Eventually, because of the sacrifices offered and endured by our men and by the entire populations of Allied countries, the enemy went down to defeat. Enemy cities were pulverized or fried to a crisp. It was something they asked for and something they got. In reverse fashion, if we keep listening to the gospel of apology and equivocation which all too many politicians and savants are preaching today in the United States, we will be asking for the same thing. And in time may achieve it.[24]

LeMay had no time for historical revisionists, especially those who were too young to have been involved in the war. He bore no personal grudge against the Germans. He worked closely with them after the war, but he did not pretend that what he saw and what actually happened did not occur.

LeMay would not see the entire Berlin Airlift through to its finish. A problem had developed back home, and its consequences would dwarf what he faced in England, in the Pacific, and in Berlin.

CHAPTER ELEVEN

SAC

IN 1948, LeMAY WAS SUMMONED BACK FROM GERMANY TO TAKE charge of the Strategic Air Command, which would become known simply by its acronym, SAC.

SAC had been started two years earlier, and was supposed to be America's nuclear punch, which would so terrify the Russians or anyone else, that they would never even think of attacking the U.S. It was a vital program, yet it was badly broken. With his track record of making the unfixable work, LeMay was the logical choice to take the helm. But as bad as he found things, General LeMay made the situation ten times worse right at the start when he said something he never should have said. When LeMay arrived, SAC's headquarters was in the process of moving from Washington to Offutt Field in Omaha, Nebraska. In 1948, placing the headquarters of the U.S. nuclear force in the middle of the country still provided more time to respond in case of an attack from the Soviet Union. Within ten years, that would no longer be true.

Upon his arrival in Omaha, LeMay was met by a group of local reporters who were understandably excited that such a huge program, along with its famous commander, was about to set up shop right in their hometown. One of the first questions put to him on his arrival was innocuous enough: "General, don't you think this will be a great thing for Omaha?"

In journalism, this is called a softball, an easy question that anyone ought to be able to hit out of the park without even thinking. Instead, LeMay responded, cigar in mouth: "It doesn't mean a damn thing to Omaha, and it doesn't mean a damn thing to me." It stopped everyone cold, including LeMay's subordinates.

LeMay was hardly stupid. He had shown absolute brilliance throughout his career. But he seemed to have a self-destructive impulse at times, and it always seemed to come out in his speech and his public behavior. Years later, he admitted that he had been impolitic in this particular instance. What he meant to say was that given the state of readiness of the Strategic Air Command, neither Omaha nor he should be impressed with the operation until SAC first proved itself. But that, of course, is not even close to what he said. "I had a great deal to learn about public utterances," he admitted. "Helen had always tried to help me on this, but I'm afraid that she hadn't made too much of an impression." One of his wife's constant refrains was "Curt, you oughtn't to say that."[1]

His assessment was right, however. SAC was a disaster. Most of its planes could not fly. Most of the crews lacked the most basic training for their new mission. A general malaise hung over the entire organization—and those were just a few of its problems. It had been organized in 1946, but perhaps because the U.S. still had a monopoly on atomic weapons, there was no sense of urgency in those early years. The wartime pressure that had pushed everyone just months earlier had evaporated. But by the time LeMay arrived in 1948, the Pentagon understood that making Strategic Air Command strong was essential for countering the Soviet threat. The logic of SAC was rudimentary—if you destroy us, we will destroy you ten times over—and in some ways, it fit perfectly with LeMay's view of the world. Do not bother anyone, but if bothered, do not be bullied. In post-war nuclear terms, it would become known as the balance of terror, or mutually assured destruction.

In theory, the Strategic Air Command was the logical vehicle to promote U.S. power around the postwar world and instill fear in the hearts of its enemies. But SAC in its infant stages was one shockingly ill-organized, ill-equipped, nonfunctioning military operation, and everyone in the upper echelons of the Air Force knew it. It is no coincidence that SAC had an appalling accident rate. Worse, nobody seemed to care. In 1947, SAC ran a simulated test. Out of the 180 planes in its command, 101 could not even get off the ground.

The perfect example of its organizational dysfunction was obvious in SAC's plan of operation. In the event of a war with the Soviets, all of SAC's B-29s would first fly from their various bases to Ft. Hood, Texas, where the nation's nuclear weapons were stored under the command of the U.S. Atomic Energy Commission. Once there, pilots would fill out the necessary paperwork, and the bombs would be brought out of their deep lockers and loaded on to the planes. From Texas, they would fly to England or Newfoundland where they would refuel. Only then would they fly off to their targets. The potential for problems was truly nightmarish if a crisis were to strike. It was obvious to LeMay, who believed in Murphy's law,[2] that no one had thought things through.

There was a flying club atmosphere in SAC, similar to the one LeMay encountered in the 1930s Army Air Corps. In an odd calculation, pilots were encouraged to take an aircraft for any cross-country weekend jaunt—to visit a girlfriend or relative—for the sole purpose of burning up gas. In the military's accounting system, all future allotments of fuel were based on what was used in the previous year. This made for some happy pilots, but hardly instilled the correct sense of mission.[3]

SAC was basically the same Twentieth Air Force from Guam that LeMay had commanded during the war. It was a natural transition, since it was the only military organization on earth with previous nuclear experience, having dropped the atomic bombs on Hiroshima and Nagasaki. SAC's bomber was still the B-29, but it did not have the capability of flying to the Soviet Union and back. If the country had been attacked and the planes were directed to drop bombs in Russia, the crews would be flying one-way missions. In case of war, Walter Boyne, a SAC colonel and later Air Force historian, was to fly to his target, the Soviet city of Tula, near Moscow. "Then [we were to] turn southwest in the hope that a successful bailout could be made somewhere in the Ukraine where, we were told, we might encounter 'friendly natives.' We were not optimistic about the outcome."[4]

No one seemed to even consider the possibility of a real conflict. Boyne remembered that when he joined SAC, there was very little sense of purpose at his first base. "Gunnery scores were fudged and the principal occupation seemed to be playing hearts in the briefing room."[5] But SAC's dysfunction was symptomatic of the entire military in those years. "In 1945 we had possessed the largest and best trained and most experienced and most effective Army and Navy in our history," LeMay wrote, not attempting to hide his sarcasm or his bitterness. "In 1948 we were going around explaining to the world that we really didn't mean it; we were sorry; and our bazookas had all been taken out to the city dump, and our airplanes had been smashed into junk."[6]

What particularly irked LeMay was that he had slogged through the early days of the War when the United States had nothing with which to fight or even defend itself. He had been forced to rack his brain to invent ways to make the few tools he was given work. He had watched men die around him because there was not time to train them and because the enemy was more advanced. And just a few years later, his country was putting its military in the same situation again, in spite of a real threat from the Soviet Union.

The marvelous military that LeMay talked about was made up mostly of civilians. And those civilians wanted nothing more than to get back to civilian life. The competing economic forces between the military and civilian sectors in postwar America created a very real division in the country. Americans were capable of forgoing luxury items in response to a global threat. They more than proved this from 1941 to 1945. But the Cold War that the United States and SAC had to fight was a new kind of war that most Americans could not grasp. Yes, it was clear the Soviet Union under Joseph Stalin was bellicose and dangerous. And the Soviets proved their expansionist intentions again and again throughout Eastern Europe and later Asia, Africa, and even the Americas, the seriousness of which world leaders, led by Winston Churchill, tried to explain. But civilians wondered—if the United States was truly at war with the Soviet Union, if the Soviets were really that great a threat, then why did everything appear to be so normal?

America was enjoying the greatest economic boom in its 170-year history. Americans were no longer told to sacrifice as they had been when fighting a more traditional enemy like Japan or Germany. In fact, battles were not being fought at all. American boys were not dying. This war encompassed a netherworld of spies and political intrigue. No one quite understood what the public's share of responsibility should be in this theoretical war. It was only natural that Americans were more interested in what was being promoted all around them—namely new homes, shiny new cars to drive on clean new highways, and that marvel of marvels, the television. After the Great Depression and then the war, this generation had more than earned its right to focus on their families and themselves. For the first time in their lives, they had some disposable income and new products to buy, and everything they heard, from advertisements to political speeches, only reinforced this rampant materialism.

The public's attitude toward the military, according to historian Boyne, ranged from condescension to contempt. The contempt came from many civilians who had a great distaste for the regimented life they had to endure for four or five years and were only too happy to leave it behind. For those who remained, condescension is probably an apt phrase. "Genteel poverty" was a term used to describe the threadbare existence of military families; vacations, good schools, elective orthodontia for children, and other perks enjoyed by civilians in comparable positions were not available to those in the military.[7] It would be the military that would have to sacrifice both financially and with their lives. It is little wonder that Air Force personnel preferred jobs in the growing commercial airline industry where they were paid ten times the salary, worked far fewer hours, and were not required to spend months away from their families. And this did not just apply to the lower echelons of the military. Even a three star general like Curtis LeMay earned the same yearly salary as a TWA pilot. These were just some of the problems facing SAC's new Commander-in-Chief.

When LeMay took over SAC, he assessed the readiness of the Air Force and was blunt in his appraisal. "I should go on record and say this flatly: we didn't have one crew, *not one crew* in the entire command who could do a professional job."[8] SAC itself was as bad as anything he had yet encountered in his career.

* * * *

DAYTON

LeMay realized at the very start that it was no use to remodel what he had inherited. It was completely broken. He had to tear it down to its foundation and completely rebuild it. So he started the process with a vivid demonstration to show everyone just how bad things were. It would become known as the Dayton Exercise, and to this day, even though many of the people involved in it have long since died, it is still a legend within SAC. For obvious reasons, the public did not learn about it at the time. Even as late as 1964, when LeMay requested the official records of the Dayton Exercise while writing his memoirs, they were still classified.

The exercise sounded fairly simple in its concept. LeMay walked into his office early one morning and issued the following order to his operations chief: "Have 'em attack Wright. The whole damn command. By radar."[9] That was all he said.

In translation, LeMay wanted the entire fleet of SAC planes to stage a practice bombing exercise on Wright Field in Dayton, Ohio. They would fly directly from every SAC base across the country, converge over Wright Field and electronically "bomb" it. The radar controller at Wright would be able to track the descent of every "bomb" to determine the accuracy of each crew. And because, as LeMay put it, "nobody seemed to know what life was like upstairs," he wanted all the planes to go in at a high altitude, where they would have to wear oxygen masks. Up until then, SAC pilots flew at low levels because they found the masks uncomfortable.

This challenge would be much easier than the real thing. SAC pilots would not have to fly into the Soviet Union, or even overseas. They were all familiar with Wright Field, but familiarity, short range, and peaceful conditions did not seem to help at all.

Because of mechanical failures, many of the planes never got off the ground. Still more had to turn back to their bases before they got anywhere near Dayton. Of the planes that actually made it all the way to Ohio, not one bomber was able to hit the target. Not one.

Now everyone at SAC and the Air Force could no longer avoid the truth. LeMay responded in his typical form. Instead of yelling or pitching a fit, he led. "I've been telling you you were in bad shape. We are in bad shape. Now let's get busy and get this fixed."[10] That was all he had to say, and as he had in the past, he included himself in the process.

Once again LeMay broke down the problem into its parts. First, he began cleaning house, and sent out a call for the best people he had worked with in the past. LeMay was cold-blooded in the way he went about his work. A lot of people were fired in that opening phase. "We don't have time to distinguish between the unfortunate and the incompetent," LeMay explained with his stinging bluntness.[11]

Tom Power (the commander of the first Tokyo raid) was on his way to England as an air attaché when LeMay turned him around. Power was a very successful commander, but not at all well liked

by the men under him. He was unusually tough and harsh, even
compared to LeMay. More than one of the officers considered him
sadistic. LeMay did not disagree. "He was sort of an autocratic bas-
tard. But he was the best wing commander I had on Guam." LeMay
found Power's style very different from his own. "[With him it was]
always 'Gaddamn it, I want this done' and 'You have to do it.' 'Go
do it.' 'Get your ass out there right now.' I maintained, 'We're a
team'. 'We have to do this.' 'You're part of this. Get going,'" LeMay
later wrote.[12]

Colonel C. S. Bill Irvine had been LeMay's maintenance chief on
Guam. He was now the only commander of a SAC group that
LeMay thought might be worth a damn—the 509th. Irvine stayed.
There was a touching scene about a year later when LeMay tried
and failed to get Irvine promoted from colonel to general. When
Irvine arrived in Omaha, LeMay was waiting for him, picked up
Irvine's bags, and started carrying them to the car. Irvine asked him
what he was doing. "If I can't get you promoted," LeMay told him,
"I can at least carry your bag."

"When you got through all that crust," Irvine recalled, "LeMay
was really a soft touch."[13]

The cool, calm, and marvelously efficient Augie Kissner came
back happily for his fourth assignment under LeMay, this time as
his Chief of Staff. Perhaps the toughest job of all went to Al
Kalberer, who would serve as the public information officer, the
man who would try to coach his boss on what to say and how to
say it to the outside world. Between Kalberer, Kissner, and Helen,
LeMay would actually demonstrate moments of true improvement
in his public comments. Or perhaps he had nowhere to go but up
after his first encounter with the Omaha press corps.

LeMay was one of the few Americans who understood how the nature of war had changed in just two years. He also understood that World War II could no longer serve as the model for any future conflicts—especially in regard to the Air Force. Nuclear weapons, along with jet planes and rockets, had changed the paradigm. The old world, in which the United States was protected by its two great oceans, was over. Unlike some, LeMay did not lament this. He always viewed technology as an ally that could advance his goals. But what made him immeasurably more effective was this ability to inject his past experience—when relevant—into this new realm.

LeMay's most crucial observation was that SAC's first mission could very well be its last. This new form of warfare would allow for no second chances. So LeMay had to create the state of readiness that was necessary to capitalize on that first and only chance to strike, should it ever be needed. To do it, he had to change the way people in SAC thought. "My determination was to put everyone in SAC in this frame of mind: *we are at war now....* So that if actually we did go to war the very next morning or even that night, we would stumble through no period in which preliminary motions would be wasted. We had to be ready to go *then*."[14] If it came to a nuclear exchange, LeMay knew there would not be the luxury of a period of adjustment as there had been in England or the Marianas.

At this period in American history—the Cold War—negative perceptions of Curtis LeMay began forming. Americans cheered when the first bombs landed in Germany, and they cheered again and looked the other way when his B-29s flew over Japan in giant formations. But at SAC in the 1950s, it was different. The U.S. nuclear strike force served a crucial purpose in stopping a Soviet advance across the globe. The collapse of the Soviet Union in 1991 was not inevitable. It required the massive arming of the U.S. military to counter the very real threat of Soviet domination. It also required a deep commitment, which not everyone was willing to make.

It was inevitable that someone like Curtis LeMay, who pushed for containment through strength, would become the target of fears swirling throughout the Cold War. The idea of instant annihilation was a real terror for Americans. So as the commander of the huge force of mighty bombers that would deliver the nuclear blow with its mushroom clouds, its fallout, and its impending nuclear winter, LeMay became a public flashpoint for groups on both sides of the frightening new reality. Those who did not view the Soviet Union as an incarnation of fascism sought any form of reconciliation between the two superpowers in order to prevent a nuclear holocaust. They marched in the streets. They denounced the U.S. military and the civilian corporations that produced weapons. In their estimation, the Pentagon, civilian contractors, and Curtis LeMay were symptoms of the greater problem, rather than the cure.

On the other side were those who accepted the new reality of the world order and viewed the Soviet Union with tremendous mistrust. This latter group—who learned in World War II that there were evil men in the world who, if left unchecked, would push their advantage—believed LeMay was doing exactly what needed to be done.

LeMay's physical image and personality reinforced negative stereotypes. To many, he was the dark knight, or as I. F. Stone bitingly referred to him, the "Caveman in the Jet Bomber."[15] And within certain political circles, the cigar chomping, monosyllabic LeMay became the perfect target. He was almost too easy to lampoon.

Cartoonists and eventually Hollywood had a field day with LeMay. But those who actually knew him and understood the rational basis for his decisions did not have the media influence that his detractors could generate.

This public debate did not concern LeMay. It was completely irrelevant to him. His chief and only consideration was giving the United States the strongest and most efficient striking force to prevent a nuclear conflict before it began. When he arrived at SAC, it was clear to him that he did not have much to offer in the way of deterrence. When he left almost a decade later, he had changed everything. SAC would be no less an achievement than the B-17 bombing campaigns in Europe or the B-29 successes in the Marianas. But to accomplish this achievement, LeMay again had to be as tough as steel. A nice guy could not do it.

LeMay completely redefined SAC along with its mission. "No other U.S. military force commander so imprinted his personality and ideals upon his organization as did LeMay," says Walter Boyne, who served under LeMay in the 1950s. "SAC became LeMay personified—but only after tremendous effort on his part."[16] Years after he left Omaha, people would comment on seeing and feeling the "LeMay aura" when they visited SAC's headquarters, which was eventually named after him.

LeMay did not accomplish this for himself or because he wanted to coax the Soviet Union into an all-out war as some have suggested. LeMay had a rock solid belief in the Constitution of the United States, which placed the military under civilian control. In spite of what his detractors said and wrote, the Strategic Air Command was under the absolute and complete control of the commander in chief of the military, not SAC. LeMay never questioned this. He performed well so the president could deal with

. adversaries from a position of power, which was, LeMay believed, the only way of dealing with adversaries.

As it had been in World War II, one of LeMay's primary concerns was looking out for the men and women under his command. From 1948 to his last day at SAC in 1957, LeMay managed to stop the hemorrhage of men and equipment that he inherited at the start. In 1948 there were 51,965 people at SAC—5,562 officers, 40,038 airmen, and 6,365 civilians. Morale was low and living conditions were appalling.

When LeMay took over SAC in 1948, the accident rate was sixty-five major accidents per 100,000 hours—a dismal record. By 1956, LeMay's last full year at SAC, the accident rate fell to nine per 100,000 hours—an 85 percent drop. "Every time a commander suffered a major accident in his wing," LeMay recounted, "he came to see me about it. We went into the matter from every angle. They did not like the idea of coming up there and standing on the unpleasant piece of carpet, but that's what I made them do. We were going to find out how the accident happened and why."[17]

General Jacob Smart, LeMay's aide in the 1950s, reiterated LeMay's firm belief in Murphy's law. Because of this, "he drove himself and others to prevent error or accident by SAC personnel." To illustrate the point, Smart says, "LeMay required all air crew members to make a detailed preflight inspection of a SAC bomber in accord with a prescribed check list. Nobody was beyond doing this. He never put himself above the rules and followed the same procedure whenever he flew a SAC bomber."[18]

Just as he disliked losing men during war, he was equally angry losing them to accidents. The worst thing a wing commander could say to LeMay was: "I don't understand it, he was a great pilot." It seemed every commander started his explanation that way. "They were never stupid pilots or bad pilots, they were always great pilots," LeMay observed. For that reason, he made the SAC safety checklist much more detailed—to make sure every pilot, especially the hotshots, followed the rules.

LeMay set up classes for navigation, radar, and bombing. There were drills. And in all cases, he left it up to the local base commanders to get their houses in order. LeMay's Dayton exercise made an impression on everyone, and he would repeat it from time to time in various forms. General David C. Jones, a future Chairman of the Joint Chiefs, was a colonel in the 1950s and served as LeMay's aide. "One of the greatest things about him was how he used psychology to lead," Jones remembered. "As long as I knew him, he never told anyone how to fix a problem...he pointed it out and left it up to the person to solve it. He had great faith in his people. And he had a great eye for choosing the right people." One particular story that Jones tells exemplifies this. One day LeMay simply walked over to Jones who was sitting at his desk and said,

"Miami, 10 a.m. tomorrow."

That's all he said.

So the next day he shows up at the flight line at 10 a.m. and says, "Cancel the plan."

Instead, we fly to another SAC base and he says, "Don't tell them I'm on board."

So we fly to the base, land, and General LeMay gets out and says he wants to see the wing commander. The commander arrives in a golf shirt and the General says, "Execute the war plan."

That means fly to England and light up nuclear weapons.

Well, we watch the base break into chaos.

After an hour and a half of watching this, he turns to me and says: "C'mon, let's go. Cancel the exercise." And we fly off.

But here's the point of the story. He never raised the subject again. He never said a thing about it to the commander or anyone else. A while later, the commander, a General, wanted to talk with LeMay and tell him everything he had done. I was only a colonel at the time, but I strongly recommended that he not raise it or talk to him about it.

About six weeks later, he gave me another order: "Savannah, 2 o'clock tomorrow."

The next day he says cancel the exercise and we fly off to another base . . . same procedure . . . no warning. But this time, it works like clockwork. That's because he knew word would spread and that he didn't have to say anything about it. People would get their houses in order.

"He was a great selector of people,"[19] Jones reiterated, still in awe fifty years later.

· · · ·

OFFUTT

Why was SAC based in Omaha? LeMay understood it was a political decision. One Senator simply had more clout than another, or was owed a bigger favor. When LeMay arrived, there was not much of anything available. Even the runway had a steep grade to it. He made his headquarters in an abandoned factory that had manufactured bombers during the war. It was sparsely furnished, but he did not expect to be spending a lot of time there.

He eventually thought Offutt and Omaha was a good decision. "My first reaction was, this is a helluva place to be going," he told historian John T. Bohn in 1971. "Although as it turned out it wasn't too bad," LeMay admitted. "It was a pretty good communications hub. It was the center of the country where we could get to our outfits, which were scattered all over the country and later all over the world, a central point. [And] the people of Omaha were the best I ever had run across as far as cooperation was concerned."[20] He was not saying that because of his earlier comments. He meant it.

Money was a continuous problem. Congress was not in the mood to overspend on defense, and balanced budgets were still popular in the 1950s. Every program had to be fought for. Besides the obvious need for a new generation of bombers to replace the World War II B-29s, LeMay's long list included everything from the fundamentals to the more prosaic. The empty factory would not do. He needed a new headquarters and command center where he could monitor all the far-flung SAC bombers. But he also needed new barracks for those of his people who were living in tar paper shacks, furniture, and even food. Once again he was back to his mess hall days, stymied by the fact that Air Force cooks started with the same basic ingredients that other cooks started with, yet produced awful meals. How was he going to compete with the more attractive private sector when the living conditions were so abysmal? It made sense to him that the attrition rate was so high.

LeMay understood that it would be a waste of time to constantly go back to Washington with his hand out. The system of getting approval for anything in the military was Byzantine. The route went like this: LeMay would send his request to the head of the Air Force (Hoyt Vandenburg at the time). After his approval, the Air Force chief sent it on to the secretary of the Air Force, who sent it on to the Secretary of Defense, who sent it on to Congress. Congress more often than not sent it back to the Secretary of Defense with questions. The request could go up and down this chain several times before it was approved or rejected. By the time all of this was done and the original request was granted, the need for it could be obsolete. LeMay eventually did get his command center. Even Congress understood it was needed. But it took five years.

Since his early days in the Air Corps, LeMay always found ways to work around the system. So instead of running to Washington, LeMay met with the town fathers of Omaha and got to know them. Together they set up a special council that would pay attention to any problems that might come up. LeMay understood that in every community, there were a few individuals who were highly successful and civic minded. As businessmen, they could appreciate that if the airmen and their families were happy with their work, they would also be better trading partners and invest in the community. They went out of their way to help in all sorts of little ways that were never even requested, even up to providing funds to help construct the new base. These Omaha citizens jumped in with an energy and determination that surprised LeMay, to the point that he credited Offutt's successful growth to their efforts.

LeMay perceived that life issues for personnel were just as crucial as the planes they flew and the ordnance they might drop. With an acute housing problem, LeMay found funds to buy prefabricated homes and had the airmen build them in their spare time. Local construction companies pitched in as well. He designed new barracks that were more like dorm rooms with two men in each as opposed to huge old barracks with a long line of cots. Crews flew on a 24-hour schedule, and if they were flying all night, they would not be able to get any sleep if other fellows were banging around the barracks during the day.

When he had to go to Washington with his new dorm room plan, he ran into an obstacle. The first question that one Congressman put to him was: "Suppose you get two 'homos' in the same room?"

LeMay sidestepped the question by saying: "I thought we weren't supposed to have any of them."[21] And that put an end to the discussion. But it reinforced his long-standing perspective— the personal lives of the men serving under LeMay were simply not an issue. "All LeMay cared about was performance," remembers Ralph Nutter. "He never asked anyone their politics or religion or anything else. He just looked at their performance."[22]

When three of these model barracks were built, they still had to be furnished. LeMay turned to Arthur Storz, who owned the local brewery. Storz had served in the Air Corps in World War I, and his two sons flew in World War II. He was one of the wealthiest men in Omaha, and he held a dinner for a large group of his friends and local businessmen one night at his brewery. After the dinner, the master of ceremonies, Morris Jacobs, who ran a local advertising company, stood up and told the group: "General LeMay has these three barracks built out at Offutt but not furnished. We're going to furnish them for him. The amount each of you is expected to give is on the envelope in front of you."[23] LeMay must have appreciated the lack of subtlety. His dormitory barracks were furnished. The Army and Navy eventually adopted similar barracks.

Air Force personnel were treated as locals from the beginning. Omaha threw parties for them. They were integrated into the community. LeMay even solved the food problem. He went to the best hotels as far as Chicago and asked if the Air Force cooks could work with their chefs for a while and watch them. He pushed the hotel owner's patriotic feelings—here was a chance for them to do their part for their country by giving the "boys" better food. It worked, although he did run into a problem with the local unions who thought he was trying to put in non-union workers. Besides working on flight problems to Russia and the correct megatonage of nuclear bombs, LeMay also had to explain his actions to the Hotel Workers of America.

·   ·   ·   ·

FAMILY LIFE

In the three years since the end of the war, Helen had moved from Cleveland to Washington to Dayton, back to Washington, then to Germany, and now to Omaha. Luckily, this would be home for the longest period in LeMay's professional life. It would also be the most consistent period of Janie's childhood. Although her father was away at least half of every year either touring other bases, in Washington, or on missions, Omaha was home. Janie went to a private school, Brownell Hall, starting in fifth grade at age ten.

The LeMays lived in a red brick house on Commander's Row at Fort Crook, which at one time had been one of the farthest outposts on the frontier. It was built in 1894, had three bedrooms, two bathrooms, and a separate apartment on the third floor. There was a large, old-fashioned kitchen, along with a formal dining room, living room, and den where they entertained a constant parade of dignitaries from Washington and overseas. More often than not, LeMay would either bring them home for lunch or have them stay overnight. He found it a more efficient way to get their business done.

Helen LeMay handled the lion's share of the entertaining, and it seemed constant. She did have help from Sergeant Boyd Waterman, who was assigned to the family as a cook and all around helper. To save money, Helen and Waterman would sometimes make dinner for over 300 rather than use a caterer.

Although his job was demanding, LeMay hoped to have Sunday afternoons at least to work on different projects that he had saved for years. He liked to putter.[24] And there had been few chances since the war began. Boxes of his collections and projects that had been kept in storage and traveled to Germany and back were now in the basement in Omaha. He guessed that he spent the first three Sundays in Omaha doing just what he wanted to do, and then never again. The boxes were not touched until he retired.

"It wasn't a normal kind of life," remembered Janie. "We didn't have weekends together. We never went on family vacations. We just couldn't do the types of things I saw my friends doing with their fathers."[25] But then, Janie did get to do things that other kids never even dreamed of. "I remember crawling down in the front of the plane with the big Plexiglas window with Dad at the controls and watched the whole world in front of me," she remembered. "That was pretty wonderful."[26]

LeMay did try to find some methods of recreation. His attempt to play golf in Omaha failed when he quickly realized that there were no telephones on the 9th hole. He could not afford to be out of touch with the base. One night he was reminiscing with Helen

for the thousandth time about that summer he rebuilt the Model-
T with a friend in college. It was the same story that used to comfort him and help him get to sleep during the war. Suddenly,
LeMay stopped in his tracks as an idea came to him. He would set
up a hobby shop on the base for anyone who might want to work
on a car—a kind of do-it-yourself garage. He found a derelict
garage, but when he sent out a notice for people interested in helping to set it up, the response was underwhelming. "LeMay and two
sergeants. We were IT. Not another soul turned up to do any work
on the place."[27] But local people in Omaha donated tools and supplies, and the concept eventually caught on. Soon there were
Hobby Shop Number 2 and Number 3, and they sprang up on SAC
bases everywhere.

LeMay would accomplish a great turnaround with the Strategic
Air Command. It would rank in achievement with anything he did
during the war. But strangely, he seemed to be more proud of the
success of his hobby shops than anything else. "Those shops were
the busiest damn places on the base. We ran a careful check at
Offutt. More people actually went into the hobby shop, and used
it, than used the Service Club."

One late night, LeMay and General Griswold, his close friend
from flight school, were working alone on a car in greasy dunga-
rees when a young airman walked in. "Hey guys," the young private called out as LeMay and Griswold looked up from under the
hood. "Could you guys help me out? My engine's gone dead, out
here in the street." It was a battery problem, the young airman
explained and asked if the "guys" could just come out and push
the car? So LeMay and Griswold went out and got the car started.
The young private waved his thanks to the two old guys in the
garage and was gone. LeMay and Griswold went back to their

project. "We hoped that the kid would never discover who had pushed his car," LeMay recalled.[28]

·   ·   ·   ·

THE TURNAROUND

Better food, improved living conditions, and happier flight crews helped, but what ultimately turned SAC around was hard work, continuous innovation, and Curtis LeMay's demand for perfection.

LeMay understood that morale would rise when a marked improvement in skill led to greater confidence, and he figured out ways to get people to want to improve themselves. "LeMay was a firm believer in the incentive plan," remembers Jim Pattillo, one of the many pilots who served under him.[29] There were just so many promotions allowed by the Department of Defense at any given time. LeMay cagily found out there were a lot of promotion vacancies following the war within the service that were never filled, and using his clout in Washington, he had many of them transferred to SAC. Then with this large number of promotions in his pocket, LeMay instituted an instant promotion system. Airmen were promoted on the spot when they did an outstanding job. If a crew managed to stay in the top 15 percent of the rating system he instituted, the entire crew was promoted. Efficiency improved. Morale improved. The entire organization began to look and act more professional. Of course, it cut both ways. When someone did something extraordinarily stupid, they were demoted or fired on the spot. Many careers came to an end under General LeMay.

There were huge logistical problems right from the start. LeMay realized the absurdity of having to go to Texas to pick up nuclear weapons from the Atomic Energy Commission long before he took over SAC, and wrote a memorandum on July 1, 1946, detailing his concerns. Nothing had changed. So rather than write more memos, LeMay staged an exercise to prove the point. Amidst an inability to get the proper signatures, lots of paper work, and loading the bombs, everyone soon realized how impractical the system was, and the Air Force was finally given the responsibility for the storage and transportation of nuclear weapons. Many of LeMay's critics have cited this alteration in the stewardship of the nuclear weapon as yet more evidence that LeMay was a dark megalomaniac who demanded control of the country's nuclear arsenal, a la Dr. Strangelove. But the change was made based on logic, efficiency, and common sense, and the failure of the nuclear exercise demonstrated how badly it was needed.

•   •   •   •

THE BOMBERS

In another indication of the length of his tenure there, LeMay saw four generations of large bombers pass through SAC. Considering how long it takes to get an airplane from the design stage to the flight line while moving in and out of Congressional budgets, this is a remarkable number. It was LeMay who led the fight on Capitol Hill for ever larger and more powerful bombers. He had friends there, and he was never shy about promoting the bomber as the logical weapon of the nuclear age. Many congressmen, senators, and even presidents made their way to Omaha for presentations and inspections.

LeMay began with the propeller-driven B-29 that he had used during the war. Next came the even larger B-36, also known as the

Peacemaker, borrowing its name from the Colt .45, the most common handgun in the old West. The plane was huge, so big that a B-29 could fit under one of its wings. It was oddly configured; its six propeller engines all faced backwards. It had been designed in 1940 when the Army Air Corps feared the United States would need an intercontinental bomber that could fly missions to Germany from the U.S. When England held on, the concept was put on hold.

The plane was not a huge success. It was used because there was nothing else as big, but the performance rating only went from disappointing to marginal—hardly a great score. The B-36 was phased out completely by 1957.

Bombers, as well as most military hardware, became obsolete as quickly as today's computers. "Alteration, alteration. Change after change." That's how LeMay put it. "The B-36 was often called an interim bomber. For my dough, every bomber which has ever been or ever will be is an interim bomber. Every weapons system is an interim system. There is no ultimate weapon."[30] The reason is obvious. Technology constantly changes. LeMay had seen it over and over again, since the time he climbed into the cockpit of the bi-wing Jenny back in high school. The next plane will always be stronger, more powerful, and will do things the old model never could do. It will amaze—until the next one surpasses it.

Many of the modern weapons systems built after the war were built with the hope that they would never be used. From 1941 to 1945, practically every weapon that was authorized by Washington and then built was tested in battle. But during the Cold War, unlike any other time in history, these weapons, especially the nuclear weapons, were built at great expense with the prayer that they would never fly off to battle.

The next plane off the assembly line was a marvel. The B-47, called the Stratojet, was the first all jet-engine bomber. It was much more powerful than its predecessor, and because the nuclear arsenal was now churning out vast numbers of weapons, the Strategic Air Command was finally reaching the potential LeMay had envisioned. The plane did have problems. It was so streamlined it was hard to stop when landing, and if a pilot had to abort a landing and take off again quickly, the engines did not always give him enough power. But the B-47's greatest feature was that its design led to the next bomber that, like LeMay, would forever be synonymous with SAC: the B-52.

The designers of the B-52 took the B-47, corrected its problems, enlarged it with thicker wings and eight more powerful jet engines, added much more advanced electronics over the years, and came up with a huge, but remarkably nimble plane with a range of 8,800 miles (although with air refueling, it can stay aloft for days). The B-52 can reach a top speed of 650 miles an hour and can reach altitudes as high as 47,700 feet.

LeMay instituted a policy of keeping B-52s in the air 24 hours a day, 365 days a year that continued from the 1950s through the late 1960s. This way, the fleet would never be caught on the ground. After the late '60s, nuclear-equipped B-52s were kept fully loaded and ready to fly, with crews on alert and within running range of the plane until the Cold War ended in 1991.

Boeing, which created and built the B-52, labeled it the Stratofortress in keeping with earlier titles such as the Flying Fortress, but no one else used that name. To its crews and the people in SAC it was the *BUFF*—the *Big Ugly Fat F----r*—or just the *52*.

In spite of its size, the huge bomber turned out to be remarkably flexible. Flying at speeds over 400 miles per hour at an altitude of just 500 feet, it could evade radar, fly along the contours of the ground, and deliver its weapons. LeMay successfully pushed for the development of larger tanker planes and greater in-flight refueling capacity that would give his bombers an unprecedented global reach.

Bearing in mind that his headquarters was, itself, vulnerable to a Soviet hit, especially after the development of intercontinental missiles, he had a command center built in a plane that could also refuel in the air and stay aloft in order to direct a nuclear war in case Washington had been knocked out.

• • • •

KOREA, CHINA, AND THE SOVIET BOMB

On August 19, 1949, the U.S. monopoly on nuclear weapons ended, without warning, years ahead of when intelligence experts had predicted. The Soviets, using spies within the highest circles of the U.S. nuclear program (the most damaging being German-born Klaus Fuchs, a brilliant theoretical physicist who was passing secrets to the Soviets throughout the Manhattan Project) and their own group of brilliant physicists led by Igor Kurchatov, detonated a plutonium implosion bomb named "First Lightning" in Kazakhstan. Overnight the nature of the Cold War, as well as SAC's mission, had changed—a nuclear standoff was no longer theoretical.

Five weeks later, the civil war in China ended in a victory for another staunch ally of Joseph Stalin's. On October 1, 1949, the

Chinese Communist party under the leadership of Mao Zedong took control of the world's most populous country.

Eight months after that, the North Koreans crossed the border and quickly overran U.S. and South Korean forces. The Korean War had begun. Although SAC was defined solely as a deterrent to nuclear war and was not to be used in conventional armed conflicts, Douglas MacArthur suddenly and desperately needed air support in Korea and there were few places to turn.

Though LeMay saw the use of bombers in Korea as a disruption to SAC's main mission, in less than a week, MacArthur had B-29s at his disposal. Two entire SAC units were transferred from California and Spokane, Washington to Japan and Okinawa under the command of General Rosie O'Donnell. In some cases, the crews did not even have time to go home and pack. The first targets were roads and rail links bringing supplies south. MacArthur was desperate in the early days of the war to stop the North Korean route that had pushed his forces almost all the way to the southern tip of the country. Later, after his successful counterattacks and the remarkable landing at Inchon, B-29s targeted industrial cities.

Many of the B-29s that were eventually used in Korea had been sitting in the Arizona desert since the end of the war. There had been no ongoing maintenance of the planes because nobody suspected that such large numbers of B-29s would ever be needed or used again. During the Korean War, some of the bombing raids could manage only twelve planes per day because of a severe lack of spare parts, a far cry from the hundreds of B-29s that LeMay had been able to send over Japan. Sixteen planes were lost to hostile fire during the war, and three times that number to crash landings returning to base.[31] The B-29s were credited with an equal number—sixteen—of MIG kills.[32]

. . . .

THE LEMAY DOCTRINE AND KOREA

LeMay studied the situation in Korea and saw things quite differently from those who directed the way the war was fought. Since the enemy forces were coming from the North, LeMay reasoned, the U.S. should bomb the North. His weapon of choice: the tried and true incendiary. LeMay wanted his bombers to hit a number of the key cities in North Korea, especially the ones that were supplying its troops. If they stopped the problem at the source, LeMay reasoned, the infiltration into the South would come to a halt. This was immediately rejected, and for the first time, the strategy of all-out war came up against the new concept of limited containment, which would become the U.S. doctrine in the nuclear age. This strategy would play out again in Vietnam and become the chief cause of a chasm that developed in the 1960s between LeMay and Robert McNamara. It would also cement the eternal image of Curtis LeMay as the crazed bomber who would first and foremost want to bomb anything in sight.

Years later, long after his retirement, LeMay defended his reasoning when he spoke to an Air Force panel in 1972. He articulated what would be considered the LeMay doctrine: that a country should think long and hard before it makes the fateful decision to go to war. But once that decision is made, and in the case of the United States, made by Congress, the war must be fought decisively to win. He was not alone in this belief. And although he was referring specifically to the North Korean conflict in his comments, he could have been talking about Vietnam as well:

So we go on and don't do it [the all out bombing campaign in Korea at the beginning] and let the war go on. Over a period of three-and-a-half or four years we did burn down every town in North Korea and every town in South Korea...And what? Killed off 20 percent of the Korean population...What I'm trying to say is if once you make a decision to use military force to solve your problem, then you ought to use it and use an overwhelming military force. Use too much and deliberately use too much so that you don't make an error on the other side and not quite have enough. And you roll over everything to start with and you close it down just like that. And you save resources, you save lives—not only your own but the enemy's too, and the recovery is quicker and everybody's back to peaceful existence hopefully in a shorter period of time.[33]

Given the radical and bizarre behavior that Pyongyang displayed over the next half-century, first under Kim Il-sung and then his son, Kim Jong-il, it is unclear whether the North Koreans would have had any logical reaction to a sustained bombing campaign. LeMay's plan may also have sparked an earlier and even greater confrontation with the Chinese or even the Russians. Yet the limited action pursued in both Korea and then Vietnam produced a certain degree of failure in the form of longer, protracted wars that caused greater suffering to civilian populations and created greater division in the U.S. .

LeMay's theory of warring nations transitioning to peaceful coexistence was not without basis. After laying waste to all of Japan, he had been awarded a medal by the Japanese—the Order of the Rising Sun, First Class—in December, 1964, less than twenty years after his firebomb raids. Though the event did not come off without some protest in the Japanese press, it certainly revealed a level of acceptance of actions pursued in wartime for the greater goal of peace.

By 1953, the Strategic Air Command under Curtis LeMay had achieved a massive retaliatory strength. There were seventeen nuclear-armed wings, which translated to 329 B-47s, 185 B-36s, 500 tankers, and 200 fighters, as well as the old standby, the B-29, which flew until the early 1960s. A global network of bases, some even built in isolated and barren locations like Greenland and North Africa, had been assembled, all within striking distance of the Soviet Union. In all, there were twenty-nine bases in the States and ten overseas.[34] Airmen would take their turns in "ready-rooms" where they would be on alert for twenty-four hours. The planes, just outside the door, were "hot," meaning they were maintained, fueled, and fully loaded with nuclear arms. The bases were secure—LeMay ended careers if he witnessed any breach in that security. Within just a few years of taking over, SAC was a well oiled and deadly machine, coiled back and ready to spring at any time of day or night.

But perhaps the most powerful aspect of the retaliatory strength the United States had in SAC was the fact that the Soviets knew the man behind it all was Curtis LeMay. The CIA made constant assessments of Soviet strength and developed psychological profiles of its military leaders; the KGB did the same. And the KGB, understanding LeMay's background in World War II, especially in the Pacific, and following his public utterances, never doubted that the commander behind it all would not hesitate for a moment if called on. Ralph Nutter relates a story that took place during the Berlin Airlift. Nutter had a friend who worked at the State Department and was in contact with the Soviets during this time. One day, one of his Soviet colleagues casually asked him if he thought LeMay could actually use the atomic bomb. The American response: "You're God damned right he would." The Soviet diplomat nodded and replied, "We think so too." Nutter believes this is a chief reason that the confrontation over Berlin during the airlift did not widen.[35]

LeMay could be secretive when he needed to be. But he understood that the whole point of deterrence was making the other side realize the power the U.S. was capable of using. Accordingly, he never tired of demonstrating the power of the Strategic Air Command.

Turning SAC around was another of many feats by the Air Force's determined general. Looking back on it, LeMay could break down his accomplishment to a simple theme: "My pattern throughout thirty-five years was painfully similar: getting heaved into something in which I'd had no previous experience." But he always fell back on a simple core philosophy that worked over and over: "When it has to be done, you just dig in and do the best you can . . . Get the best people you can around you who will help. Decide on the course of action. Get busy on it and keep out of your subordinates' way. Actually, it seems like the simplest thing in the world: to be excruciatingly honest always with yourself, and with everyone who's working for you."[36]

He recalled when, at Ohio State back in the 1920s, a German military officer came to speak to his ROTC class. The German could never understand just how the Americans won the First World War, because he thought there was no discipline amongst American troops. "First you have to give them the order and then you have to explain why. That is not a good way. Nein. How did you ever get anything done?"[37] the German officer wondered aloud.

LeMay disagreed. "My notion has been that you explain why, and then you don't need to give any order at all. All you have to do is get your big feet out of the way, and things will really happen. Forever I took the same course. Get the team together. 'There's the goal, people. Go ahead.'"[38]

LeMay never stopped tinkering with SAC's overall design, always thinking of new and better ways to innovate. He was aware that SAC crews might someday have to parachute into very harsh environments, so he set up the Air Force Survival School outside of Reno, Nevada. By the time he left SAC, more than 20,000 airmen had taken the seventeen-day course that taught them how to survive on their own in the world's most difficult environments.[39] Even astronauts would come to take the survival course, including the original Mercury Seven.

He developed an elite corps of military police to protect SAC bases, always afraid of the possibility of a domestic attack. More than half a century later, LeMay's Cold War mentality may appear excessive in hindsight. But it was up to a commander to think of every possible way that his forces could be immobilized. The criticism after Pearl Harbor, and then sixty years later, after September 11, was that our intelligence services had not foreseen the possible moves an enemy might make. They had not been creative in their thinking and, unfortunately, the results were national tragedies. LeMay always tried to stay one step ahead of the opposition. Fifty years later, some people dismiss his concerns as paranoia because the Cold War ended successfully for the United States. But that was never preordained, and in the 1950s and '60s it was especially uncertain. If any of the scenarios that LeMay was concerned about actually occurred, he would have been criticized for not anticipating the unimaginable.

LeMay definitely held strong views, which he had developed over long and difficult years, not just from his experience in SAC. He was always a staunch anti-Communist, and during the early McCarthy era, before the Soviets really had any nuclear capability, he was one of those who believed that subversion was a real threat, noting, "The Russians didn't threaten us [with nuclear weapons shortly after the war]. But I was worried about fifth column activity. Sabotage."[40] That's why he pushed to secure SAC bases.

LeMay had appeared as a hero on the covers of *Time*, *Newsweek*, *U.S. News & World Report*, *Parade*, and *Look* in the 1940s and 1950s, but the national mood had shifted, and by the 1960s when the Vietnam war was creating a divide throughout the country between conservatives and liberals, he came down on the wrong side of the political debate in the eyes of the new generation of writers and producers who were gaining influence in the media.

There have been books written and movies made that portray Curtis LeMay as an independent force unto himself—the one breach in our constitution that the founding fathers were unable to anticipate, the one member of government with no check or balance. In Stanley Kubrick's brilliant and frightening 1964 film, *Dr. Strangelove*, LeMay is seen in two characters: first the cigar-smoking General Jack D. Ripper, who sends his wing of nuclear armed B-52s against the Soviet Union all on his own because he has become completely paranoid; and then as the George C. Scott character, General Buck Turgidson, the head of the Air Force in the Pentagon who, instead of seeing Ripper's act as a disaster, sees it as

an opportunity. In the famous scene that takes place in the Pentagon War Room, the president asks for Turgidson's assessment of
the situation if the U.S. goes ahead with an all-out nuclear strike.
Turgidson pushes for it, but in a bizarre moment of his own strange
reality, he confesses: "Sir, I'm not saying we won't get our hair
mussed, but [we'd lose] no more than 10–20 million killed
tops. . . Uh, depending on the breaks." In the final scene of the film,
the world comes to an end in a long sequence of evocative nuclear
explosions to the music of "We'll Meet Again."

These portrayals were actually quite off the mark. LeMay
answered to the Joint Chiefs and to the President. He was the one
person who never forgot it and who always respected the chain of
command. "Our job in SAC was not to promulgate a national policy or an international one. Our job was to produce. And we produced."

There is a final irony to the *Dr. Strangelove* story that does
involve Curtis LeMay. Up until 1957, U.S. nuclear weapons actually did not have an effective safety net, and in some cases just one
person had access to a weapon. That means one man could have
possibly triggered an unauthorized detonation on his own. This
was noticed by a young researcher at the Rand Corporation named
Fred Ikle. Ikle raised this potential problem in his first briefing to
a group of generals at the Pentagon. "My knees were shaking," Ikle
recalls, looking back over half a century. None of this seemed to
interest the people who were present, except for a colonel who
thought his boss would want to know about it. That colonel's boss
was LeMay. "Luckily General Curtis LeMay, who was not at the
meeting, got wind of it and it hit him. He got moving on it and he
changed the procedure," Ikle explained. Because of Ikle's observa-

tion and LeMay's ability to move mountains, U.S. nuclear weapons thereafter were under the direction of two-man teams, adding one more crucial safeguard.

"He had a competence in getting things done," recalls Ikle. "Today, all you have are meetings and then meetings about meetings."[41]

Contrary to popular perception, LeMay never stepped outside the chain of command or even tried to advance his personal views. As he later wrote, "We in SAC were not saber-rattlers. We were not yelling for war and action in order to 'flex the mighty muscles we had built.' No stupidity of that sort. We wanted peace as much as anyone else wanted it."[42] However, he strongly disagreed with the policy that promised the Soviets that the U.S. would never use nuclear weapons first. He believed the entire purpose of having a nuclear arsenal was its threatened use, not its actual use. And by promising not to use it, what was the sense in even having it? Despite this view, however, he stuck to his job. Years after his retirement, he insisted to biographer Thomas Coffey that he never advocated preemptive war with the Soviets, saying, "I never discussed the problem with President Truman or with President Eisenhower. I never discussed it with General Vandenberg when he was Chief of Staff. I stuck to my job at Offutt and in the Command. I never discussed what we were going to do with the force we had or what he should do with it, or anything of that sort. Never discussed it with topside Brass, military or civilian."[43]

Over the past sixty years, political beliefs have changed remarkably. In 1945, an astounding 85 percent of the American public supported the use of the atomic bombs on Japan (practically a quarter of the population—23 percent—thought even more atomic bombs should be dropped). By 1995, those who favored the use of atomic bombs in Hiroshima and Nagasaki dropped to 55 percent.[44] The celebrity general on the cover of *Time* magazine in August 1945, who had also been brilliantly and heroically profiled in the *New Yorker* just two months earlier, had become a demonic clown in the eyes of many Americans by the 1960s.

LeMay saw the fascist and then Communist enemies he faced throughout his career as the same schoolyard bullies who would not listen to reason until brought to it by force. "I can't get over the notion that when you stand up and act like a man, you win respect . . . though perhaps it is only a fearful respect which leads eventually to compliance with your wishes. It's when you fall back, shaking with apprehension, that you're apt to get into trouble."[45]

To LeMay, SAC was the sheriff who protected the small western town. It was the cop on the beat. He truly believed SAC's motto: "Peace is our profession."

CHAPTER TWELVE

WASHINGTON

THERE ARE SOME PEOPLE IN THE PUBLIC SPOTLIGHT WHO GENERATE controversy yet are very thin-skinned. LeMay was not one of them. He had skin as tough as a rhino's and a keen understanding of the press and how it worked, so he came to expect criticism. He never took it personally because he understood it was just part of the process. His daughter, Janie, says that he just did not care what other people said or thought and everything in his public life backs that up. "Whatever you do, somebody's going to criticize you. Forget criticism," was the advice he gave to Air Force personnel.[1]

At the same time, there was also a part of LeMay that seemed to go after criticism. It was as if he wanted or even needed people to dislike him. His gruff exterior, his intemperate and sarcastic remarks, or his complete silence in situations where conversation was called for hint at an innate hostility that would become more acute as he aged.

His son-in-law, Dr. James Lodge, suggests that part of this may have been due to a hearing problem that worsened as he aged. This may have come from his early flying days in open cockpits. LeMay could read lips and follow a conversation, but it was more difficult in crowded rooms. "Loss of hearing can lead to frustration," explains Dr. Lodge, "and frustration can lead to anger."[2] But in the greater picture, LeMay understood that given his job, he was a sitting duck when it came to negative opinions.

"Point is, the person in public life is bound to receive a lot of half-witted criticism. He's a natural-born target for it. It is unnecessary to go to any extraordinary lengths to maintain a picture of lily-white purity and innocence. If you let things like that worry you, very soon you run out of worrying time. There are too many real problems up there on the board," he remarked in his memoir.[3]

Years later, long after various critics voiced their opinions about him, LeMay took the opportunity to set the record straight in his memoirs. One case, where critics had charged that he used Air Force jets and therefore taxpayer dollars for his own benefit, he called hogwash. "Sure as death and taxes, some character who runs a newspaper column, or some politician who has a bigger mouth than he has a fund of correct information—he gets up and starts raving about Air Force people using Air Force airplanes on trips for their personal pleasure."[4] He was forced to be away from Omaha at least half of every year and almost never had time for family vacations. He made no bones about using work-related inspections to Alaska or Maine to take a day or two off for a side trip to hunt or fish.

Sometimes, he even had fun with the criticism. Once, when he was the head of SAC, a reporter who did not know his subject very well began to look into the possibility that General LeMay was using an Air Force jet at government expense to go to San Francisco regularly to attend the opera. LeMay had never been to an opera in his life—anywhere. "If there was one next door tonight, I wouldn't go."[5]

LeMay never deviated from regulations. He was exceedingly honest, to the penny. In October 1946, he received a check for $12.50 for an article he had contributed to the *Encyclopedia Britannica*. As soon as it arrived in his office, he turned it around and sent it to the Army Air Force Aid Society. His need to follow the rules extended beyond money. On a hunting trip to shoot Canadian Geese wintering on an island off the Texas coast, he watched the geese flock to the water's edge. When his rowboat neared the island, he realized that the geese had been baited. Disgusted, LeMay turned around and returned to the mainland without firing a shot. He would never shoot an animal if it was not a fair shot.[6]

After his success in the war, a number of wealthy and famous people befriended LeMay. In one case, the New York toy manufacturer Louis Marx constantly sent him boxes of toys that Marx thought the General would be interested in. Every time he sent a package, Marx specified that the toys were "for your own personal use." And LeMay sent every shipment on to Air Force children. When Marx asked if he could send some cosmetics to Helen and Janie, LeMay wrote back saying it was too soon after the last gifts, but so as to not offend Marx, he made up the excuse, "We must keep the ladies unspoiled if possible." LeMay's responses were always graciously to thank Marx, but quietly suggest that he send fewer gifts.

Marx and his wife even named one of their sons Curtis and asked LeMay to be his godfather. Later, Mrs. Marx asked him for some advice he could pass on to his godson. LeMay's response showed an insight that extended far beyond an airplane. "During my travels to various parts of the world," he wrote to Mrs. Marx in 1958, "I have discovered that extremely few Americans, including myself, are bilingual. On the other hand, a good percentage of the foreigners we visit fluently speak at least two languages. It is a shame that this situation exists and I really feel our education system should endeavor to make the coming generations at least bilingual." He advised the young man to study Russian or Chinese.[7]

At Christmas time, there were cigars, cigar cutters, along with a variety of smoking accessories from various people, and even a bathrobe and slippers from the radio and television personality, Arthur Godfrey. Unlike many of the others who courted LeMay, Godfrey seemed to have had a real friendship with him. They shared an interest in flying, hunting, and their political beliefs seemed to run in tandem. Sometimes, LeMay would come to New York with Helen and stay in Godfrey's apartment. They also took a hunting trip to Africa.

There were often letters from Hollywood inviting him to screenings of films pertaining to the Air Force. After the screening of the new film *12 O'Clock High* at the end of 1949, he wrote to producer Darryl F. Zanuck: "I do not feel qualified to predict how the public or the critics will receive the picture, but I do know that every airman who served in England in the early days of the war will be forever grateful to you and 20th Century Fox for producing it." And there were letters from Jimmy Stewart, who flew under him in the Eighth Air Force in the War. Stewart treated LeMay the way one might expect someone would treat a former commanding officer—with great respect and deference.

Most of the invitations and requests for dinners, lunches, hunt clubs, and various social events were declined with a polite note, owing to a pressing work schedule. "Work before pleasure, you know,"[8] he would often write.

As difficult as it was for LeMay to talk to people, his writing showed thoughtfulness and even caring. This was certainly not the silent LeMay people knew. He could also be self-deprecating and even humorous. In a letter to his wartime aide Theodore Becke-meier, who was practicing law in St. Louis after the war, LeMay wrote in August 1946: "Dear Beck: Kenyon College, for some unknown reason, conferred a Doctor of Laws degree on me at their spring commencement. Not to worry. I'm not seriously thinking of taking the bar exam and will probably still need the services of a good lawyer."[9]

Although LeMay could not interact in large social settings, he could carry on conversations with people with whom he shared interests. If the topics were automobiles, flying, or even ham radios, he could be an avid conversationalist, especially with younger people. He loved hobbies and lamented that he never had more time for them. Many people sent requests for autographs for their collections. He always wrote back providing the autograph and added graciously that it was a privilege to add his name to their collection. He always wished them luck with their hobby. Joan Whitney of San Francisco served with the Red Cross in the War and began collecting songs and parodies. She wrote to him wondering if he knew the origins of the line: "Throw your mask away, you fly for Curt LeMay." He wrote back saying he tried but could not find any information and was unfamiliar with the song, but he added that her hobby "sounds like an interesting endeavor."[10] The correct answer to this question, however, had to do with the low level incendiary raid over Tokyo on March 9, 1945. When LeMay ordered the planes to fly at 5,000 feet, some talented crewman wrote a jingle explaining why oxygen masks would not be necessary.

Even celebrities like Claire Booth Luce, the Congresswoman and wife of the powerful media titan, Henry Luce, were not immune. She wrote that she and her husband had been going over war photographs from the files of *Life* magazine, which Henry Luce owned, and came across what she called "an extraordinarily fine candid study" of LeMay and was "overcome with the well known 'fan' complex." Luce asked him to autograph it for her wall at their country estate in Connecticut.[11]

LeMay was always available to anyone who served under him during the war. Five years after the war, Ralph Nutter, who had flown twenty-seven missions over Germany and then voluntarily served in the Marianas, was facing a personal crisis. One of his sons had a brain injury from a playground accident, his wife was having medical problems, and he had just started a new law practice. Nutter was trying to hold his family together when he learned he was going to be called up for active duty in Korea. He called LeMay and explained that it would destroy his family. LeMay responded, "Don't worry, leave it to me." Nutter was never called up. "He saved my life...twice," Nutter remarked.[12] And when D.H. Loughridge, a physics professor, was nominated for president of the University of Southern California in 1946, Loughridge asked for a letter of recommendation. LeMay asked for his service record and when he found that all was in order and that Loughridge had flown with him, he sent off a stellar letter of recommendation. Whenever anyone came by, especially from the 305th, LeMay made time to see them, and this continued during his years in Washington. He answered almost every letter personally.

Robert Rosenthal, the young pilot who stood up in the dramatic moment after the Munster mission in 1943 when he was the only surviving pilot in his group of thirteen to return, wrote to him in 1947. Rosenthal had gone back to Germany, this time as a lawyer working for the United States Department of Justice in the Nuremburg trials. While there, he met and fell in love with a woman on his staff and they were married. Along with his wedding announcement, he added this note:

Dear Sir:

The last time I reported to you was in 1943 regarding a trip I took to Munster. This time I would like to announce the results of my mission to Nuremburg. Hope you can come by and visit. Rosie.

LeMay's response:

Dear Rosenthal: Extend my congratulations on recent marriage. Apparently you have been better received in Nuremberg Germany, than in Munster. Please give my very best regards to any like yourself, who are still wandering around over the target area. Curtis LeMay.[13]

And in a letter just before he was sent to Germany in 1947, he wrote to a former colleague, Colonel Albert Price:

I suppose you have seen my new assignment in the newspapers. By a touch of fate, I now have to help build up what we tore down during the war.[14]

William Blanchard was the doctor who diagnosed his Bell's Palsy in Syracuse in 1942. Four years later, LeMay wrote a surprisingly candid and self-critical letter on April 18, 1946. In almost all of his letters, he called people by their last names, but with Blanchard he included his title:

> Dear Dr. Blanchard: It is indeed gratifying to me to find there are still some people left who do not believe that their Army is made up of stupid and selfish individuals as portrayed by some of the radical elements of the country.
>
> Being only human, I can look back over the war and find many mistakes and criticize myself for actions that seemed perfectly sound at the time. The only fault I can find with this decision is that it was not done soon enough.[15]

In his letter to Blanchard, it is doubtful that by "mistakes" he is referring to his destruction of the enemy. More probably, they have to do with losing his own men. LeMay was not one to spend a lot of time in self-reflection; there just was not the time for such luxury. But throughout the war and later, he thought that if he had only worked a little harder or been a little smarter, more men could have returned to enjoy their families and postwar life.

LeMay was also the recipient of hundreds of crank letters. Many of them are impossible to decipher, written in strange scrawls, or so tiny that they are a marvel of miniaturization. But sometimes the letters would appear normal until further down. A polite lady in Kansas wanted to alert LeMay to the sky arc that would drag human beings aloft and the fact that she was no longer able to control it. There were letters concerned about the Communist-Zionist conspiracy that had control of the president's mind. When these letters did make their way to LeMay's desk, one can see his handwritten label that simply says: "crank file" or just "crank." After one particularly strange message, from a man in San Diego announcing the invention of a design for rotary motion that will render the Air Force obsolete, LeMay wrote at the top: "WHEW!!"[16]

His physical appearance seemed to change along with his uniform. When LeMay came off his B-17 after a mission over Germany, he was filmed wearing that classic World War II bomber jacket, he still had his "May West" life preserver over his front, and he wore a visor cap with big fluffy ear flaps, not unlike those worn by schoolboys. He was indistinguishable in rank from the young sergeant who stood behind him. And he seemed more approachable. But ten years later, in all his public appearances, he wore the new light blue Air Force uniform with a field of medals on the front that immediately made him far less accessible.

This separation from the men below inevitably comes with command. LeMay understood this. Part of him still remembered and even longed for the days when that was not so, yet another part of him enjoyed the status he had attained.

·   ·   ·   ·

REASSIGNMENT

Nine years is an unusually long time to stay in one senior posting in the military. At SAC, LeMay had more than proven his abilities again. By 1957, he was considered the most effective officer in the Air Force. The next move up seemed obvious to everyone in military circles.

The Joint Chiefs of Staff at the Pentagon represent the heads of each military branch—the Army, Navy, Marines, and Air Force, who advise the Secretary of Defense and the President. When a crisis occurs, the Chiefs converge on the White House. They work together to develop potential war plans for the President's approval and advise the Defense Chief on what weapons systems will be needed in the years ahead. Each Chief has a Vice Chief who runs his particular branch of the service on a day-to-day basis to free up the Chief to concentrate on global issues. In 1957, General Thomas D. White, also a four star General, became Chief of the Air Force. There seemed to be no question of who his understudy would be.

The Vice Chief has to develop a good working relationship with the Chief if the posting is to succeed. The understudy must be able to think like his boss, execute orders for him, in essence, be the other half of his brain. White and LeMay knew each other only slightly, having met once, briefly, during the war. From all indications, LeMay served well. When there were questions, he asked White.

Although LeMay was exceedingly careful never to overreach his authority and always made sure his boss's wishes were carried out, there were still strong differences between them. LeMay did not like White's willingness to compromise. LeMay was more aggressive and would only reach an accommodation when it looked like his argument was lost and there was no other alternative. "If you believed in something, God Damn it, you go in there and fight for it," he later told a biographer.[17]

The Washington assignment created a more normal life for LeMay and his family in contrast to his previous postings and the long periods away from home. Janie was already in college, not far away at the University of Maryland, and she was home for occasional weekends and vacations. The LeMays moved to a detached colonial house at Fort Myer, just across from the Jefferson Memorial near the Pentagon. The Whites lived on the other side of the same house. Although the two generals respected each other professionally, they were not personal friends and did not mix socially. White was much smoother on the Washington social circuit and was aware of his subordinate's limitations. "LeMay has almost no social graces," he observed in his notes.[18]

LeMay could not completely avoid the Washington social circuit, as much as he tried. Helen made up for many of her husband's shortcomings, but there were still stories that circulated. Once, it was said that LeMay frightened dinner companions in Georgetown with predictions of thermonuclear war with the Soviets, although it is hard to imagine LeMay expending that many words in a social setting.

The origins of LeMay's difficult tenure in Washington can be traced to this difference in style. Washington moves forward on politics and compromise. Unlike a battle, where an aggressive and decisive personality is necessary, the most successful generals who have made the transition to Washington—and many generals have not been able to make this transition—learned quickly that accommodation is the only route to take. LeMay's strong character worked in England and on Guam during the war. It proved to be successful and even brilliant at the Rand Corporation, in the Berlin Airlift, and at SAC. But his combative nature and his inability to transition into this very different environment proved to be the first unsuccessful assignment in his career.

He did find other ways to succeed, but they rarely came from compromise, and in the highly charged political atmosphere in

Washington he would make enemies. Just as he understood how to maneuver around roadblocks in the military to accomplish his goals, he would use the same tactics at the Pentagon. But the military can be much more forgiving, especially when success follows the approach of a maverick. End runs may lead to some victories, but in Washington, they also leave a trail of memory and dislike.

In one case, LeMay thought the pay raises for military personnel from enlisted men all the way up to the top generals were too low. He was correct in his complaint. The Air Force, which needed highly skilled minds to handle increasingly sophisticated equipment, could never compete with the civilian sector, especially when the lowest ranking Airman received $78 a month. Even LeMay, at the highest rung of the service, was earning $1,221 a month. While $15,000 a year in 1957 was considered a very good salary, it was nowhere near anything in the public sector with the same degree of responsibility.

So LeMay wangled an invitation to the Texas ranch of Lyndon Johnson, the powerful Senate Majority Leader. Johnson was as blunt as LeMay when the question finally came up. LBJ told him he did not stand a chance of getting a pay raise for the military, given the fiscal mood of Congress in 1957. Undeterred, LeMay went to his friend, Arthur Godfrey, who used his forum on radio and television to push for pay raises. When the letters started coming in from people across the country, the military got its raise.[19] There are few people who were able to outplay Lyndon Johnson, but LeMay was not above an end run around Congress when it came to improving anything in the Air Force. But at the same time, LBJ was not someone to cross.

LeMay had a keen understanding of the symbiotic relationship between the press corps and Congress and understood how to play one off the other. Later that year, after the Soviets launched Sputnik, Congress set off on a whirlwind of hearings to find out why the U.S. fell behind. White and LeMay were both called to testify, but LeMay deflected the space race question by casually turning the argument to a lack of funds, mentioning that SAC planes had to stop flying because they had to wait for their fuel allotment. This was a slight exaggeration, since LeMay had only been ordered to slow down his practice missions to save gasoline, which he refused to do anyway. (That same year, SAC planes burned up 1,500,000,000 gallons of jet fuel.[20])

It was not that LeMay did not see space as vital for the future. He had argued for a U.S. satellite right after the war in 1946, but was rejected because Congress did not want to spend the money.[21] Eleven years later, as Sputnik sent beeps down to earth, there was suddenly more than enough money for the U.S. rocket programs.

In the first three and a half years of his Washington tour, the White House was occupied by a military hero, Dwight Eisenhower. The Commander in Chief was trained at West Point and spent his career in the Army. When matters came up that required the attention of the Joint Chiefs, or during their regular meetings, a certain telegraphy was apparent in the room—concepts did not have to be defined before moving on to decisions. And in spite of occasional flare-ups, the world remained calm for the most part. The Cold War was at a stalemate. Both sides were learning to live with the tension of possible armed conflict set against the desire to preserve the status quo.

• • • •

THE NEW FRONTIER

The Eisenhower administration and the 1950s ended on a cold Friday in January 1961 when a much younger president was sworn into office. John F. Kennedy was, in almost every way, the antithesis of LeMay. Although he was also forged by the Second World War, Kennedy was eleven years younger. He came from an extraordinarily wealthy family, and his childhood had been a series of elite schools, world travel, and personal connections to the powerful. Kennedy was a strong cold warrior, running on a platform that the United States should never flinch from demonstrating its strength, but his domestic policies were much more liberal than LeMay's. There was an enormous difference in the style of the two men. Kennedy's grace was natural, and he was adored by the press. Even if LeMay had tried, and he did not, he would never have the ability to produce a popular image. However, the greatest divide between these two men came in Kennedy's appointment of Robert S. McNamara to the position of Secretary of Defense. McNamara had worked under LeMay as a statistician for the Army Air Forces in Europe and then in the Marianas. He had gone from there to become the highest paid executive in the country as the president of Ford. Now, reversing the earlier dynamic, McNamara would be LeMay's boss. It was not a match made in heaven.

It took almost no time for these differences to boil to the surface. In March, just two months into the new administration, LeMay was called into a meeting at the Pentagon with the Joint Chiefs. He would represent the Air Force because White was out of town. LeMay noticed that there was something odd about the meeting right from the start. To begin with, there was a civilian in the room who pushed aside a curtain to reveal landing areas for a military engagement on the coast of Cuba. LeMay had been told absolutely nothing about the operation until that moment. All eyes turned to him when the civilian, who worked for the CIA, asked which of the three sites would provide the best landing area for planes.

LeMay explained that he was completely in the dark and needed more information before he would hazard a guess. He asked how many troops would be involved in the landing. The answer, that there would be 700, dumbfounded him. There was no way, he told them, that an operation would succeed with so few troops. The briefer cut him short. "That doesn't concern you," he told LeMay.[22]

Over the next month, LeMay tried unsuccessfully to get information about the impending invasion. Then on April 16 he stood in for White—again out of town—at another meeting. Just one day before the planned invasion, he finally learned some of the basics of the plan. The operation, which would become known as the Bay of Pigs, had been conceived during the Eisenhower administration by the CIA as a way to depose Cuban dictator Fidel Castro. Cuban exiles had been trained as an invasion force by the CIA and former U.S. military personnel. The exiles would land in Cuba with the aid of old World War II bombers with Cuban markings and try to instigate a counterrevolution. It was an intricate plan that depended on every phase working perfectly. LeMay saw immediately that the invasion force would need the air cover of U.S. planes, but the Secretary of State, Dean Rusk, under Kennedy's order, had cancelled that the night before. LeMay saw the plan was destined to fail, and he wanted to express his concern to McNamara. But the Secretary of Defense was not present at the meeting.

Instead, LeMay was able to speak only to the Under Secretary of Defense, Roswell Gilpatric. LeMay did not mince words.

"You just cut the throats of everybody on the beach down there," LeMay told Gilpatric.

"What do you mean?" Gilpatric asked.[23]

LeMay explained that without air support, the landing forces were doomed. Gilpatric responded with a shrug.

The entire operation went against everything LeMay had learned in his thirty-three years of experience. In any military operation, especially one of this significance, a plan cannot depend on every step going right. Most steps do not go right and a great deal of padding must be built in to compensate for those unforeseen problems. It went back to the LeMay doctrine—hitting an enemy with everything you had at your disposal if you have already come to the conclusion that a military engagement is your only option. Use everything, so there is no chance of failure. Limited, half-hearted endeavors are doomed.

The Bay of Pigs invasion turned out to be a disaster for the Kennedy administration. Kennedy realized it too late. The Cubans did not rise up against Castro, and the small, CIA-trained army was quickly defeated by Castro's forces. The men were either killed or taken prisoner. All of this made Kennedy look weak and inexperienced. A short time later, Kennedy went out to a golf course with his old friend, Charles Bartlett, a journalist. Bartlett remembered Kennedy driving golf balls far into a distant field with unusual anger and frustration, saying over and over, "I can't believe they talked me into this."[24] The entire episode undermined the administration and set the stage for a difficult summit meeting between Kennedy and Soviet Premier Nikita Khrushchev two

months later. It also exacerbated the administration's rocky relationship with the Joint Chiefs, who felt the military was unfairly
blamed for the fiasco in Cuba.

This was not quite true. Kennedy put the blame squarely on the
CIA and on himself for going along with the ill-conceived plan.
One of his first steps following the debacle was to replace the CIA
director, Allen Dulles, with John McCone. The incident forced
Kennedy to grow in office. Although his relationship with the military did suffer, the problems between Kennedy and the Pentagon
predated the Bay of Pigs. According to his chief aid and speechwriter, Ted Sorensen, Kennedy was unawed by Generals. "First,
during his own military service, he found that military brass was
not as wise and efficient as the brass on their uniform indicated . . .
and when he was president with a great background in foreign
affairs, he was not that impressed with the advice he received."[25]

LeMay and the other Chiefs sensed this and felt that Kennedy
and the people under him simply ignored the military's advice.
LeMay was especially incensed when McNamara brought in a
group of brilliant, young statisticians as an additional civilian
buffer between the ranks of professional military advisers and the
White House. They became known as the Defense Intellectuals.
LeMay used the more derogatory term "Whiz Kids." These were
people who had either no military experience on the ground whatsoever or, at the most, two or three years in lower ranks. In
LeMay's mind, this limited background could never match the
combined experience that the Joint Chiefs brought to the table.
These young men, who seemed to have the President's ear, also
exuded a sureness of their opinions that LeMay saw as arrogance.
This ran against his personality—as LeMay approached almost

everything in his life with a feeling of self-doubt, he was actually surprised when things worked out well. Here he saw the opposite—inexperienced people coming in absolutely sure of themselves and ultimately making the wrong decisions with terrible consequences.

This feeling of distrust cut both ways. Carl Kaysen was Deputy National Security Adviser to President Kennedy. Kaysen had first encountered LeMay in Europe during the War when he was part of an OSS group that helped pick targets for the Eighth Air Force. Almost two decades later, in August of 1961, Kaysen said he encountered the LeMay "aura" when he and a small group of advisers went to visit SAC Headquarters in Omaha. LeMay had already left for Washington, and Tommy Power was in charge, but LeMay's presence could still be felt. "The atmosphere was tight and tense . . . it was as if they were saying: 'What the hell are you civilians doing here? This is not your business. It's the military's business.'"[26] The general tone of the meeting astounded Kayson, especially since he and his group represented the Commander-in-Chief. It was clear that the sour feelings between the administration and the military had trickled down the chain of command.

All of these factors might have been overcome. However, the ultimate problem that arose between Curtis LeMay and the White House during his tenure in Washington came as the result of his very prickly relationship with McNamara.

•   •   •   •

MCNAMARA

By the time LeMay reached the Pentagon, he was much more sure of himself than he had been as a young commander in England and later in the Pacific. The success of his visions, along with age and experience, bolstered this confidence. He was still as determined as ever to have his way, but now a new air of tenacity had entered his personality. He had also become used to getting his way, whether it was with subordinates, or even congressmen and senators.

Now, for the first time in memory, he had encountered someone who was as smart, self-reliant, and fearless as he was himself. Robert McNamara had very clear ideas of what he wanted to do at the Pentagon. He had been given a clear mandate by the President. McNamara had a brilliant mind for numbers, and he was determined to take control of the unwieldy Defense Department and its industrial counterpart that Dwight Eisenhower had himself warned about in the final days of his administration. He went after huge and costly programs from planes to ships with the cool hand of a disinterested third party. His belief structure appeared to be based only on data and logic. For the first time, the Defense Department did not run its chief; the chief was determined to run the Defense Department.

As for LeMay, the entire relationship went downhill at the very beginning. The Joint Chiefs tried to talk to McNamara. As LeMay later told biographer Tom Coffey, "It was like talking into a brick wall. We got nowhere. Finally it was just a waste of time and effort."[27]

McNamara and LeMay would disagree on almost everything. McNamara wanted the Air Force to concentrate on missiles, which were more cost effective. LeMay wanted a new generation of supersonic bombers (the B-70), which would replace the B-52. But the arguments would go beyond individual programs to every major geo-political issue of the day—the Soviet Union, Cuba, and Vietnam. Even for Washington, which has witnessed strong personal rivalries, the LeMay-McNamara struggle would be epic. To his credit, McNamara would later be much more generous in his appraisal of LeMay. "Without question, Curtis LeMay was the finest combat commander the U.S. has ever produced," he said in an interview.[28] LeMay was not as kind. In 1968, three years after his retirement, he wrote a book in which the sole purpose was to attack McNamara and the Defense Intellectuals, mincing no words even in its title: *America Is in Danger*. The genesis of this struggle began in those early days in 1961.

LeMay clearly did not fit into the profile of the New Frontier. "Every time the President had to see LeMay, he ended up in a sort of fit," remembered Roswell Gilpatric, Undersecretary of Defense. "I mean he would just be frantic at the end of a session with LeMay because, you know, LeMay couldn't listen or wouldn't take in, and he would make what Kennedy considered . . . outrageous proposals that bore no relation to the state of affairs in the 1960s."[29] This observation is corroborated by McNamara.[30]

Given this already hostile atmosphere, it seemed clear that when Thomas White's term was over with the Joint Chiefs in June of 1961, LeMay would probably leave as well. So it came as a real shock when Kennedy appointed LeMay as the new Air Force Chief to replace White. And it came with McNamara's recommendation. Years later, Gilpatric said LeMay was appointed because the administration feared a revolt within the Air Force if LeMay had been cast aside.

LeMay discounted that. "Everyone realized the president picks whomever he wants. There wouldn't have been a revolt."[31]

Although McNamara agrees with Gilpatric's assessment that Kennedy did not enjoy his encounters with LeMay, he says LeMay was chosen for two very clear reasons. "First, because he was such a fine commander and second, because we—the president and I—thought, I don't want to use the word control . . . reason . . . we thought we could reason with him."[32]

But there is another, darker, explanation for Kennedy and McNamara's choice. It can be seen in McNamara's first response—LeMay's qualities as a fine commander. The possibility of an all-out nuclear war with the Soviets in 1961 was very real. And if that nightmare scenario ever unfolded, the president wanted someone with LeMay's cool and experienced hand by his side. Kennedy spoke to *Time* magazine correspondent Hugh Sidey about this. "It's good to have men like Curt LeMay and Arleigh Burke (Chief of Naval Operations) commanding troops once you decide to go in. But these men aren't the only ones you listen to when you decide whether to go in or not. I like having LeMay at the head of the Air Force. Everybody knows how he feels. That's a good thing right now."[33]

LeMay was sworn into office at the White House by the Secretary of the Air Force Eugene Zuckert on June 8, 1961, with Kennedy standing between them. Helen was there with Janie. It has often been noted that Defense Secretary McNamara was conspicuously not in attendance, which led to speculation that because of the rift between them the Defense Secretary was absent on purpose. "Nothing of the sort," remembers McNamara. "I was out of town, I don't remember where, but it couldn't be helped. I recommended him."[34]

LeMay's Vice Chief was Frederic Smith, Jr., an officer who went through cadet school with LeMay back in 1928. Smith was nominated by the Secretary of the Air Force, Eugene Zuckert, with LeMay's approval. Zuckert was impressed with Smith's understanding of computers, which Zuckert wanted the Air Force to become more proficient with, and there was another reason. Even though Smith was reluctant because he thought their personalities would not match, General Lauris Norstad told him it would be good for the Air Force, because Smith would be "a mellowing influence" on LeMay.[35]

Smith's first worries turned out to be correct: it was an ill fit, and he was soon gone. LeMay made the next selection himself, William F. McKee, known in the Air Force by his unflattering nickname, "Bozo." LeMay's choice surprised everyone, because Bozo McKee was one of the only high-ranking Air Force officers who was not a pilot. George Marshall transferred McKee to the Air Force during the war because he thought Hap Arnold needed more logistical help. McKee proved to be brilliant at his job and moved up the chain.

When LeMay first offered him the job, McKee said no thanks. "Why the hell do I want to be vice chief?" McKee was not intimidated by the LeMay aura. He was more than content with his present job—head of Air Force logistics at Wright Patterson in Ohio. LeMay told him he had no choice, he would start as soon as he packed his bags. The relationship worked very well. Nothing LeMay said or did ever deterred McKee; he answered him as an equal. Both men were in agreement on the major issues. LeMay left McKee alone to run the Air Force and never second-guessed him.

Less than two months after the Bay of Pigs, Kennedy met Khrushchev in Vienna. It did not go well at all. Khrushchev surmised that Kennedy was inexperienced from his handling of the

Bay of Pigs. Kennedy tried to push Khrushchev to stop Communist expansion in Europe, but the Soviet Premier was in no mood
to be pushed around. Khrushchev refused, threatened, and bullied.
"Force will be met by force," he blustered to Kennedy. "If the U.S.
wants war, that's its problem."

"Then, Mr. Chairman, it will be war," Kennedy replied. "It will
be a cold, long winter."[36]

Two months after the summit, the construction of the Berlin
Wall began.

LeMay concentrated on technology in those years. The U.S. Air
Force had always had a special knack for looking forward and
developing programs years ahead of its potential adversaries. As
early as 1963, LeMay was already looking at outer space for a
global satellite communications system, a missile defense shield
(later known as Star Wars), smart bombs, and pilotless aircraft.
Some projects were stopped cold by Robert McNamara. An atomic
airplane that was in the early stage of development came across the
Defense Secretary's desk. When he saw there was little advancement year after year, he killed the program . . . and saved one billion dollars. McNamara also stopped the supersonic B-70 bomber
program that was LeMay's pet project.

LeMay pushed hard for the B-70. He wanted 150 of these planes
capable of flying at 80,000 feet in SAC's fleet as soon as possible.
LeMay's experience was based on the development of the B-17,
when a few far thinking men had pushed for the program that
eventually helped save the U.S. at the start of World War II.
McNamara thought guided missiles were more cost-effective and
that the B-52 would suffice. This was the setup for a battle between
the two men, which would culminate in a crisis.

McNamara stopped the order for the 150 B-70s, offering just enough funding for North American Aviation to develop two prototypes for testing. Had LeMay's concept gone through, it would have been a huge program, costing close to $5 billion to initiate and involving not just North American Aviation, but eighteen subcontractors and thousands of jobs across twenty-five states. To the shock of the White House, LeMay tried another end run, going to Carl Vinson, the wily old congressman of Georgia and the head of the Congressional Armed Services Committee. Vinson was first elected to Congress in 1914 and became one of the greatest advocates for national defense. On March 1, 1962, Vinson announced that the House Armed Services Committee authorized the Secretary of the Air Force to spend the full $491,000,000 for the development of the bomber.

"This was more than just a fight over a bomber," said Ted Sorenson. "Never before had the Congress sought to tie the president's hands on a discretionary military matter in this fashion."[37]

The crisis was eventually worked out several weeks later in a private walk in the White House Rose Garden when the President charmed the courtly old southern congressman into relenting. To this day, no one knows what transpired or how Kennedy got Vinson to back down, but shortly afterwards, the request was withdrawn. LeMay tried twice more to raise the issue with Congress but failed both times.

Later that year, just before Christmas, LeMay stayed home, complaining that he was not feeling well. This was highly unusual. He was rarely sick and when he was, he never let it interfere with work. After two days in bed, he went to the hospital at Andrews Air Force Base, where doctors discovered he had suffered a heart attack. He remained in the hospital until February 12, 1962. The inactivity drove LeMay and everyone around him slightly crazy. When he was released, he and Helen went on an extended vacation to Hawaii so he could rest.

Upon his return, LeMay made an appointment to see President Kennedy at the White House. His purpose was to try, one more time, to explain his perspective on the B-70 strategy. It was an uphill battle anyway, since McNamara was a White House insider. Kennedy steered the topic away from the bomber program and talked more about military problems around the globe. LeMay left the meeting frustrated that he had not been able to get his point across.

On the other side of the globe, another long-simmering military problem was beginning to get more public attention. At the start of 1962, the U.S. had 16,000 military advisors training the South Vietnamese army in its fight against the Viet Cong and the Communist government based in Hanoi. In early February, the Pentagon set up a permanent U.S. military presence in Saigon—the Military Assistance Command in Vietnam (MACV). The U.S. military presence in a country that most Americans knew very little about would only grow from that point on. In April, LeMay went to Vietnam for an inspection tour and met with the head of MACV, General Paul Harkins, as well as the President of South Vietnam, Ngo Dinh Diem. While MACV was concentrating its efforts in the South, LeMay saw that the real problem was clearly coming from the North. LeMay made the same recommendation he made twelve years earlier, for Korea—if the U.S. intended to stop this infiltration, a massive bombing campaign of the North would do the trick. LeMay zeroed in on the port facility in Haiphong, where the weapons and supplies were coming in from the Soviet Union, and proposed bombing it. He believed this would put a halt to the guerrilla war in the South, but the plan was much too bold for the tentative steps that the Kennedy Administration was making in Vietnam in 1962.

Ten years and 59,000 American lives later, the U.S. did exactly what LeMay had suggested. From December 19 to 29, 1972, the Air Force and Navy conducted Linebacker II, the largest concentrated bombing since World War II. The bombing of the North Vietnamese capital, Hanoi, and the port of Haiphong was conducted by tactical fighters, along with 741 B-52 sorties. Ten B-52s were shot down, five crash-landed in Laos and Thailand, thirty-three B-52 crewmen were killed, thirty-three were captured, and twenty-six were rescued. After years of stops and starts, the massive bombing finally pushed the North Vietnamese to hammer out a negotiated settlement that gave the U.S. a way to extricate itself from its tortured involvement.

Decades later, the political debate over this conflict remains unresolved. Kennedy aide Ted Sorensen strongly disagreed with the suggestion that the conflict may have ended sooner had LeMay's plan been followed ten years earlier, "I don't know how you can say this so many years after the fact, especially when you consider that the Vietnamese had been fighting for their independence since forever and the idea that some bombs in Hanoi or Haiphong would have brought them to the table is ludicrous."[38]

But former Secretary of Defense, James Schlesinger, countered Sorensen's view. "That's ridiculous, the myth that it was a civil war. What destroyed Vietnam was that 18 divisions came down from the North in 1975. There was nationalism in Hanoi but not in the South and it was the North imposing its view on the South."[39]

Schlesinger also points out that had the strikes taken place earlier when LeMay suggested them, the Soviet surface-to-air missiles would not have been in place, saving the U.S. planes and crews that were shot down a decade later.

It was around this time that the most famous quote attributed to LeMay would come out, a quote that stuck long after his death. In his autobiography, *Mission With LeMay*, written with the help of novelist McKinley Kantor, LeMay gave Kantor his quotes, stories, and ideas, and Kantor helped shape them into written form. The drafts of the book were sent to LeMay for his approval before the book was published. The book is very much in LeMay's voice, and it is well done. But there is one quote on page 565 concerning Vietnam that Kantor invented: "My solution to the problem would be to tell them frankly that they've got to draw in their horns and stop their aggression, or we're going to bomb them back into the Stone Age. And we would shove them back into the Stone Age with Air power or Naval power—not with ground forces."[40]

To this day, when LeMay's name comes up, most people remember that quote, asking "Isn't he the guy who wanted to bomb Vietnam back to the Stone Age?" Much later, LeMay admitted to friends that he never said those words. "I was just so damned bored going through the transcripts that I just let it get by," he told friends and family.[41] Since he put his name on the book, he was responsible, but the quote most likely stayed with him simply because it sounded like something he could have said.

Vietnam highlighted the greatest difference between LeMay's philosophy of war and McNamara's. The Defense Secretary pushed for what he called flexible response from the very start of the U.S. involvement in the conflict: namely, offering the enemy a way out; however, if they show aggression, match the aggression, but only proportionately. Consequently, the full weight of the growing American military was never brought to bear on the North. Ground would be fought over in the South and then abandoned only to be fought over again and again, always with more casualties. The North would be bombed and then the bombing would be halted. It was a completely different strategy than the one the U.S. used in World War II.

LeMay thought flexible response was counterintuitive; it ran completely against his doctrine of war. If a war is not worth winning, LeMay's answer was simple: do not get involved in the first place. Consequently, as LeMay watched the troop levels expand along with U.S. casualties, he grew more and more angry. The focal point of that anger was McNamara. As the conflict dragged on, he also grew furious with Lyndon Johnson because he believed McNamara and LBJ lied to the American people about the war. While the Vietnam War deeply divided the country, it would create major fissures within the government as well.

CHAPTER THIRTEEN

CUBA, KENNEDY, AND JOHNSON

BY THE SUMMER OF 1962, LeMAY HAD SETTLED INTO HIS JOB AT the Pentagon. Bozo McKee was running the Air Force, which freed LeMay to work with the Joint Chiefs, testify before Congress, and continue his fight for the B-70 bomber. He had made his peace with life in Washington, and he was feeling more energetic after his heart attack. By that summer he could put in the same number of hours at work again. Helen became active in a number of Air Force women's organizations. The two had time for dinner together, and Helen could even accompany him on some of his trips.

Janie had been married the summer before in a large wedding with a reception at Fort Myer. Helen had been instrumental in every detail, including the match, originally pushing Janie to meet James Lodge, Jr., a young Army doctor. The newlyweds settled in Washington at first, where Dr. Lodge worked as a pediatrician at

Walter Reed hospital. LeMay had been away a good part of Janie's life. He was gone throughout World War II, and during the SAC years. He missed a great deal of the ordinary, day-to-day events that are hardly dramatic, but which make up a life. In his autobiography, LeMay was uncharacteristically sentimental thinking back about Janie as a little girl. He seemed to take great pleasure from one of those nondescript moments, when Janie was a Brownie Scout, Helen was the leader, and an entire troop of little girls came bounding in and out of the large house during his posting in Wiesbaden Germany. "It was comical to see her, along with a German butler and a German governess, running that aggregation," he recalled. "'Course, I didn't witness much of it firsthand; but every now and then we'd hear the noise, and see them swarming in or out of the place." Like any father who is suddenly escorting his beautiful young daughter down the aisle of a church, the person in his mind was not the woman in the white gown, but the little girl. "I shut my eyes and see the whole thing again."[1]

In the summer of 1962, negotiations on a treaty to ban above ground nuclear testing dominated the political world. The treaty involved seventeen countries, but the two main players were the United States and the Soviet Union. Throughout the 1950s, with the megaton load of nuclear bombs growing, nuclear fallout from tests had become a health hazard, and by the 1960s, it was enough to worry scientists. Kennedy, in particular, was pushing for a ban and was optimistic about succeeding.

LeMay was less sanguine because the U.S. had already been limiting its above ground tests while the Soviets had been increasing their own. Just eight months earlier, on October 31, 1961, the Soviets tested the fifty megaton "Tsar" Bomb, the largest nuclear device to date ever exploded in the atmosphere (the test took place in the Novaya Zemlya archipelago in the far reaches of the Arctic Ocean and was originally designed as a 100 megaton bomb, but even the Soviets cut the yield in half because of their own fears of fallout reaching its population). LeMay did not see any military advantage for the U.S. to sign such a treaty. He doubted the countries would come to an agreement and felt vindicated when the talks deadlocked by the end of the summer. The agreement was ultimately signed the following spring, though, and remains one of the crowning achievements of the Kennedy Administration.

Completely unnoticed that summer was the sailing of Soviet cargo ships bound for Cuba. Shipping between Cuba and the USSR was not unusual since Cuba had quickly become a Soviet client state. With the U.S. embargo restricting Cuba's trade, the Soviets were propping up the island with technical assistance, machinery, and grain, while Cuba reciprocated in a limited way with return shipments of sugar and produce. But these particular ships were part of a larger military endeavor that would bring the two powers to the most frightening standoff of the Cold War.

Sailing under false manifest, these cargo ships were secretly bringing Soviet-made, medium range ballistic missiles to be deployed in Cuba. Once operational, these highly accurate missiles would be capable of striking as far north as Washington, D.C. An army of over 40,000 technicians sailed as well. Because the Soviets did not want their plan to be detected by American surveillance planes, the human cargo was forced to stay beneath the deck during the heat of the day. They were allowed to come topside only at night, and for a short time. The ocean crossing, which lasted over a month, was horrendous for the Soviet advisers.

The entire idea was dreamed up by Soviet Premier Nikita Krushchev earlier in the year as a way of putting the Soviets on nuclear par with the United States. It began with a Soviet problem; the mighty intercontinental ballistic missiles (ICBM) that Krushchev constantly glorified did not work. The huge missiles were inaccurate and unstable. The fuel was so volatile that the rockets had to be stored unfueled, which, in the event of a nuclear attack, added a step in returning fire. The Soviets also lacked the huge punch that the U.S. had in SAC, as well as Polaris missiles in its submarines. Khrushchev thought that the Americans would eventually exploit the ICBM's weakness in a first strike. So he thought that if he could position his much more accurate medium range missiles right next door to the United States, he could quickly stalemate the Cold War. Ever the chess player, the Russian Premier had come up with what he thought was a bold move.

Concerns about just such an escalation had been coming from Republican Senator Kenneth Keating of New York, but they were dismissed by the Kennedy administration. Krushchev had given Kennedy his word that he would never place offensive missiles in Cuba, and Kennedy believed him. John McCone, the new CIA director who replaced Allan Dulles after the Bay of Pigs disaster, was also skeptical of Krushchev's promises. McCone was smart and cagey and a good choice to head the Intelligence Agency. He tried to think like Krushchev and, knowing what he knew about the Soviet weakness with its ICBM, he thought the placement of short-range missiles in Cuba was extremely likely. McCone pushed for more U-2 reconnaissance flights over Cuba, which Kennedy at first rejected. He feared the flights would be too confrontational. McCone did not give up until Kennedy relented.

Before leaving for a planned trip to Spain in September 1962, LeMay, who had been watching these developments, ordered that the fuel and ordnance dumps be filled in the southern sector of the U.S. He was always on the lookout for trouble, committed to making sure everything was ready, just in case.

The first unmistakable evidence of the Soviet missiles came from a U-2 reconnaissance flight over the island on October 14, 1962, that showed the first of twenty-four launching pads being constructed to accommodate forty-two R-12 medium range missiles that had the potential to deliver forty-five nuclear warheads almost anywhere in the eastern half of the United States.

But the Soviet operation in Cuba actually went far beyond the missiles. There was also a military force to protect the weapons with SA-2 surface-to-air missiles (which would prove to be deadly to U.S. fighters just a few years later in Vietnam), forty MIG-21 fighters, warehouses of equipment and food, and even three hospitals and a bakery.[2]

Kennedy suddenly saw that he had been deceived by Krushchev and convened a war cabinet called ExCom (Executive Committee of the National Security Council), which included the Secretaries of State and Defense (Rusk and McNamara), as well as his closest advisers. At the Pentagon, the Joint Chiefs began planning for an immediate air assault, followed by a full invasion. Kennedy wanted everything done secretly. He had been caught short, but he did not want the Russians to know that he knew their plan until he had decided his own response and could announce it to the world.

The head of the Joint Chiefs, General Maxwell Taylor, came to Bozo McKee and suggested he get LeMay back from Europe as soon as possible, but because the phone lines were not secure,

LeMay could not be told the reason. Without batting an eye, McKee told Taylor he knew just how to do it. He would call LeMay and tell him that the B-70 bomber was about to be killed in Congress. Taylor smiled. When LeMay got the message, he blew up on the phone and demanded to know just who was killing it. McKee said he would not go into it on the phone, and LeMay was back in the office the following morning, still fuming.

"Listen," McKee told LeMay as he came into the office, "nobody's mentioned the B-70 since you've been gone. We're about to get in a war."

"What?!" LeMay responded.

"It's Cuba," said McKee.[3]

At first, Kennedy favored an air strike against the SAM sites and the nuclear missiles. He was still smarting from the Bay of Pigs, and this caught him right in the middle of a mid-year congressional election. Kennedy knew the standing of the U.S. throughout the world would deteriorate rapidly if he did nothing. But the thought of a possible all-out nuclear war with the Soviets was unacceptable as well, even if the U.S. was to emerge as the ultimate victor. LeMay always believed that the U.S. and the USSR would eventually come to a shooting war. His experience with the Russians in the war, withholding weather information and crews, as well as his deep abhorrence of Communism and the forced takeover of countries in the postwar years reinforced his belief.

In light of this belief, his reasoning was simple: if the U.S. was going to fight the Soviet Union eventually, it should do it now while it had the strong advantage. In the meetings between the Joint Chiefs and the president, he pushed this line. Although it would take the Army time to gather the forces for an all-out invasion, he told Kennedy that the Air Force could start pounding the missiles at any time. Kennedy would eventually back away from this scenario, always worried that the situation, once loose, would get out of control. And there was always the real worry that if even one missile got through, it would create unimaginable devastation in the United States. But while LeMay did not believe that the Russians would retaliate, he did believe that a political solution would be construed as appeasement.

Kennedy shared his decision to pursue negotiation and a naval blockade of Cuba while keeping the option of an all-out invasion on the table with the Joint Chiefs on Friday, October 19. The heads of the military, General Earle Wheeler of the Army, Admiral George Anderson of the Navy, General David Shoup of the Marines, and LeMay of the Air Force, along with the head of the Joint Chiefs, Maxwell Taylor, saw the blockade as ineffective and in danger of making the U.S. look weak. As Taylor told the president, "If we don't respond here in Cuba, we think the credibility (of the U.S.) is sacrificed."[4]

Of all the Chiefs, Kennedy and his team saw LeMay as the most intractable. But that impression may have come from his demeanor, his candor, and perhaps his facial expressions, since he was not the most belligerent of the Chiefs. Shoup was crude and angry at times. Admiral Anderson was equally vociferous and would have the worst run-in with civilian leadership when he told McNamara directly that he did not need the Defense Secretary's advice on how to run a blockade. McNamara responded, "I don't give a damn what John Paul Jones would have done, I want to know what you are going to do—now!" On his way out, McNamara told a deputy, "That's the end of Anderson." And in fact,

Admiral Anderson became Ambassador Anderson to Portugal a short time later.[5]

There is no question that LeMay was forceful in all the meetings and was never afraid to disagree with the President, but he never exceeded his authority. He saw his role as twofold: to make sure the Air Force was ready to attack if needed, and to offer advice to the President when asked. Just as LeMay always pushed his subordinates to never be afraid of offering opposing ideas, he thought the last thing the president needed in these crucial moments was a Yes-Man.

LeMay demonstrated that belief the next time the Joint Chiefs met to discuss the Cuba situation with the president, raising the concern that the missiles would quickly be hidden in the woods once the communists learned that the Americans had discovered their scheme. Then, perhaps impolitically, he offered his own political judgment to the President, saying it would not just be seen as weakness around the globe, but right here at home among Americans as well.

"You're in a pretty bad fix, Mr. President." LeMay concluded.

"What did you say?" Kennedy responded.

"You're in a pretty bad fix," LeMay repeated himself.

"You're in there with me—personally," Kennedy half-heartedly joked back.[6]

After Kennedy left the room, the microphones of his secret recording equipment remained on as McNamara reviewed everything with the Generals. It was there that Shoup of the Marines opened up with a barrage of curses. Shoup told LeMay that in his forceful answers to the President, "You pulled the rug right out from under him. Goddamn."

"Jesus Christ. What the hell do you mean?" LeMay asked, clearly surprised that anything he said could have been interpreted that way.

Shoup explained that he completely agreed with LeMay's political point, but then went on in a crude and caustic expansion of his thoughts.

"If only somebody could keep them from doing the goddamn thing piecemeal," Shoup lamented. "That's our problem. You go in there and friggin around with the missiles . . . you're screwed."[7]

LeMay differed from Kennedy and McNamara on the basic concept of nuclear weapons. Back on Tinian, LeMay thought the use of the Hiroshima and Nagasaki bombs, although certainly larger than all other weapons used, were really not all that different from other bombs. He based this on the fact that many more people were killed in his first incendiary raid on Tokyo five months earlier than with either atomic bomb. "The assumption seems to be that it is much more wicked to kill people with a nuclear bomb, than to kill people by busting their heads with rocks," he wrote in his memoir.[8] But McNamara and Kennedy realized that there was a world of difference between two bombs in the hands of one nation in 1945 and the growing arsenals of several nations in 1962.

Upon entering office and taking responsibility for the nuclear decision during the most dangerous period of the Cold War, Kennedy came to loathe the destructive possibilities of this type of warfare. McNamara would sway both ways during the Cuban Missile Crisis, making sure that the military option was always there and available, but also trying to help the President find a negotiated way out. His proportional response strategy that would come into play in Vietnam in the Johnson Administration three years later was born in the reality of the dangers that came out of the Cuban crisis. "LeMay would have invaded Cuba and had it out ... but with nuclear weapons, you can't have a limited war," McNamara remembered. "It's completely unacceptable ... with even just a few nuclear weapons getting through ... it's crazy."[9]

As Kennedy told his Chief of Staff, Kenny O'Donnell, "These brass hats have one great advantage in their favor. If we listen to them, and do what they want us to do, none of us will be alive later to tell them that they were wrong."[10]

Over the next two weeks, the negotiations dragged on with great tension and difficulty. On one particular day, when a U-2 flight was shot down and its pilot killed by an over eager Soviet missile battery, an invasion began to look more likely.

There was one more problem. While Krushchev and Kennedy were negotiating a way to step back from the brink, there was a real lag in communications. In 1962, there was no direct phone line between the two countries (the "hotline" would be set up afterwards in response to this problem). Messages would be sent to the U.S. embassy in Moscow or the Soviet Embassy in Washington, translated, and sent by hand to the White House or Kremlin. As the two leaders tried to avoid a no-win confrontation, the most menacing character turned out to be the one with the most to lose: Fidel Castro. The Cuban dictator seemed to be just itching for a fight with the Yankees.

Finally, Nikita Krushchev, who created the crisis, brought it to an end by backing down and agreeing to remove the weapons. As a political officer in the Red Army during the worst of World War II, at the siege of Stalingrad, the Soviet leader understood what could happen if things got out of hand. As his son, Sergei

Krushchev, remembered his father saying, "Once you begin shooting, you can't stop."[11]

In an effort to help him save face, Kennedy made it clear to everyone around him that there would be no gloating over this victory. Castro, on the other hand was quite different in his response. When he learned that the missiles were being packed up, Castro let loose with a tirade of cursing at Krushchev's betrayal. "He went on cursing, beating even his own record for curses," recalled his journalist friend, Carlos Franqui.[12]

There was also a feeling of letdown among the Joint Chiefs. They thought the U.S. had capitulated and, in the end, looked weak. They also did not trust the Russians to stand by their promise to dismantle and take home all the missiles. The Soviets had a long track record of breaking most of their previous agreements. LeMay considered the final negotiated settlement the greatest appeasement since Munich. By breaking his word to Kennedy and placing missiles in the western hemisphere, Krushchev secured the ceremonial removal of the United States' antiquated medium range missiles from Turkey in exchange for retrieving the missiles in Cuba. It was a hollow gesture as they were scheduled to be removed already, but it allowed Krushchev to save face internationally. Castro continued to be a thorn in the side of the United States. But ultimately, he was mostly inconsequential. More than four decades later, Kennedy's blockade and negotiated settlement stand as the best-case scenario.

As a postscript to the Cuban Missile Crisis, LeMay's two-year term with the Joint Chiefs was over the following May of 1963 and the President could easily have ended his career by offering retirement after thirty-five years of service, a substantial length of time.

But once again, Kennedy and McNamara surprised Washington by reappointing LeMay to another term, though they limited it to a year. Admiral Anderson of the Navy was out after his blowup with McNamara during the crisis. But LeMay, who constantly fought the administration in policy and procurement, remained. There was much speculation as to why. Bozo McKee offered, perhaps, the simplest and probably the most correct explanation to biographer Thomas Coffey: "[Kennedy] had no basis on which to fire him. Both Kennedy and McNamara knew LeMay was a great soldier. And he had a lot of support on the Hill. They weren't about to run into that."[13]

Still, for all the thorniness, McNamara, being the original cost-benefit analyst, would not have put up with the grief LeMay caused him if there was not some gain. Throughout the Cuban Missile Crisis, LeMay offered a point of view that the President shied away from. But if things had gone terribly wrong—and this possibility was very real—both Kennedy and McNamara knew that the Air Force would deliver the deciding blow against the missiles, the bases, and Castro. And they wanted LeMay's experience and competence at the helm if it ever became necessary.

• • • •

KENNEDY, JOHNSON, AND THE
FINAL DAYS IN WASHINGTON

LeMay's battles with Defense Secretary McNamara did not let up in 1963. He used every persuasive power he knew to convince the President to build the new bomber. He worked the congressional side as well. He was unrelenting. But McNamara was becoming more than a Defense Secretary to the President. Except for the president's brother, Attorney General Robert Kennedy, McNamara became John F. Kennedy's most trusted cabinet official. If McNamara would not put the new bomber in the 1964 Defense Budget, it was unlikely the president would overrule him. That did not mean that LeMay would stop fighting for it. It just meant that the likelihood of the U.S. spending 9 to 10 billion dollars for the B-70 supersonic bomber was nil.

In spite of political battles, real life would intrude in the capital bringing out very different sides of these participants. In the summer of 1963, two deaths saddened the city. The Kennedys lost an infant son just two days after his birth from a lung ailment. In an exchange of personal notes, LeMay showed heartfelt sorrow for the first couple, which the President responded to with a personal note.

In the same week, the publisher of the *Washington Post* and a giant force in the capital, Philip Graham, committed suicide. Graham had served in the Army Air Forces during the War and had risen from private to major. He was rich, powerful, and successful. He had also been struggling with manic depression. In her grateful response to LeMay's note, Philip Graham's widow, Katharine, added the line: "As you know, he was a *great* admirer of yours." LeMay had few social skills. But he had honed one during the war, which probably he least wanted to excel at—writing condolence notes.

LeMay spent much of his time running the Air Force and inspecting bases. He made another trip to Vietnam that year and was still unhappy with what he saw. One of the consequences of the strategic success of the Cuban Missile Crisis was that it emboldened the civilian leaders, especially McNamara, in practicing the theory

of flexible-response or gradual warfare, something LeMay disliked
down to his very bones. The situation in Saigon was deteriorating
with the Diem regime's violent crackdown on Buddhist protestors.
Kennedy's position would ultimately be unknown. In an interview
with Walter Cronkite on the occasion of the expansion of the *CBS
Evening News* in September, 1963, Kennedy gave two conflicting
answers about the American presence in Vietnam. He was clear
that the U.S. would not allow Vietnam to fall to the Communists,
giving the indication that he would stick with his commitment.
But in the same interview, he also said that in the end it was South
Vietnam's war to win or lose; they would have to do the fighting.
This was one of the president's last comments on Vietnam, and historians would argue the question for years to come.

On November 22, 1963, while on a hunting trip in Michigan,
Curtis LeMay heard that President Kennedy had been assassinated
in Dallas. He immediately flew back to Washington. LeMay remembered a lot of people in Washington worrying that the entire series
of events might be some sort of attempted coup, a theory he never
took seriously. LeMay was just too practical and, knowing the military as he did, he believed the United States was the least suscep-
tible country in the world to a military takeover "because the
American military profession is itself steeped in the tradition of civil
supremacy over the military... [and] the armed forces of the United
States have repeatedly fostered and protected this principle."[14]

In his first meeting on November 29, their new Commander-
In-Chief, Lyndon Johnson, announced that he wanted the Joint
Chiefs to focus on budget austerity. Later in December, they
met with Johnson again at his ranch in Texas just before Christmas. While there, LeMay got into the ongoing argument with

McNamara over the bomber and its projected cost. By this time, even LeMay was getting the picture that his new bomber would never be produced.

One more time, in the spring of 1964, LeMay's tenure came up for renewal. He firmly believed that he would be let go and forced into retirement. That seemed a definite possibility when LBJ pulled him aside at a White House event in April and asked him who he thought should replace him. Johnson, ever the politician, threw out the idea of an ambassadorship. LeMay's answer showed his very forthright nature, as well as his common sense. He told the President "it didn't make much sense to stop doing something I knew something about to take on something I knew nothing about."[15]

Johnson, who had the capacity to cajole and bully anyone into almost anything, was not deterred by LeMay's response and came up with a few more suggestions that were as pointless as the first. Then the president got to the core of the matter when he asked LeMay if he had "made any other commitments." This struck LeMay as almost obscene, since he was not allowed to "make other commitments" while on active duty.

What Johnson was clearly fishing for was whether LeMay was going to help Barry Goldwater in the upcoming election. It demonstrates how differently these two men came to their decisions. LeMay played by the rules set up by the military. Johnson lived and breathed politics and deal-making. But Johnson knew that in addition to being friends, LeMay's politics were aligned with Goldwater's, who had served in the Army Air Force during the War. Just a few days after that meeting, LeMay was summoned back and to his surprise—and everyone else's, including McNamara—Johnson reappointed LeMay for another year.

Lyndon Johnson gained his office by accident, and he was not about to take any chances with his own election. The last thing he needed was LeMay campaigning with Goldwater as a private citizen and railing against his former boss. Any personal insecurity that Johnson felt would quickly evaporate after his historic landslide over Goldwater in November 1964. Johnson was sworn in on the steps of the Capitol in January 1965, no longer under the Kennedy shadow and very much his own man. LeMay's days were numbered.

The last year of LeMay's tenure in Washington would be severely limited. It was clear to everyone that he would not be reappointed again. He did his job, but the fights with McNamara went nowhere and even began to die down. Neither McNamara nor Maxwell Taylor consulted with him. He was ignored. LeMay watched in complete frustration as the huge buildup in Vietnam proceeded with the North Vietnamese able to ferry supplies to the South and wage the war on their terms. "We should stop swatting flies," he told an official at the State Department in his blunt style, "and go after the manure pile."[16]

LeMay made speeches and collected awards in those final months. He also spoke to the press in that last year. He still would not give up on the new bomber and complained about the way the war in Vietnam was conducted. He did it publicly because none of the people above him would listen to him. And then, finally, it was over.

•   •   •   •

RETIREMENT

LeMay held his final staff meeting on February 1, 1965. He praised his subordinates and advised them always to push the

Chief and never compromise. "Stick to your guns" if you know you are right. "It takes a long time here to get things done; however, water wears away stone. Right prevails in the end in our form of government."[17] He still believed that. There was an official ceremony in the East Room of the White House with the President and Vice President in attendance.

Everyone knew that LBJ had eased LeMay out, yet he was in attendance to publicly praise the General. In his remarks, LBJ made the odd analogy that in the same month of October 1929, the stock market crashed and Curtis LeMay got his wings. The stock market crash, according to the President, taught Americans that the price of success is constant vigilance and understanding. And Curtis LeMay, he said, devoted his career to teaching Americans that the price of peace is preparedness and vigilance as well.

After receiving his fourth Distinguished Service Medal from the Undersecretary of Defense, Cyrus Vance, LeMay spoke to the gathering. He was much shorter in his remarks, which were directed towards the President. "I wish I could say I was leaving and retiring with a world free of problems," he told the audience. "Unfortunately, that is not true." But LeMay assured President Johnson that he was leaving him with the strongest Air Force and best commanders to help when he would have to tackle these burdens.

Later that day, at Andrews Air Force Base, there was a display of all the planes LeMay had come in contact with, including the Consolidated P-1 biplane he flew as a cadet at Kelly Field in 1928. It was a cold, overcast day. After all the tumultuous events that had taken place in the past thirty-seven years, the ceremony may have seemed anticlimactic and even a bit staged, but LeMay seemed genuinely to appreciate and even enjoy it.

"Being in the military is not a very real life because a lot of things that everyone else has to deal with are taken care of for you," observed Janie LeMay Lodge, referring to the fact that life outside the military womb can be a rude awakening for someone who spent his entire adult life on the inside. "My father had never written a check to pay a bill."[18] Even though it had been clear for at least a year that he was leaving, LeMay had made few plans for retirement. Perhaps he could not believe that it would actually happen.

The usual course for men of high rank who leave the service is to decide between the many job offers that flow in. Some retired officers gravitate towards academic institutions and nonprofit organizations. Others take jobs with the industries that service the military who want these men precisely because of their expertise, their command experience, and their contacts. It is a time when these men can finally reap the financial rewards from the private sector that were unavailable to them in the service. LeMay's salary as Chief of Staff of the Air Force was only $25,680 a year. But LeMay was essentially the CEO of a business with over 2 million employees and a budget in the billions of dollars. And in his position, LeMay had to deal with life and death issues, and his decisions impacted not just everyone in the United States, but throughout the entire world.

Yet the offers did not flow in. In fact, they did not come in at all. Between his bluntness, his demeanor, and the negative press he received, the major aeronautic companies shied away from him. At the same time, LeMay did not feel it was appropriate that he turn around and work for a defense contractor. "He earned a lot of money for companies like Boeing," recalled Janie LeMay Lodge, "but he thought it was just wrong to work for them. He had a very strong sense of right and wrong."[19]

The LeMays rented a home temporarily in Washington until they could decide their next move. He had been working with novelist McKinley Kantor on a biography since 1953. Kantor had flown with the 305th during the War as a correspondent. Because of that connection, and the fact that he liked his writing, LeMay contacted him early on for help. LeMay understood what he could do and where he fell short, and he knew he could not write a book on his own. It came out later in 1965, titled *Mission with LeMay*, and was published by Doubleday. It is written very much in LeMay's terse voice, and it goes through his life honestly, paying special attention to the period between Pearl Harbor and the Japanese surrender on the U.S.S. *Missouri*. LeMay did not shy away from the truth about his father and the difficulties he encountered as a boy. He was unusually poignant in talking about the loss of the men under his command, and his devotion to his country and the military is clear throughout. He also took pot shots at McNamara whenever possible. But in 1965, the country was going through tectonic shifts in social mores, and the military was falling into disfavor. The book was only a moderate success. One suspects that if it had been published twenty years earlier, in 1945, the market would have been different.

Once it was over, his performance as Joint Chief was analyzed by the military as well. Several generals thought his lack of political acumen and his inability to compromise led to his first career failure. Thomas White, the Air Force chief before LeMay, thought it was LeMay's inability to see the world beyond black and white— a common way to view a battle plan, but not the way to deal with Washington's many hues of gray—that led to his downfall. "True, [he] lost many battles in the nearly four years he was chief of staff. But many of the losses would have come about in any case because of the McNamara upheaval in all the military services . . . Whatever one may think of him as a person, he deserves to be rated as one of America's 'greats.'"[20]

Others were less kind. "I did not admire him and he was one of the worst Chiefs we had," said one retired general who cited LeMay's prejudice in favor of SAC above all other parts of the Air Force. Others agreed that his heavy emphasis on bombers left the tactical side of the Air Force weaker.[21]

A job offer finally came in from a privately-owned electronics company on the west coast. The chief selling point was that it was located in the San Fernando Valley of Los Angeles. The LeMays bought a magnificent home in Bel Air—the first home he ever owned in his life—and his retirement seemed to be set. The job was described as that of an adviser to the owner, Mihal Patrichi. LeMay would not have to run the company on a day-to-day basis. However, from day one, it was a bad fit, "a complete disaster as far as I was concerned," remembered LeMay.[22]

"That just didn't work at all," Janie Lodge recalls of his time with Network Electronics.[23] Still, LeMay stuck it out for a little over two years, believing he had made a commitment. He did continue speaking out, whenever he had the opportunity, on his three basic themes: the necessity of a strong military to protect the U.S. from the Soviet threat; criticizing Secretary of Defense McNamara and the "Defense Intellectuals" who supported the flexible response strategy used in Vietnam; and against a general moral weakness that seemed to be growing in the 1960s.

In 1968, he pushed those thoughts further when he published a small book with Major General Dale O. Smith entitled *America Is in Danger*. Forty years later, the book serves as an interesting defense study, demonstrating LeMay's often radical thinking and trying—yet again—to explain why it was not in the interest of a country to admit it would never use nuclear weapons first. Years before serious questions were raised concerning intelligence flaws that led to September 11 and the 2003 war in Iraq, LeMay criticized the usefulness of the information brought forth by U.S. spy agencies. He also took one more shot at the growing movement of pacifists taking part in the national discourse. "Anyone who seeks an absolute end to the possibility of war might as well resign from the human race,"[24] he wrote, as blunt as ever.

In his frustration with the civilian influence in the Pentagon, he pointed out that they had added a jargon to the language that makes understanding the military almost impossible for the layman. "Gobbledygook has become the union card of the defense intellectuals," he wrote in his book.[25] LeMay also tried to expand the thinking of the military establishment. "It is a strange phenomenon of our land," LeMay wrote, "that professional judgment is respected and given corresponding weight in every area of human endeavor but that of the military."[26] He warned the Defense establishment not to be afraid to debate the unthinkable, "which permits the screwball idea to come forth and which tolerates the maverick officer."[27] He pointed out that Grant, Jackson, and Billy Mitchell were among them. He does not say so, but he himself is on that list as well. And these are the officers who go against the grain to come up with the winning strategies.

LeMay firmly believed that the Soviet Union was no different from Nazi Germany and highlighted that historically, the United States found itself unprepared for nearly every war it entered. As he also believed that, despite the existence of nuclear weapons, the

U.S. and the USSR would eventually fight World War III, not in a cold war, but in a very hot war, he was upset that the theorists who wanted to scale down weapons systems in order to check the arms race held sway in the Pentagon. Though the Cold War between 1945 and 1990 did not end up escalating to Armageddon, it is precisely the arms race, ratcheted up by Ronald Reagan, that finally brought down the Soviet empire.

It should come as no surprise that the eight-year-old boy who woke up earlier than his father to feed his family, and the officer who worked harder than anyone on his staff during the war to figure out how to save one more crew and hit one more target, had trouble sitting back and playing golf under the California sun. The same man who felt responsibility weighing on him as a child would now find one last endeavor in his long and distinguished career. In making this final choice, he would, like many military men before him, fall on his sword, but in a cruel twist, destroy his own legacy. This last act would erase almost every positive action that had come before.

CHAPTER FOURTEEN

WALLACE

FOR SOMEONE WHO HAD BEEN BORN IN POVERTY IN THE EARLY part of the twentieth century, who struggled to succeed at everything he ever accomplished, and who watched thousands of young men die around him to save their country, the year 1968 must have been perplexing. Indeed, Curtis LeMay was hardly alone in his bewilderment. As the tempo of the sixties began to outpace any sense of normalcy, Americans found no solace in the institutions that had brought them security in the past. Many families were ripped apart by the sequence of events. Generations argued. Races fought each other. The domestic peace that Americans had taken for granted was no longer a guarantee. And in the middle of all this, Americans had to elect a new president.

There were many causes of this upheaval: the revolt of the huge baby-boom generation, the anti-war movement, a new drug culture, and the sexual revolution. But the two main conflicts centered around race and the war in Vietnam. By the 1960s the United States finally began to pay its long overdue bill to its black citizens. The process of giving black citizens the same rights as whites started ever so slowly when the first troops returned home in 1945, eighty-two years after Lincoln signed the Emancipation Proclamation.

Although the Armed Forces were still segregated during the war, mixing was inevitable. Men of different color began to acknowledge each other, many for the first time. Friendships were forged on ships and on military bases. Prior to that, most neighborhoods were so completely segregated that the chances of a white man coming to know a black man as a friend, especially in the North, were slim. This sociological transformation during the war went beyond race. It included all groups—from Baptists from Mississippi who had never met Jews from New York to Irish Catholics from Chicago and Mormons from Utah—these men shared something unique: the bond of camaraderie created in war. Stereotypes and ignorance, the cornerstones of bigotry, slowly began to break down. But when these servicemen returned home, they came back to the same world they left, one which included their old segregated neighborhoods.

It was at this point that the unequal treatment of blacks in America could no longer be ignored. In 1948, President Truman ordered the integration of the military. It occurred with surprising order. Just one year earlier, the handsome, modest, and enormously talented Jackie Robinson took the field for the Brooklyn Dodgers, and this titanic change of opportunity in professional sports provided black heroes to white boys and girls. In each case, the pathfinders—whether in a barracks or at second base in

Brooklyn—encountered difficult times, but eventually, the transition took hold. In 1954, the Supreme Court ordered the desegregation of America's public schools, which did not really come to pass for many years. Through it all, there was a reaction of equal and opposite proportions against this slow undoing of the old ways, not just in the South, but in the North as well. The resistance to the civil rights movement of the 1950s and 1960s had ugly and, at times, deadly consequences.

There was a brief moment in the beginning of 1964, shortly after the assassination of John F. Kennedy, when polls showed that a majority of America's white working class expressed sympathy with the idea that poor blacks should be given a chance to work their way out of poverty.[1] In the afterglow of his huge landslide victory that year, Lyndon Johnson unveiled his plan for a Great Society with a plan that began with a War on Poverty for all poor Americans. Yet within just four years of that electoral triumph, it all lay in shambles. The Vietnam War, urban riots, the angry voices of black revolutionaries, and escalating welfare costs alienated much of the white middle class.

In the face of what whites saw as progress in the passing of the Voting Rights Act, the integration of public schools, and federal poverty programs, the devastating riots in Watts, California in 1965 and Detroit, Michigan in 1967, and accompanying social unrest confused and angered them. Whole neighborhoods with homes and businesses had been burned to the ground. Among middle class whites—those young men who defended their country just twenty years earlier, and who had suffered through terrible poverty themselves during the depression—the divide between blacks and whites grew larger. Seismic shifts in the strata of society leave people feeling unsettled. And if a country is unlucky, there will be someone waiting in the wings to exploit this anger and fear.

•   •   •   •

THE SCHOOL HOUSE DOOR

George Corley Wallace, Jr. was born in Clio, Alabama in 1919. His family was at the bottom of the state's social ladder. But, like LeMay, he had ambition and drive instilled in him by his mother. He worked his way through college and law school. He was a sergeant in the Army Air Forces, serving under General LeMay in the Pacific, and flew combat missions on B-29s over Japan until he fell ill with spinal meningitis. Wallace returned home with a medical discharge and a disability pension. Politics in the Southern tradition came naturally to Wallace. Even when he was in the Marianas, he began sending Christmas cards to voters—people he had never met. A series of elected offices finally brought him to the Governor's mansion in Montgomery in 1962. Yet even with this great honor, there was no reason that Wallace should ever have been a national figure. Few Americans could name the governor of any other state except their own.

But on June 11, 1963, Governor Wallace stood in the doorway of the University of Alabama in a symbolic attempt to deny entrance to the first three black students attempting to register for classes. Wallace failed. The federal government in the form of an assistant attorney general, Nicholas Katzenbach, ordered him to stand aside, and he had no choice but to move. The black students entered and the process of desegregation began at the university. That should have been the end of it all. But television cameras captured the event, flashing the image across the country. Within hours Wallace became not just a symbol for the South's intransigence, but a national figure.

Wallace was ambitious, he was tireless, and his political instincts were sharp. When he traveled through the North just one year after his standoff with the Kennedy Administration, he sensed an approval of his actions from other Americans far from his native state. When he took the advice of some supporters and entered a few presidential primaries in 1964, he experienced a surprising popularity with voters as far North as Wisconsin. Some of this can be attributed directly to racism—there was strong support for segregation all over the country. There was also a group of voters—smaller than the first—who were attracted to the populism he professed, and there were others who were completely dissatisfied with their government because of high taxes and a sense of having nothing in common with those whom they perceived to be the elites in the big cities who controlled their lives. Government leaders seemed too weak-kneed to solve the social upheaval in the country, and Wallace certainly did not appear to be weak-kneed.

Over the next four years, the push and pull of the civil rights movement was a constant sight on Americans' television screens. That and Vietnam dominated headlines until the chaotic year of 1968. Within hours of the assassination of Martin Luther King, Jr. in Memphis, on April 4, 1968, huge riots exploded in dozens of cities across the country. While the assassination shocked most Americans, this reaction to it frightened them as well. Photographs of machine gun positions manned by U.S. soldiers on the steps of the Capitol Building in Washington flashed across the country. In 1968, Americans were accustomed to seeing these images coming from Vietnam, but not their own capital.

Wallace instinctively understood that he could tap into the growing fear among white voters. He had money and an organization to help him run. Some of the money came from questionable contracts that the state of Alabama gave out for its work programs while he was governor. But money also started to roll in from individuals far from Alabama who sent five and ten dollar bills that began to add up to a large sum. Wallace even had a political party—the American Independent Party—and he declared his candidacy for President in the turbulent year of 1968.

George Wallace sidestepped a head-on campaign about race and used the slogan "Law and Order," even though everyone knew what he meant. After the assassination of Robert Kennedy in June and the riots surrounding the Democratic convention in Chicago in August, Wallace found himself not far behind the Democratic nominee and sitting Vice President, Hubert Humphrey. Polls began to show a possibility that none of the candidates might receive an electoral majority, which would then throw the decision to the House of Representatives.

As the election came down to the final stretch in the first days of autumn, Wallace's crowds were growing and his poll numbers were rising. Money poured into his headquarters. Douglas Kiker, a correspondent for NBC News who traveled with the campaign and was from Georgia himself, observed:

> It is as if somewhere, sometime a while back, George Wallace had been awakened by a white, blinding vision: they all hate black people, all of them. They're all afraid, all of them. Great God! That's it! They're all Southern! The whole United States is Southern! Anybody who travels with Wallace these days on his

presidential campaign finds it hard to resist arriving at the same conclusion.[2]

By the beginning of October, just one month before Americans would cast their votes, it looked as if a third party candidate could actually be a real contender. Most polls put him at 21 percent of the vote, but many of the reporters following the election were unsure. They thought the number could actually be higher. The Nixon campaign ceded Wallace between 90 and 100 Electoral votes. Three British journalists who put together one of the best election histories of that year, Lewis Chester, Godfrey Hodgson, and Bruce Page, wrote that at the end of September as "he left Chicago and flew to Grand Rapids, Michigan, Wallace looked as dangerous as Lee on his march to Gettysburg."[3]

In order for Wallace to get on the ballot in some states, he needed a running mate. Wallace did not particularly want a running mate. He enjoyed being the sole practitioner of his divisive political message. He alone had the capacity to raise crowds into a frenzy, and he clearly relished taunting the inevitable hecklers who followed him from city to city. (More than once, bullies in the crowd who came to support Wallace physically attacked these protestors.) Wallace liked working alone.

The small group of directors who ran his campaign, almost all of them from Alabama, came up with several different names. Wallace wanted Governor John Connolly of Texas, who declined. One suggested J. Edgar Hoover, the director of the FBI. In September, the campaign seemed to strike a deal with A. B. "Happy" Chandler, the former governor of Kentucky and former baseball commissioner, but a last-minute problem arose. Chandler had been a racial moderate, and when asked to refute his record, he politely told Wallace and the campaign he would not. Wallace was stuck. A wealthy contributor in Indiana first put out the name Curtis LeMay. Wallace liked it. LeMay had national standing from his long Air Force career, he had tremendous experience, and he was certainly politically conservative. He understood there were a large number of voters who served in the military and would be attracted by LeMay. But when the campaign first approached LeMay, he said, flatly, no thanks.

"He was the worst person possible to go into politics," explained his daughter, Janie.[4] LeMay had a very long list of areas where he excelled masterfully. But he knew he was not a politician. He did not like making speeches. He did not want to be subjected to reporter's questions. In fact, he did not like reporters, period, at least not the new breed of journalists who, unlike the reporters he had encountered during the war, were more interested in controversy. There was also another reason for his refusal. He did not particularly like Wallace or his racist politics.

LeMay was not a racist. There is absolutely nothing among his extensive papers, or any anecdotes over his very long career with slurs about any group or religion. Even in his criticism of liberals, he never pointed to any minority group. Many of the top World War II generals, including General Patton and General Stilwell, could not completely pass this test. Furthermore, LeMay had supported the Secretary of the Air Force, Stuart Symington, in initiating integration after World War II. Leaders in the Air Force determined that segregating units by race was wasteful and reduced productivity while excluding a huge talent pool.

LeMay firmly believed in rewarding excellence and stamping out incompetence. It was his method of motivation and as well as a way to remove dead wood. A person's looks, religion, or politics were inconsequential. When the desegregation order came down, LeMay did not question it. Instead, in his usual fashion, he figured out how to make it work best. LeMay understood that there would be resistance at first from many white officers and enlisted men, especially those from the South. In order to mitigate this, he ordered his assistants to find the most qualified black airmen. Just as Dodger owner Branch Rickey waited until he found Jackie Robinson, an exceptionally strong human being who could withstand the inevitable insults that would come his way, LeMay would use these black airmen as the trailblazers. He knew the white officers and men would eventually come on board.

On the face of it, LeMay had no incentive to team up with Wallace, or support him in any way. However, when the Wallace people came back to LeMay for a second try, the head of the campaign, Seymore Trammel, wisely hit on the one consequential factor that worried LeMay: the possibility of Humphrey winning and continuing the Kennedy-Johnson-McNamara policies in Vietnam and the Cold War. This appealed to LeMay's ongoing belief in defending his country. He believed that the "Defense Intellectuals" were going to cut the U.S. deterrent until the Soviets would be able to win a general war. He also thought the policy in Vietnam would lead to more deaths and a possible defeat. Here was one last chance to rise up and do battle.

LeMay was intrigued by the idea. He was politically conservative and had real worries about the direction that Johnson had taken the country. He feared that Humphrey would follow in Johnson's footsteps. And he figured that by running with Wallace, he would draw votes from Humphrey in the South and help elect Richard Nixon while securing a platform from which to talk about his own ideas. While he was still disgusted with Wallace's brand of racial politics, he became willing to overlook them, failing to understand in a stunning display of political naïveté that by running with Wallace, he would be condoning those politics.

LeMay shocked everyone around him when he finally said yes—and agreed to join a campaign that played off America's worst impulses. His friends from the military tried to dissuade him. There were strong letters that came from every corner. Old timers like Spaatz, Eaker, and others told him to steer clear of Wallace. And his family was not interested either.

LeMay would later say that he believed of the three candidates running, Richard Nixon offered the greatest opportunity to lead the country out of Vietnam and deal wisely with the Soviets. And though he thought he might draw votes from Humphrey in the South, there is little evidence that he was able to do this, although it was clear from the very start that his entry to the race least benefited the man he was supposed to help—George Wallace.

He was tentative about his decision, though, which was not like him. When he and his family flew to Pittsburgh on October 3, 1968, to join Wallace for the announcement and press conference, the campaign was still so unsure that LeMay would actually go through with it that they had a replacement standing by—the former governor of Louisiana and the composer of the song "You Are My Sunshine," Jimmie H. Davis.

In LeMay's acceptance speech at the press conference, he provided insight into another reason he may have had for running. He told reporters that he and Helen were more than happy with their retirement. They finally had a home of their own. He did not miss the eighteen-hour days and the constant strain of command, which left him always waiting for the phone to ring. But he also said it finally occurred to him "that nobody cared where I was going any more. Nobody wanted to know."[5] Retirement, it seemed, was difficult for someone used to being in charge and at the center of things for so long.

What followed next was one of the more extraordinary moments in a political year filled with them. It was breathtaking in its brevity and in its impact. British political observers Hodgson, Chester, and Page, who were present, described it this way:

> It was over in seven minutes flat. One reporter was so stunned that he forgot to switch on his tape recorder. A CBS reporter, broadcasting live, had to take a grip on himself not to shake his head with sheer astonishment as he listened. A veteran British reporter who had slipped out for some refreshment at the bar came back in as LeMay finished. "Did I miss anything, old boy?" he asked. He sure did.[6]

Everything George Wallace had feared, and every reason Wallace wanted to run alone played out in front of him. Everything he had worked for and felt within his grasp suddenly dissolved, like a handful of sand in an ocean wave.

Instead of explaining why he felt compelled to run, or why George Wallace was a good alternative to Richard Nixon or Hubert Humphrey, LeMay, inexplicably, chose to use this national platform, his first in years, to explain his philosophy of war and why every weapons system—including nuclear weapons—should be used to win wars rather than have prolonged and gradual conflicts like the one taking place in Vietnam. A person with any political acumen would have chosen fifty topics to cover before talking about the use of nuclear weapons. And nobody in the crowd was more flummoxed by what came out of LeMay's mouth than George Corley Wallace, who tried to step in and salvage what might be left of his campaign.

"General LeMay hasn't advocated the use of nuclear weapons, not at all," Wallace tried to interject. But LeMay came right back and replied: "I gave you a discussion on the phobia that we have in this country about the use of nuclear weapons."

Wallace jumped in again, and again LeMay answered.

The Wallace campaign had shown clear signs up until that moment that it was being run by amateurs. This press conference, which should have been a rote introduction of a running mate instead turned into what could best be described as a segment from a political version of the Keystone Cops. Everyone knew LeMay was no politician, but this press conference went beyond what they might have considered to be a worst case scenario. If LeMay wanted to destroy the chances of Hubert Humphrey taking the White House, he may have succeeded in doing exactly that to Wallace.

It can be seen in the polls of that year that Wallace crested to his strongest numbers ten minutes before that press conference began in Pittsburgh. From that moment on, he would only go downhill. The great political writer of the twentieth century, Theodore White, watched the change in mood towards Wallace. "Down he went, gurgling, first in the Harris poll, then in the Gallup poll, followed by every other index.... And the peril with which he had threatened the two-party system appeared, for the year 1968 at least, to have been smothered by the much-maligned electoral system ordained by the United States Constitution."[7]

It is White's observation that LeMay was the poorest choice for Wallace because he ran counter to an important psychological element of the Wallace campaign that few picked up on. The people who backed Wallace, White believed, were the enlisted men of the great crusade twenty years earlier, and if they had come to hate anyone in that war, it was not so much the Germans or even the Japanese, but the generals who made their lives miserable while they were in the service. "Meeting Curtis LeMay, as I had in Asia, one could not but instantly respect him then, and later, in retrospect, recognize how great a debt the Republic-in-arms owed him. But one could not love him; and the men of his command loathed the harsh, unsparing, iron discipline by which he made the United States Air Force the supreme instrument of annihilation it became in the skies of Japan."[8]

LeMay cannot be given full credit for Wallace's downfall. In that final month of October, Hubert Humphrey finally broke away from Lyndon Johnson's reputation and began moving up in the polls. He went after Nixon as the disastrous Chicago convention (which turned into riots that made Humphrey look powerless) began to recede in the collective memory. Humphrey finally stood alone, his own man. And he began to put real amplification behind his rhetoric. "Let's lay it on the line," Humphrey told factory workers in Detroit, "George Wallace's pitch is racism. If you want to feel damn mean and ornery, find some other way to do it, but don't sacrifice your country."[9] Humphrey also began to receive strong Labor Union support that particularly opposed Wallace and his base of white factory workers. They were reminded, over and over, that workers in Alabama with the same jobs earned $2,000 less per year than they did in places like Akron and Detroit and Los Angeles.

The reaction to LeMay's decision to run with Wallace was clear
and strong. His boss at Network Electronics Corporation, Mihal
Patrichi, called him a no-good bum (LeMay would never return to
the job). A former colleague at the Pentagon, said, "He's not helping us a damn bit." His friend and former Republican nominee,
Senator Barry Goldwater admitted: "I hope he hasn't made a mistake, but I think he has." And his own 91-year-old mother-in-law
back in Ohio, Maude Maitland, said, "I idolize Curt, but I'm very,
very disappointed."[10]

Within the Air Force, the feeling was almost unanimously negative. LeMay was still respected by the vast majority of the men
who had served under him at the Pentagon; they feared the
destruction of his reputation and subsequent harm to the military
itself. Many of the generals in command had called Symington,
LeMay's former boss, hoping he might have some influence in persuading LeMay not to run. Symington, who understood the Air
Force and politics in Washington simply smiled and told the generals not to worry. "Wallace will be spending all of his time,"
Symington wisely told them, "saying 'What General LeMay *meant*
to say was. . . .'"[11]

Telegrams poured in. Many supported him and thanked him for
running (the majority of which were from the South). Some of the
men who served under him were less kind. A former sergeant
under his command from Valparaiso, Florida suggested that he
"consult a psychiatrist before committing to Wallace."[12]

Perhaps the most stinging commentary came from the political
cartoonist of the *Los Angeles Times*, Paul Conrad. On the front page
of the October 6, 1968, edition, millions of readers saw the image
of Wallace and LeMay in uniform standing together at a podium,

smoking cigars, and up above the clouds, a smiling Adolf Hitler and Hermann Goering with the caption reading: "It brings to mind der good old days . . . yah, Herr Goering?" The irony came full circle as LeMay, a legitimate American hero, was compared to the most evil, maniacal villain of our time—someone he risked his own life to defeat.

Mercifully, LeMay had come into the Wallace campaign late. There was only one month for him to do what he disliked in the first place. The Wallace people were grateful for this as well. Once, when a reporter asked him about legalized abortion and the use of birth control, two essential platforms for Wallace's support from the conservative right, LeMay did not back away for a second. "I favor them both," he candidly responded. His political handlers visibly winced.[13]

But within that month of campaigning, there were moments— and they were few—when a very different side of LeMay came through. They came when he separated himself from prepared speeches by the Wallace campaign, and when he spoke from his heart. He may have realized that he had made a serious mistake in running at all, and at that point he had nothing else to lose. In an attempt to explain his feelings about war, he told the Women's Press Club in Washington, D.C.:

> In my mind's eye I can still see planes flying next to me blow up in the air and then go down in a ball of flame. I can recall walking the floor of the operations office watching the clock until we knew that their gas had run out and there were no more chances of their coming home. I remember meeting the returning missions and seeing the red flare come out of the plane

indicating wounded on board and pulling them out—those that were still alive—and getting them to the hospital. I remember in the Chengdu Valley in China the pile of bodies wrapped in blankets and stacked against the operations shack waiting for burial. These are the things I remember about the war and I don't like any part of it.[14]

And there was an extraordinary speech delivered just before the election to, of all places, Yale University, where he confronted the image that he himself helped create.

I have been labeled a warmonger by those who oppose the Wallace-LeMay candidacy... [the other candidates] have tried to create the image of LeMay, the big bomber general, with a thunderbolt in one hand, a nuclear warhead in the other and a kind of wild gleam in his eye anxious to plunge this country into a nuclear war if given half a chance.

LeMay then launched into a call to arms on behalf of the environment that was as radical as anything Al Gore or Ralph Nader could possibly say forty years later. He went after deforestation and the use of insecticides... every mile of highway that ruins fifty acres of farmland... air pollutants "belched from exhaust of 90 million automobiles, trucks, tractors, and airplanes"... he even talked about the need for population control. And finally, LeMay said that the U.S. must take the lead "toward the end of the savage orgy of ecological rape of mother nature that has been raging since the renaissance in the so-called civilized countries." He called on the country to get the best minds behind the effort, create an agency as great as NASA, and make "a last ditch stand not for the political but for human survival."[15] If Yale students had come to the speech with the idea of protesting, they were stopped in their tracks by its content.

The entire riotous campaign came to an end on Tuesday, November 5, when 71 million Americans cast their votes. Richard Nixon barely squeaked past Hubert Humphrey, winning with 43.4 percent of the popular vote against Humphrey's 42.7 percent...a difference of only 500,000 votes out of 71 million cast. Wallace/LeMay garnered just under 13 percent or 9.9 million votes. Nixon was farther ahead in the electoral count, winning thirty-two states against Humphrey's thirteen states plus the District of Columbia. The Wallace-LeMay ticket carried five states, all in the South: Georgia, Mississippi, Louisiana, Arkansas, and, of course, Alabama, for a total of 46 Electoral votes against Humphrey-Muskie's 191 and Nixon-Agnew's 301.

There were repercussions of LeMay's decision to run with Wallace besides his destroyed reputation. In the immediate days after Nixon's inauguration on January 20, 1969, the IRS called his son-in-law, Dr. James Lodge, in Lincoln, Nebraska, and ordered him to come in the next day. He was told that his entire pediatric practice was being audited. IRS agents also came to LeMay's home and asked to see his financial records. He let them into the house, but when they passed a display case that held many of his medals and one of agents asked LeMay where he had purchased them, he kicked them out.[16] Mr. Nixon was sending a message to the retired general, just in case he wanted to get back into third party politics.

The association with Wallace would stay with Curtis LeMay for the rest of his life. For a new generation of Americans who knew little about his brilliance and courage in World War II or the great effort in the creation of the Strategic Air Command, it would be the run with Wallace that would most often come up when LeMay's name was mentioned. If it was not Wallace, it was the Kantor-authored quote about bombing Vietnam "back to the stone age" from LeMay's 1965 autobiography.

He did little to dispel this negative image. He told friends and family that he did not care what people said about him. He would not talk to reporters, and after a while, they stopped calling. If LeMay felt badly about the phone not ringing immediately after his retirement, the 1968 campaign knocked that out of him.

Ralph Nutter lived nearby in Santa Barbara, and the two men who flew together so long ago stayed in touch. Once, after the election, Nutter asked, "General, why the hell did you ever run with Wallace . . . you know it hurt you."

"Yeah," responded LeMay, "I know that, but Johnson lied to me so God-damn many times I figured Humphrey would do the same thing. I just didn't want to see him in office."[17]

Helen and Curtis LeMay spent their last years in California. The home in Bel Air with its four acres of land became too much to take care of, and they moved to a smaller house in Newport Beach, Orange County. Because Helen had an ongoing problem of congestive heart failure, their travel was restricted. Other than his monthly trips to Washington for the meeting of the board of the National Geographic, the couple stayed mostly at home, fifteen minutes from Janie and Jim Lodge and their grandson Charles.

"That was a great time for them," remembers Janie. "Mother belonged to the garden club and they had a lot of friends and a busy social life." Of course that was Helen's doing. Curtis still preferred to putter around the house or work on the various cars in the garage. He also read almost every book in the Newport Beach Library.

In retirement, LeMay enjoyed being on the board of the National Geographic, which he had admired since they provided detailed maps of South America that the military did not possess for his historic flight in 1938. "He would take a nonstop flight from LAX to Dulles [for board meetings]," Janie says. "He would be met by a staff car, taken to the Pentagon for a briefing" (offered to all former Chiefs). He would spend the night in a hotel, have breakfast and then go straight to the meeting at National Geographic. He rarely stayed for the whole meeting, opting instead to get back to Dulles to catch the early flight back to Los Angeles.

"I think he did the whole trip in less than twenty-four hours." Janie says. "I kept telling him he should stay an extra day and have dinner with friends. But he hated Washington so much that he wanted to get back home as soon as possible."[18]

He developed a group of friends he went hunting with, and target shooting. They would meet every day at a sort of club house. There was a retired pilot for United Airlines, the owner of High Time Liquor and Tobacco Depot, and another retiree who owned a small machine shop. "The four of them were inseparable," Janie Lodge recalls. "They fixed appliances, loaded shotgun shells and played cards. The washroom was filthy."

He spent a great deal of time with his grandson, Charles Lodge, taking him on fishing and hunting trips. Charles Lodge remembers his grandfather's very calm and supportive method of teaching. "Whether he was showing me how to shoot guns at the shooting range each weekend or showing me how to change the oil in his car or helping me with math homework, his approach was to show me one example and then let me try the processes and experience the mistakes or successes as they came," recalled Charles. "He also knew when to push me a little harder so both of us could see what I could do."[19]

He stopped flying shortly after he retired. His hearing was getting worse and he was meticulous about following all the rules concerning his pilot's license. Flying had been one of his great joys, but he accepted this new reality without question.

He gave oral histories for the Air Force. He spoke with Air Force historians on everything from the effects of bombing in World War II to his time with the Joint Chiefs. He still saw it as his obligation to teach a new generation of fliers, to help them learn from the past, and perhaps more importantly, to accomplish a task within a large, unwieldy bureaucracy. If a young pilot or commander in the future could perform better or avoid a problem LeMay had already encountered, then it was worth the effort. He would never be called avuncular and he always kept his edge, but historians were surprised when they met him. They had been intimidated by the many stories that preceded him, but they found him helpful and forthcoming.

One of these talks was given to the Air Force Planning Committee, a group of about 250 people who looked into future needs of the Air Force. It was run in the early 1980s by General Perry Smith. "[LeMay] didn't look that great by then... he had hearing aids in both ears," recalled Smith. "He told some interesting stories about his war experiences" always trying to emphasize the severe problems of going to war with inexperienced crews. "He told one story about sending his group on a mission only to see them return after about forty-five minutes. He asked why they came back and they said the lead navigator got lost and none of the other navigators could find their way to Germany. He didn't want that kind of thing to happen again."[20]

He stayed out of politics completely. "I can't ever remember discussing politics with him when we got together," Janie recalled. "I know he had opinions. But he just didn't talk about it . . . or didn't want to talk about it."

Once, his grandson befriended another boy in his class who was Japanese. He was living in the States because his father had been sent there by his company. When Thanksgiving arrived, Janie invited the family to join them for their dinner. She explained it would be a very small group, just the Lodges, her parents, and her son's godfather. Her father was perfectly comfortable with the family at the holiday table.

LeMay lived long enough to witness something he never thought imaginable. After his efforts with the Berlin Airlift, he watched the Berlin Wall come down on November 9, 1989, and the reunification of the two Germanys. After his years of planning and defending his country against the very real possibility of a nuclear attack from Russia, he was able to see the beginning of the collapse of the Soviet Union, but not its final demise. His prediction that the two superpowers would ultimately fight a war was, thankfully, quite wrong.

On the night of October 1, 1990, Helen fell asleep in front of the television set in the living room as she sometimes did. She heard her husband get up to go to the bathroom around midnight. On his way back, he collapsed from a massive heart attack and died instantly. After the dangerous missions over Europe and Japan, and the thousands of flying hours, Curtis LeMay died at home in his bedroom just one month shy of his eighty-fourth birthday.

The media reaction to LeMay's death was, not surprisingly, complicated, and in some ways it fit the pattern of how the man was perceived throughout his life. The *New York Times* talked about his willingness to use nuclear weapons in the very first sentence of its obituary, and it mentioned the "back to the Stone Age" comment regarding Vietnam. It also went into great detail on his exploits in World War II and the Cold War. That evening on ABC News, anchor Peter Jennings noted only the Stone Age comment and LeMay's run with Wallace. There were enough phone calls of complaint after the show that the ABC anchorman was forced to add an unusual addendum the following night to mention LeMay's distinguished record in World War II, the Berlin Airlift, and SAC, but as if to make his point one more time, Jennings repeated the Stone Age comment and the run with Wallace.

A private funeral was held at March Field for family and civilian friends, which added a wonderful symmetry since it was there that he first arrived for cadet school sixty-two years earlier. Then the family (minus Helen who stayed behind because of her heart condition—she would die less than two years later) and casket were flown on a huge KC135 Air Force transport for LeMay's final flight to the Air Force Academy in Colorado Springs.

A formal military service with honors was accorded him at the Academy. All the cadets attended in the magnificent chapel with its seventeen soaring and very modern spires. General John Chain, Jr., the Commander-in-Chief of SAC, offered an accurate and stirring eulogy that emphasized LeMay's courage, his determination, and his vision. Chain began with a quote from Supreme Court Justice Louis Brandeis: "Those who won our independence believed liberty to be the secret of happiness—and courage to be the secret of liberty."

There was one part of the service that LeMay would not have enjoyed. The service included not one, but three very long religious homilies. "I swear," recalled Janie thinking about the three sermons, "if my father could have gotten up out of that casket, he would have walked right out."[21]

After the service the hearse had gone around the side of the chapel to wait as the guests and cadets exited. When it was time to move on to the cemetery, Janie and some of the other family members were surprised to see a huge buck, which had strolled onto the Academy grounds from the nearby woods, standing right next to the hearse, almost in homage to the departed hunter. As they approached it, the buck jumped over the hearse and bounded off.

As taps were played by the military honor guard at the grave, just after a 21-gun salute to the fallen warrior, a sound could be heard, growing in intensity. Within seconds, a huge B-52 bomber flew on a direct path over the grave, followed by a squadron of jet fighters. It was slightly more than three-quarters of a century after the Wright brothers' plane flew over LeMay in his backyard in Columbus, sparking the young boy's imagination. The modern plane, with its jet engines roaring, saluted the man who had seen its promise.

Ralph Nutter remembers that after LeMay named him chief navigator in England, he found out about his law background. LeMay told him that he did not like people who talked a lot, and lawyers talk too much. But then he added that he judged people by their actions, not by their words. "The irony," recalled Nutter after

LeMay's death, "is that he's been judged all these years by what he said and not by what he did."[22]

Curtis LeMay understood that if he was going to do his job well, he would have to give up any chance at being liked. Not just by the enemy combatants and civilians whom he destroyed by the thousands, but by his own men, whom he pushed without letup. It was the only way to make them victorious and help save their lives.

He may have gone further than necessary in establishing his relentless persona. It seemed to come naturally to him. But if he had given it any thought, the loss of personal popularity was without a doubt more than worthwhile if it meant his enemies would be vanquished, his country would survive, and as many of those young men serving under him as was humanly possible would come home and lead normal lives again.

For LeMay, the ultimate realist, it was a bargain he readily accepted.

ACKNOWLEDGMENTS

FOUR YEARS AGO, MY WIFE AND I WERE SITTING IN A PLAY AT Lincoln Center that had absolutely nothing at all to do with World War II or bombers or the man who is the focus of this book. In fact, it was a romantic musical set in Italy. I've long ago given up trying to figure out the patterns of our thoughts and this is a perfect example of why I stopped. My mind wandered during the play and I kept coming back to, of all things, a quote from a college lecture years ago. "You might not agree with his politics," the professor told our class, "but if you have a son serving in combat, you want him serving under someone like LeMay." It was the first positive thing I ever heard about Curtis LeMay, and I thought if you could entrust your child's life to this man there had to be more to him than the one-dimensional caricatures I had seen in *Dr. Strangelove* and political journals and cartoons.

I began this journey the next day by calling my friend, Chuck Nash, a retired Naval Captain and aviator, who put me in touch with his wonderful network of military contacts. One call led to another. Along the way, I luckily stumbled on Herman Wolk, the former chief historian for the U.S. Air Force. Herm guided and encouraged this effort, answering constant and probably stupid questions from a writer who never served in the Air Force and never flew a plane.

Janie LeMay Lodge and her husband Jim not only gave me access to her father's papers, but opened up their home to me as well. I became a boarder in their guest room as I spent days going over the personal effects that make up a life of great consequence. One of the other great benefits of working on LeMay was coming to know his family. The other great benefit was befriending Ralph Nutter, who plays a major role in this book. Ralph Nutter is a retired California Superior Court Judge, a die-hard liberal, a Harvard alum, and at the age of twenty-two he was Curtis LeMay's lead-navigator, first in Europe and then in the Pacific. It is Judge Nutter, as feisty and quick as ever, who exemplifies everything great in his generation. Flying twenty-eight missions over Europe and willing to give up his life for his country to defeat a dark tyranny that threatened mankind—this is the stuff of legend. Judge Nutter also gave me the best advice for handling the criticism he expected would ensue for trying to tell a story that disagrees with preconceived notions. "Build your case like a lawyer." The Judge advised me. "Just stick with the facts. You'll be all right."

The people who helped me stick to the facts were the men who served under General LeMay during the war and afterwards . . . in particular, Col. Jim Pattillo, General Paul Carlton, and General

Jacob Smart—all B-17 and B-29 pilots. (It was Jacob Smart, who has since passed away, who sent me one of my favorite notes: "I'm sorry this took so long, but my typing skills are not great, I have a very demanding care-giver and I am on the wrong side of 96!") There was Mike Kruge who I literally bumped into coming home from work one night. Mike Kruge flew twenty-five missions over Europe and, like Judge Nutter, was part of the original group that LeMay brought to England in the fall of 1942. All of these men helped set the record straight. Sitting with them and listening to their stories, I felt like the luckiest guy in town.

Authors always thank their spouses and families. The reasons are both obvious and subtle. Curtis LeMay took over our lives for the better part of four years. My wife, Lisa Krenzel, does not share my fascination with World War II, but she fully understands the merits of fairness and patriotism and recognizes a great story when she sees one. Her field is medicine, but what lurks behind her MD is an editor of great talent who kept pushing me because she believed in this project and saw things when I did not. And it is my wife, more than anyone else, who I thank for getting this from a random wandering of the mind at a play to the bound book you hold in your hands.

At various stages I received tremendous professional help and advice from friends—Barbara Marcus, Jeffrey Krenzel, Dr. Phil Herschenfeld, Dr. Archie Krenzel, Michael Connor, Henry Dunow, Mark Reiter and Michael Denneny. My friend, Gwen Sarnoff, shared her late father, Dan Miller's diaries with me. Perhaps of greatest importance, I called David Horowitz when I was looking for a publisher and he said: "Why don't you give Harry Crocker a call over at Regnery?" I did and I'm so glad for that. Between Harry and the marvelously talented Anneke Green, this book was shaped and formed with great care.

Finally, my father died in 2002, an elderly and frail man who, unless you knew him when he was young, you would never have guessed was once a strong, young captain who went through the war in Europe from Normandy to Germany. He held most of his stories to himself. But he shared one with me that still gives me chills. After two weeks of horrific weather during the worst of the Battle of the Bulge, the skies suddenly cleared one morning. He told me the men around him heard the sound before they actually saw it. But as they looked up, they watched in awe as the entire sky filled with planes from one end to the other. (He actually waved his hand across as he told me this.) And they were all going in one direction. "I couldn't imagine one country could build so many airplanes." He recounted as if he was still standing there on that frozen soil, "That was the moment I realized that we won the war." And then, almost as an afterthought, he added: "It was the most religious experience of my life."

I think about my Dad a lot. And I think about all those young men in the skies and on the ground and at sea. And the gratitude I feel I will never be able to repay.

March 2009, New York City

NOTES

PROLOGUE

1 I. F. Stone, "Curtis LeMay: Cave Man in a Jet Bomber," in Karl Weber, ed., *The Best of I. F. Stone* (Public Affairs, 2006), 326–38.
2 Ralph Nutter to Author, May 7, 2008.
3 Kenneth D. Rose, *One Nation Underground: The Fallout Shelter in American Culture* (NY: New York University Press, 2001), 20.
4 Ralph Nutter to Author, May 8, 2008.

CHAPTER ONE

1 Curtis LeMay and MacKinlay Kantor, *Mission With LeMay: My Story:* (NY: Doubleday & Co., 1965), 13.
2 Curtis LeMay and MacKinlay Kantor, *Mission With LeMay: My Story,* 14.
3 Ibid.
4 Ibid.
5 Patarica Hauger to Author, October 22, 2006.

6   Ibid.

7   Jane LeMay Lodge to Author, June 22, 2006.

8   Ralph Nutter to Author, April 24, 2006.

9   Curtis LeMay and MacKinlay Kantor, *Mission With LeMay: My Story*, 15.

10 Ibid., 17.

11 Patarica Hauger to Author, October 22, 2006.

12 Jane LeMay Lodge to Author, May 5, 2008.

13 Curtis LeMay and MacKinlay Kantor, *Mission With LeMay: My Story*, 28.

14 Thomas M. Coffey, *Iron Eagle: The Turbulent Life of General Curtis LeMay* (NY: Avon Books, 1988), 193.

15 Curtis LeMay and MacKinlay Kantor, *Mission With LeMay: My Story*, 19.

16 Ibid., 20.

17 Thomas M. Coffey, *Iron Eagle: The Turbulent Life of General Curtis LeMay*, 20.

18 Ibid.

19 Curtis LeMay and MacKinlay Kantor, *Mission With LeMay: My Story*, 30.

20 A simple radio receiver that works without batteries or household electric current. For more information see http://www.electronics-tutorials.com/receivers/crystal-radio-set.htm.

21 Curtis LeMay and MacKinlay Kantor, *Mission With LeMay: My Story*, 30.

22 Ibid.

23 Ibid., 32.

24 Ibid.

25 Ibid., 36.

26 Thomas M. Coffey, *Iron Eagle: The Turbulent Life of General Curtis LeMay*, 196.

27 Curtis LeMay and MacKinlay Kantor, *Mission With LeMay: My Story*, 41.

28 Ibid., 43.

29 Ibid., 45.

30 Ibid., 47.

31 Ibid., 46.

CHAPTER TWO

1 Ibid., 52.

2 Ibid.

3 Ibid., 54.

4 General Paul Carlton to Author, December 6, 2006.

5 Curtis LeMay and MacKinlay Kantor, *Mission With LeMay: My Story*, 55.

6 Ibid., 56.

7 Ibid., 58.

8 Ibid.

9 Ibid., 65.

10 Ibid., 62.

11 Ibid., 76.

12 Ibid., 79.

13 Ibid.

14 Ibid., 80.

15 Ibid.

16 Ibid., 83.

17 Ibid., 86.

18 In 1933, Goering was Minister of Civil Air transport, which served as a false front for the German air force, which was banned by the Treaty of Versailles.

19 Curtis LeMay and MacKinlay Kantor, *Mission With LeMay: My Story*, 87.

20 Ibid., 88.

21 Ibid., 89.

22 Ibid., 90.

23 Another form of navigation was being developed at that time in which pilots in flight honed in on a radio beam that emanated from their destination. LeMay concentrated on celestial navigation.

24 Curtis LeMay and MacKinlay Kantor, *Mission With LeMay: My Story,* 97.

25 Edward A. Keogh, "A Brief History of the Air Mail Services of the U.S. Post Office Department," in "Saga of the U.S. Air Mail Service," 1927, http://www.airmailpioneers.org/history/Sagahistory.htm.

26 Curtis LeMay and MacKinlay Kantor, *Mission With LeMay: My Story,* 102.

27 Ibid.

28 Ibid., 103.

29 Patarica Hauger to Author, July 27, 2006.

30 Thomas M. Coffey, *Iron Eagle: The Turbulent Life of General Curtis LeMay,* 228.

31 Jane LeMay Lodge to Author, May 5, 2008.

32 Curtis LeMay and MacKinlay Kantor, *Mission With LeMay: My Story,* 115.

33 Ibid., 121.

34 Ibid., 118.

35 Ibid., 124.

CHAPTER THREE

1   Ibid., 131.

2   General Jacob Smart to Author, March 19, 2006.

3   Colonel James Pattillo (retired) to Author, May 6, 2008.

4   Curtis LeMay and MacKinlay Kantor, *Mission With LeMay: My Story*, 130.

5   Ibid., 131.

6   Ibid., 135.

7   Ibid., 132.

8   Jorg Friedrich, *The Fire: The Bombing of Germany, 1940-1945* (NY: Columbia University Press, 2006), 2.

9   Donald L. Miller, *Masters of the Air: America's Bomber Boys Who Fought the Air War Against Nazi Germany* (NY: Simon and Schuster, 2007), 39.

10 Curtis LeMay and MacKinlay Kantor, *Mission With LeMay: My Story*, 137.

11 Ibid., 146.

12 Thomas M. Coffey, *Iron Eagle: The Turbulent Life of General Curtis LeMay*, 237.

13 Ibid., 238.

14 Curtis LeMay and MacKinlay Kantor, *Mission With LeMay: My Story*, 151.

15 Ibid., 140.

16 Ibid., 173.

17 Ibid., 139.

18 Bill Sault to Author, July 21, 2006.

19 Curtis LeMay and MacKinlay Kantor, *Mission With LeMay: My Story*, 187.

20 Ibid., 188.

21 Ibid., 192.

22 Ibid., 198.

23 Ibid., 201.

24 Ibid.

25 Ibid., 204.

26 Ibid.

27 Ibid., 205.

CHAPTER FOUR

1 Thomas Fleming, "Pearl Harbor Hype," George Mason University, History News Network, July 5, 2002, http://hnn.us/articles/89.html.

2 Richard F. Hill, *Hitler Attacks Pearl Harbor: Why the United States Declared War on Germany* (CO: Lynne Rienner Publishers, 2002), 128.

3 Personal Interview, Gert Kozak, October 20, 1981.

4 Front page headline of the *New York Times*, December 12, 1941, http://graphics8.nytimes.com/packages/pdf/topics/germany_timeline/12-12-1941.pdf.

5 Curtis LeMay and MacKinlay Kantor, *Mission With LeMay: My Story*, 208.

6 Bill Sault to Author, July 21, 2006.

7 Curtis LeMay and MacKinlay Kantor, *Mission With LeMay: My Story*, 207.

8 Representative Jeannette Rankin of Montana cast the lone dissenting vote.

9 Lead editorial, *New York Times*, December 9, 1941.

10 Ralph Nutter to Author, April 26, 2006.

11 Curtis LeMay and MacKinlay Kantor, *Mission With LeMay: My Story*, 210.

12 Ibid.

13 Ibid., 211.

14 Ibid., 207.

15 Thomas M. Coffey, *Iron Eagle: The Turbulent Life of General Curtis LeMay*, 21.

16 Mike Kruge to Author, November 14, 2006.

17 Bill Witson to Author, April 27, 2006.

18 Curtis LeMay and MacKinlay Kantor, *Mission With LeMay: My Story*, 219.

19 Ibid., 218.

20 Ibid.

21 Ibid., 217.

22 Curtis LeMay, letter to Helen LeMay, March 17, 1942.

23 Barbara W. Tuchman, *Stilwell and the American Experience in China*, 1911-1945 (NY: Grove/Atlantic, Inc., 1970), 230.

24 Curtis LeMay and MacKinlay Kantor, *Mission With LeMay: My Story*, 216.

25 Ralph H. Nutter, *With The Possum and The Eagle: A Memoir of a Navigator's War Over Germany and Japan* (TX: University of North Texas Press, 2005), 6.

26 Ibid., 9.

27 Bill Witson to Author, April 27, 2006.

28 Mike Kruge to Author, November 14, 2006.

29 Ralph H. Nutter, *With The Possum and The Eagle: A Memoir of a Navigator's War Over Germany and Japan*, 12.

30 Curtis LeMay and MacKinlay Kantor, *Mission With LeMay: My Story*, 217.

31 Ralph H. Nutter, *With The Possum and The Eagle: A Memoir of a Navigator's War Over Germany and Japan*, 13.

32 Curtis LeMay and MacKinlay Kantor, *Mission With LeMay: My Story*, 222.

33 Bill Sault to Author, July 21, 2006.

34 Ralph H. Nutter, *With The Possum and The Eagle: A Memoir of a Navigator's War Over Germany and Japan*, 14.

35 Curtis LeMay and MacKinlay Kantor, *Mission With LeMay: My Story*, 227.

36 Curtis LeMay, letter to Helen LeMay, October 21, 1942.

37 Bill Sault to Author, July 21, 2006.

38 Curtis LeMay and MacKinlay Kantor, *Mission With LeMay: My Story*, 228.

39 Mike Kruge to Author, November 14, 2006.

40 Although planes were used in fighting in World War I, they never flew as high as the bombers in World War II.

41 Donald L. Miller, *Masters of the Air: America's Bomber Boys Who Fought the Air War Against Nazi Germany*, 2.

42 Curtis LeMay and MacKinlay Kantor, *Mission With LeMay: My Story*, 247.

43 Ibid., 231.

44 Mike Kruge to Author, November 14, 2006.

45 Curtis LeMay and MacKinlay Kantor, *Mission With LeMay: My Story*, 230.

46 Richard G. Davis, *Carl A. Spaatz and the Air War in Europe* (Department of the Air Force, 1993), Appendix 13.

47 Curtis LeMay and MacKinlay Kantor, *Mission With LeMay: My Story*, 231.

48 Ibid.

49 Ibid., 233.

50 Mike Kruge to Author, November 14, 2006.

51 Curtis LeMay and MacKinlay Kantor, *Mission With LeMay: My Story*, 231.

52 Kit Carson, *The B-17 Flying Fortress*, The History Channel (A&E Television Networks, 2003).

53 Curtis LeMay and MacKinlay Kantor, *Mission With LeMay: My Story*, 237.

54 Ibid.

55 Ibid.

56 Doris Kearns Goodwin, *No Ordinary Time: Franklin and Eleanor Roosevelt: The Home Front in World War II* (NY: Simon and Schuster, 1995), 13.

57 Mike Kruge to Author, November 13, 2006.

58 Bill Sault to Author, July 21, 2006.

59 Bill Witson to Author, April 27, 2006.

60 Curtis LeMay and MacKinlay Kantor, *Mission With LeMay: My Story*, 241.

61 Ibid., 242.

62 Ibid.

CHAPTER FIVE

1 Eric Larrabee, *Commander In Chief: Franklin Delano Roosevelt, His Lieutenants, and Their War* (MD: U.S. Naval Institute Press, 2004), 594; Heinz Knocke, *I Flew for the Fuhrer* (London: Greenhill Books, 1997), 88–9; and Adolf Galland, *The First and the Last* (Cutchogue, NY: Buccaneer Books, 1990), 180–81.

2 Dr. Albert Atkins, *Air Marshal Sir Arthur Harris and General Curtis E. LeMay: A Comparative Analytical Biography* (IN: 1st Books Library, 2002), 29.

3 Jorg Friedrich, *The Fire: The Bombing of Germany, 1940-1945*, 20.

4 Mike Kruge to Author, November 13, 2006.

5 Donald L. Miller, *Masters of the Air: America's Bomber Boys Who Fought the Air War Against Nazi Germany*, 316.

6 Ibid., 317.

7 In a famous incident, General Patton struck a soldier who was suffering from "battle fatigue" in Sicily, which he interpreted as cowardice.

8 Curtis LeMay and MacKinlay Kantor, *Mission With LeMay: My Story*, 358.

9   Ralph Nutter to Author, May 8, 2008.

10 Curtis LeMay and MacKinlay Kantor, *Mission With LeMay: My Story,* 357.

11 Ibid., 361.

12 St. Clair McKelway, "A Reporter with the B-29s: The Cigar, the Three Wings, and the Low-Level Attacks," *New Yorker* Magazine, June 23, 1945.

13 Ralph Nutter to Author, May 8, 2008.

14 Donald L. Miller, *Masters of the Air: America's Bomber Boys Who Fought the Air War Against Nazi Germany*, 241.

15 Ibid., 49.

16 Ibid., 149.

17 Ralph Nutter to Author, April 24, 2006.

18 Ibid.

19 Ibid.

20 Curtis LeMay, Air Force Oral History, transcript K105.5-30, p.11.

21 Ralph Nutter to Author, April 24, 2006.

22 Mike Kruge to Author, November 13, 2006.

23 Max Domarus, *Hitler: Speeches and Proclamations 1932–1945—The Chronicle of a Dictatorship* Vol. 3 (Mundelein, IL: Bolchazy-Carducci Publishers, 2004), 2086.

24 Michael Walzer, *Just and Unjust Wars: A Moral Argument with Historical Illustrations* (NY: Basic Books, 2000), 256.

25 Dr. Albert Atkins, *Air Marshal Sir Arthur Harris and General Curtis E. LeMay: A Comparative Analytical Biography*, xx.

26 Ibid., 24.

27 Ibid., 26.

28 James Parton, *Air Force Spoken Here: General Ira Eaker and the Command of the Air* (KS: Sunflower University Press, 1989), 140; and Donald L. Miller, *Masters of the Air: America's Bomber Boys Who Fought the Air War Against Nazi Germany*, 57.

29 Thomas M. Coffey, *Iron Eagle: The Turbulent Life of General Curtis LeMay*, 66.

30 Donald L. Miller, *Masters of the Air: America's Bomber Boys Who Fought the Air War Against Nazi Germany*, 57.

31 Dr. Albert Atkins, *Air Marshal Sir Arthur Harris and General Curtis E. LeMay: A Comparative Analytical Biography*, 25.

32 Ralph Nutter to Author, May 6, 2008.

33 Curtis LeMay and MacKinlay Kantor, *Mission With LeMay: My Story*, 282.

34 Thomas M. Coffey, *Iron Eagle: The Turbulent Life of General Curtis LeMay*, 68.

35 Ibid.

36 Ibid., 66.

37 Curtis LeMay and MacKinlay Kantor, *Mission With LeMay: My Story*, 276.

CHAPTER SIX

1 Ralph Nutter to Author, May 7, 2008.

2 Personal story, Phil Herschenfeld to Author, April 21, 2008; and Linda Kasten to Author, December 2, 2008.

3 Mike Kruge to Author, November 13, 2006.

4 Donald L. Miller, *Masters of the Air: America's Bomber Boys Who Fought the Air War Against Nazi Germany*, 192.

5 Thomas M. Coffey, *Iron Eagle: The Turbulent Life of General Curtis LeMay*, 82.

6 Ibid.

7 Donald L. Miller, *Masters of the Air: America's Bomber Boys Who Fought the Air War Against Nazi Germany*, 193.

8 Ibid., 194.

9 Ibid., 195.

10 Thomas M. Coffey, *Iron Eagle: The Turbulent Life of General Curtis LeMay*, 83.

11 Pinetree was the headquarters of the Eighth Air Force.

12 Curtis LeMay and MacKinlay Kantor, *Mission With LeMay: My Story*, 293.

13 Ibid., 295.

14 Ibid., 294.

15 Donald L. Miller, *Masters of the Air: America's Bomber Boys Who Fought the Air War Against Nazi Germany*, 199.

16 Robert Jackson, *Bomber! Famous Bomber Missions of WWII* (NY: St. Martin's Press, 1980), 117.

17 Donald L. Miller, *Masters of the Air: America's Bomber Boys Who Fought the Air War Against Nazi Germany*, 197.

18 Thomas M. Coffey, *Iron Eagle: The Turbulent Life of General Curtis LeMay*, 89.

19 An acronym standing for "Situation normal . . . all fucked up."

20 Thomas M. Coffey, *Iron Eagle: The Turbulent Life of General Curtis LeMay*, 91.

21 Albert Speer, *Inside The Third Reich* (Ishi Press, 2009), 284.

22 Ibid., 286.

23 Thomas M. Coffey, *Iron Eagle: The Turbulent Life of General Curtis LeMay*, 94; and LeMay-Hopper Interview, September 7, 1943, 21.

24 Thomas M. Coffey, *Iron Eagle: The Turbulent Life of General Curtis LeMay*, 101.

25 Ibid., 97.

26 Ibid., 99.

27 Ibid., 100.

28 Donald L. Miller, *Masters of the Air: America's Bomber Boys Who Fought the Air War Against Nazi Germany*, 210.

29 Thomas M. Coffey, *Iron Eagle: The Turbulent Life of General Curtis LeMay*, 98.

30 Ibid., 70.

31 Ibid., 98.

32 Donald L. Miller, *Masters of the Air: America's Bomber Boys Who Fought the Air War Against Nazi Germany*, 247–48.

33 Ibid., 248.

34 Bartlett would write the screenplay for the 1950 film *12 O'Clock High* with Colonel Beirne Lay, Jr., who flew the Schweinfurt-Regensburg mission.

35 Curtis LeMay and MacKinlay Kantor, *Mission With LeMay: My Story*, 303.

36 Any airman who flew 25 combat missions and survived was allowed to return to the States and spend the rest of the war at training bases. Mathematically, the odds were against surviving to that number. Later, it was increased to 35 missions, making it even more difficult.

37 Donald L. Miller, *Masters of the Air: America's Bomber Boys Who Fought the Air War Against Nazi Germany*, 254.

38 Albert Speer, *Inside The Third Reich*, 290.

39 Donald L. Miller, *Masters of the Air: America's Bomber Boys Who Fought the Air War Against Nazi Germany*, 272.

40 Veteran's History Project, http://www.loc.gov/vets/.

41 Curtis LeMay and MacKinlay Kantor, *Mission With LeMay: My Story*, 298.

42 Ibid., 283.

43 Donald L. Miller, *Masters of the Air: America's Bomber Boys Who Fought the Air War Against Nazi Germany*, 276.

44 Ibid., 267.

CHAPTER SEVEN

1 Herman Wolk to Author, January 30, 2008.

2 Curtis LeMay and MacKinlay Kantor, *Mission With LeMay: My Story,* 321.

3 Ibid., 315.

4 Ibid.

5 Ibid., 318.

6 Curtis E. LeMay papers, Diary of Theodore Beckmeier, Library of Congress, Washington, D.C., Container B-7.

7 Curtis LeMay and MacKinlay Kantor, *Mission With LeMay: My Story,* 323.

8 The Manhattan Project cost $2.4 billion.

9 Eric Larrabee, *Commander In Chief: Franklin Delano Roosevelt, His Lieutenants, and Their War,* 580; and Thomas Collison, *The Superfortress Is Born* (NY: Duell, Sloan & Pearce, 1944), 44.

10 Eric Larrabee, *Commander In Chief: Franklin Delano Roosevelt, His Lieutenants, and Their War,* 611; Vern Haugland, *The AAF Against Japan* (NY: Harper, 1948), 416.

11 Daniel Miller, Jr., private diary, 2.

12 Eric Larrabee, *Commander In Chief: Franklin Delano Roosevelt, His Lieutenants, and Their War,* 580.

13 Letter from General Hansell to Major James M. Boyle, U.S. Air Force Academy, 1965.

14 Curtis LeMay and MacKinlay Kantor, *Mission With LeMay: My Story,* 323.

15 Irving Brinton Holley, *Buying Aircraft: Material Procurement for the Army Air Forces* (World War II) (Darby, PA: Diane Pub Co, 2001); and Curtis LeMay and Bill Yenne, *Superfortress: The Boeing B-29 and American Air Power in World War II* (Yardley, PA: Westholme Publishing, 2006), 48.

16 Curtis LeMay and Bill Yenne, *Superfortress: The Boeing B-29 and American Air Power in World War II*, 98.

17 Ralph H. Nutter, *With The Possum and The Eagle: A Memoir of a Navigator's War Over Germany and Japan*, 167.

18 Curtis LeMay and MacKinlay Kantor, *Mission With LeMay: My Story*, 343.

19 Curtis LeMay and Bill Yenne, *Superfortress: The Boeing B-29 and American Air Power in World War II*, 28.

20 Ibid., 33.

21 Boeing History, "The War Years: 1939–1945, The Boeing Airplane Co.... Superfortress Goes to War," http://www.boeing.com/history/narrative/n025boe.html.

22 Curtis LeMay and Bill Yenne, *Superfortress: The Boeing B-29 and American Air Power in World War II*, 60.

23 Ibid., 61.

24 Ibid.

25 Ibid., 62.

26 Ibid., 63.

27 *Target Tokyo*, directed by Clark Gable, (RareAviation, 1945), United States War Department.

28 Curtis LeMay and Bill Yenne, *Superfortress: The Boeing B-29 and American Air Power in World War II*, 66.

29 Ibid.

30 Ibid., 72.

31 Curtis LeMay and MacKinlay Kantor, *Mission With LeMay: My Story*, 339.

32 Curtis LeMay and Bill Yenne, *Superfortress: The Boeing B-29 and American Air Power in World War II*, 81.

33 Curtis LeMay and MacKinlay Kantor, *Mission With LeMay: My Story*, 324.

34 Ibid., 322.

35 Ibid., 324.

36 General Paul Carlton to Author, December 12, 2006.

37 Curtis LeMay and MacKinlay Kantor, *Mission With LeMay: My Story,* 329.

38 Ibid., 330.

39 Ibid.

40 Ibid., 331.

41 Ibid., 336.

42 Daniel Miller, Jr., private diary.

CHAPTER EIGHT

1 Richard Rhodes, *The Making of the Atomic Bomb* (NY: Simon and Schuster, 1995), 588.

2 Ibid.

3 Richard. B. Frank, *Downfall: The End of the Imperial Japanese Empire* (Random House, 1999), 4.

4 "Victory in the Pacific," *The American Experience*, PBS, November 7, 2005, http://www.pbs.org/wgbh/amex/pacific/.

5 Curtis LeMay and Bill Yenne, *Superfortress: The Boeing B-29 and American Air Power in World War II*, 104.

6 Ibid., 125.

7 Ibid.

8 Ibid.

9 Ibid., 105.

10 Ibid.

11 Ibid., 125.

12 General Paul Carlton to Author, December 12, 2006.

13 Richard. B. Frank, *Downfall: The End of the Imperial Japanese Empire*, 57.

14 Ralph Nutter to Author, May 7, 2008.

15 Ralph H. Nutter, *With the Possum and the Eagle: A Memoir of a Navigator's War Over Germany and Japan*, 218.

16 Ibid., 222.

17 Ralph Nutter to Author, May 7, 2008.

18 Ralph H. Nutter, *With the Possum and the Eagle: A Memoir of a Navigator's War Over Germany and Japan*, 156.

19 Jeremy Isaacs, *The World At War*, Episode # 24, "The Bomb," Thames Television documentary, 1974.

20 Ralph H. Nutter, *With the Possum and the Eagle: A Memoir of a Navigator's War Over Germany and Japan*, 223.

21 Ibid., 156.

22 St. Clair McKelway, "A Reporter With the B-29s: The Doldrums, Guam, and Something Coming Up," *The New Yorker*, June 16, 1945.

23 At that point in the war, crewmen were allowed to return to the States if they survived 25 missions. It was later raised to 35. Nutter completed an extra two missions with the British to study their radar navigation.

24 Ralph H. Nutter, *With the Possum and the Eagle: A Memoir of a Navigator's War Over Germany and Japan*, 156.

25 Ibid., 173.

26 Ibid., 230.

27 Curtis LeMay and MacKinlay Kantor, *Mission With LeMay: My Story*, 347.

28 Richard. B. Frank, *Downfall: The End of the Imperial Japanese Empire*, 86.

29 Robert McNamara to Author, September 19, 2005.

30 Curtis LeMay and MacKinlay Kantor, *Mission With LeMay: My Story*, 338.

31 Ibid., 339.

32 Thomas M. Coffey, *Iron Eagle: The Turbulent Life of General Curtis LeMay*, 134.

33 Curtis LeMay and MacKinlay Kantor, *Mission With LeMay: My Story*, 338.

34 St. Clair McKelway, "A Reporter with the B-29s: The Doldrums, Guam, and Something Coming Up," *The New Yorker*, June 16, 1945.

35 Ibid.

36 Ibid.

37 Ibid.

38 Thomas M. Coffey, *Iron Eagle: The Turbulent Life of General Curtis LeMay*, 160.

39 Curtis LeMay and MacKinlay Kantor, *Mission With LeMay: My Story*, 341–42.

40 Afterwards, a number of different people claimed that they came up with the idea of low-level bombing before LeMay and Power worked it out. But ultimately, as commander, LeMay was responsible if the plan failed. If there was a major loss of B-29s with little damage done to Japan, LeMay fully understood his career would end, marred with the unnecessary slaughter of more Americans.

41 Curtis LeMay and MacKinlay Kantor, *Mission With LeMay: My Story*, 352.

42 Ibid., 347.

43 Ibid.

44 Richard Rhodes, *The Making of the Atomic Bomb*, 591.

45 Michael S. Sherry, *Rise of American Air Power: The Creation of Armageddon* (New Haven, CT: Yale University Press, 1989), 279.

46 Ralph H. Nutter, *With the Possum and the Eagle: A Memoir of a Navigator's War Over Germany and Japan*, 236.

47 Ibid., 237.

48 Ibid., 240–41.

49 Ibid., 242.

50 General Glen Martin, Air Force Oral History Project, Transcript dated February 6–10, 1978, 352.

51 Curtis LeMay and MacKinlay Kantor, *Mission With LeMay: My Story,* 379.

52 St. Clair McKelway, "A Reporter with the B-29s: The Cigar, the Three Wings, and the Low-Level Attacks," *The New Yorker,* June 23, 1946, 36.

53 Richard. B. Frank, *Downfall: The End of the Imperial Japanese Empire,* 7.

54 Ibid., 9.

55 Ibid., 13.

56 Richard Rhodes, *The Making of the Atomic Bomb,* 590.

57 Richard Rhodes, *Dark Sun: the Making of the Hydrogen Bomb* (NY: Simon & Schuster, 1996), 21.

58 United States Strategic Bomb Survey #96, p.95. For more information see http://www.ibiblio.org/hyperwar/AAF/USSBS/IJO/index.html#pageVI .

59 Richard. B. Frank, *Downfall: The End of the Imperial Japanese Empire,* 10.

60 Eric Larrabee, *Commander In Chief: Franklin Delano Roosevelt, His Lieutenants, and Their War,* 621.

61 Ralph H. Nutter, *With the Possum and the Eagle: A Memoir of a Navigator's War Over Germany and Japan,* 243.

62 Richard. B. Frank, *Downfall: The End of the Imperial Japanese Empire,* 337.

63 Ibid., 89.

64 Ibid.

65 Ibid., 163.

CHAPTER NINE

1   Ibid., 15.

2   Ibid.

3   Richard. B. Frank, *Downfall: The End of the Imperial Japanese Empire*, 17.

4   Ibid., 18.

5   Curtis LeMay and MacKinlay Kantor, *Mission With LeMay: My Story,* 381.

6   Robert McNamara to Author, September 19, 2005.

7   Ralph H. Nutter, *With the Possum and the Eagle: A Memoir of a Navigator's War Over Germany and Japan*, 245.

8   Thomas M. Coffey, *Iron Eagle: The Turbulent Life of General Curtis LeMay*, 166.

9   Front page headline, *New York Times*, March 10, 1945.

10 Lead editorial, *New York Times*, March 12, 1945.

11 Colonel James Pattillo (retired) to Author, May 10, 2008.

12 Ralph Nutter to Author, May 9, 2008.

13 Richard Rhodes, *The Making of the Atomic Bomb*, 597.

14 Thomas M. Coffey, *Iron Eagle: The Turbulent Life of General Curtis LeMay*, 168.

15 Richard. B. Frank, *Downfall: The End of the Imperial Japanese Empire*, 77.

16 Ibid., 81.

17 Ibid., 79.

18 Curtis LeMay and MacKinlay Kantor, *Mission With LeMay: My Story: My Story*.

19 Richard. B. Frank, *Downfall: The End of the Imperial Japanese Empire*, 162.

20 Ibid., 161.

21 Curtis LeMay, letter to Helen LeMay, July 21, 1945.

22 Thomas M. Coffey, *Iron Eagle: The Turbulent Life of General Curtis LeMay*, 174.

23 Ibid.

24 Ibid., 175.

25 Eric Larrabee, *Commander In Chief: Franklin Delano Roosevelt, His Lieutenants, and Their War*, 578.

26 Thomas M. Coffey, *Iron Eagle: The Turbulent Life of General Curtis LeMay*, 176.

27 Ibid.

28 Seymour Tabacoff to Author, January 22, 2007.

29 Morton Camac to Author, July 5, 2006.

30 Seymour Tabacoff to Author, January 22, 2007.

31 Curtis LeMay, letter to Helen LeMay, July 30, 1945.

32 Richard. B. Frank, *Downfall: The End of the Imperial Japanese Empire*, 153.

33 Curtis LeMay and MacKinlay Kantor, *Mission With LeMay: My Story*, 375.

34 Ibid.

35 Curtis LeMay, letter to Helen LeMay, July 10, 1945.

36 Richard. B. Frank, *Downfall: The End of the Imperial Japanese Empire*, 154.

37 Curtis LeMay and MacKinlay Kantor, *Mission With LeMay: My Story*, 279.

38 Ibid., 388.

39 Thomas M. Coffey, *Iron Eagle: The Turbulent Life of General Curtis LeMay*, 181.

40 Seymour Tabacoff to Author, January 22, 2007.

41 Curtis LeMay and MacKinlay Kantor, *Mission With LeMay: My Story*, 389.

42 Ibid.

43 Ibid., 390.

44 Barbara W. Tuchman, *Stilwell and the American Experience in China, 1911-1945*, 522.

45 Ibid.

46 Curtis LeMay and MacKinlay Kantor, *Mission With LeMay: My Story*, 390.

47 Ibid.

CHAPTER TEN

1 *Pictorial History of the Second World War*, Vol. V (NY: Wm. H. Wise and Co., 1944), 2162.

2 Curtis LeMay, letter to Helen LeMay, September 18, 1945.

3 Thomas M. Coffey, *Iron Eagle: The Turbulent Life of General Curtis LeMay*, 249–50; from LeMay-Coffey Interview February 2, 1984.

4 Walter J. Boyne, *Beyond the Wild Blue* (NY: Thomas Dunne Books, 2007), 31.

5 Richard Rhodes, *Dark Sun: The Making of the Hydrogen Bomb*, 227.

6 Air Force Oral History Project, October 1, 1975.

7 Thomas M. Coffey, *Iron Eagle: The Turbulent Life of General Curtis LeMay*, 254.

8 Air Force Oral History Project, October 1, 1975.

9 Ibid.

10 Ibid.

11 Jane LeMay Lodge to Author, May 7, 2008.

12 Dr. James Lodge to Author, May 8, 2008.

13 Thomas M. Coffey, *Iron Eagle: The Turbulent Life of General Curtis LeMay*, 255.

14 Walter J. Boyne, *Beyond the Wild Blue*, 29.

15 Curtis LeMay and MacKinlay Kantor, *Mission With LeMay: My Story,* 403.

16 Thomas M. Coffey, *Iron Eagle: The Turbulent Life of General Curtis LeMay*, 259.

17 Ibid., 260.

18 Curtis LeMay and MacKinlay Kantor, *Mission With LeMay: My Story*, 408.

19 Ibid., 401.

20 Ibid., 415.

21 Ibid., 416.

22 Ibid., 417.

23 Ibid., 416.

24 Ibid., 420.

CHAPTER ELEVEN

1 Ibid., 430.

2 Anything that can go wrong, will go wrong.

3 Walter J. Boyne, *Beyond the Wild Blue*, 104.

4 Ibid., 40.

5 Ibid., 102.

6 Curtis LeMay and MacKinlay Kantor, *Mission With LeMay: My Story*, 431.

7 Walter J. Boyne, *Beyond the Wild Blue*, 46.

8 Curtis LeMay and MacKinlay Kantor, *Mission With LeMay: My Story*, 429.

9 Ibid., 432.

10 Thomas M. Coffey, *Iron Eagle: The Turbulent Life of General Curtis LeMay*, 278.

11 Tom Compere, *The Air Force Blue Book* (Indianapolis, IN: Bobbs-Merrill, 1959), 57.

12 Thomas M. Coffey, *Iron Eagle: The Turbulent Life of General Curtis LeMay*, 276.

13 Ibid., 281.

14 Curtis LeMay and MacKinlay Kantor, *Mission With LeMay: My Story*, 437.

15 I. F. Stone, "Curtis LeMay: Cave Man in a Jet Bomber," in Karl Weber, ed., *The Best of I. F. Stone*, 326.

16 Walter J. Boyne, *Beyond the Wild Blue*, 99.

17 Curtis LeMay and MacKinlay Kantor, *Mission With LeMay: My Story*, 439.

18 General Jacob Smart to Author, March 19, 2006.

19 General David C. Jones to Author, August 12, 2005.

20 Thomas M. Coffey, *Iron Eagle: The Turbulent Life of General Curtis LeMay*, 276.

21 Ibid., 295.

22 Ralph Nutter to Author, May 9, 2008.

23 Thomas M. Coffey, *Iron Eagle: The Turbulent Life of General Curtis LeMay*, 296.

24 Curtis LeMay and MacKinlay Kantor, *Mission With LeMay: My Story*, 449.

25 Jane LeMay Lodge to Author, June 2006.

26 Ibid.

27 Curtis LeMay and MacKinlay Kantor, *Mission With LeMay: My Story*, 451.

28 Ibid., 452.

29 Colonel James Pattillo (retired) to Author, May 9, 2008.

30 Curtis LeMay and MacKinlay Kantor, *Mission With LeMay: My Story*, 473.

31 Walter J. Boyne, *Beyond the Wild Blue*, 87.

32 Ibid., 88.

33 General Curtis LeMay, Oral History, Air Force Oral History Project, 592, p.54ff.

34 Dr. Albert Atkins, *Air Marshal Sir Arthur Harris and General Curtis E. LeMay: A Comparative Analyitical Biography*, 47.

35 Ralph Nutter to Author, May 17, 2006.

36 Curtis LeMay and MacKinlay Kantor, *Mission With LeMay: My Story*, 456.

37 Ibid., 457.

38 Ibid.

39 Thomas M. Coffey, *Iron Eagle: The Turbulent Life of General Curtis LeMay*, 324.

40 Ibid., 311.

41 Fred Ikle to Author, August 16, 2005.

42 Thomas M. Coffey, *Iron Eagle: The Turbulent Life of General Curtis LeMay*, 331.

43 Curtis LeMay and MacKinlay Kantor, *Mission With LeMay: My Story*, 482.

44 Richard. B. Frank, *Downfall: The End of the Imperial Japanese Empire*, 332.

45 Curtis LeMay and MacKinlay Kantor, *Mission With LeMay: My Story*, 482.

CHAPTER TWELVE

1 Jane LeMay Lodge to Author, March 31, 2008.

2 Dr. James Lodge to Author, May 5, 2008.

3 Curtis LeMay and MacKinlay Kantor, *Mission With LeMay: My Story*, 484.

4 Ibid.

5 Ibid.

6 General Jacob Smart to Author, March 19, 2006.

7   Curtis E. LeMay Papers, Library of Congress, Washington, D.C.,
    Container A-3.

8   Curtis E. LeMay Papers, Library of Congress, Washington, D.C.

9   Ibid.

10 Ibid.

11 Curtis E. LeMay Papers, Library of Congress, Washington, D.C.,
    Container B-43.

12 Ralph Nutter to Author, May 9, 2008.

13 Curtis E. LeMay Papers, Library of Congress, Washington, D.C.,
    Container B-43.

14 Ibid.

15 Ibid.

16 Library of Congress, LeMay Collection, Archives Box B132.

17 Thomas M. Coffey, *Iron Eagle: The Turbulent Life of General Curtis
    LeMay*, 346.

18 Ibid.

19 Ibid., 347.

20 Curtis LeMay and MacKinlay Kantor, *Mission With LeMay: My
    Story*, 498.

21 Thomas M. Coffey, *Iron Eagle: The Turbulent Life of General Curtis
    LeMay*, 350.

22 Ibid., 354.

23 Ibid., 355.

24 Robert Dallek interview from "The Kennedys" on *The American
    Experience*, PBS, 2003, http://www.pbs.org/wgbh/amex/kennedys/
    sfeature/sf_dallek.html.

25 Ted Sorensen to Author, November 22, 2005.

26 Carl Kaysen to Author, November 22, 2005.

27 Thomas M. Coffey, *Iron Eagle: The Turbulent Life of General Curtis
    LeMay*, 372.

28 Robert McNamara to Author, September 19, 2005.

29 Roswell Gilpatric, Kennedy Library Oral History Program, June 30, 1970. For more information, visit http://www.jfklibrary.org/Asset-Viewer/Archives/RLGPP.aspx.

30 Robert McNamara to Author, September 19, 2005.

31 Thomas M. Coffey, *Iron Eagle: The Turbulent Life of General Curtis LeMay*, 358.

32 Robert McNamara to Author, September 19, 2005.

33 Thomas M. Coffey, *Iron Eagle: The Turbulent Life of General Curtis LeMay*, 358.

34 Robert McNamara to Author, September 19, 2005.

35 Thomas M. Coffey, *Iron Eagle: The Turbulent Life of General Curtis LeMay*, 361.

36 Richard Reeves, *President Kennedy: Profile of Power* (NY: Simon and Schuster, 1993), 171.

37 Gordon Frank Sander, "The B-70 Fight," World Affairs Board, November 4, 2006, http://gordonsander.com/2000/03/the-b-70-fight/.

38 Ted Sorensen to Author, November 22, 2005.

39 James Schlesinger to Author, April 25, 2008.

40 Curtis LeMay and MacKinlay Kantor, *Mission With LeMay: My Story*, 565.

41 Jane LeMay Lodge to Author, May 6, 2008; and Ralph Nutter to Author, May 9, 2008.

CHAPTER THIRTEEN

1 Curtis LeMay and MacKinlay Kantor, *Mission With LeMay: My Story*, 528–29.

2 Max Frankel, *High Noon in the Cold War: Kennedy, Kruschev, and the Cuban Missile Crisis* (NY: Presidio Press, 2005), 15–16.

3 Thomas M. Coffey, *Iron Eagle: The Turbulent Life of General Curtis LeMay*, 390.

4 Ernest R. May and Philip D. Zelikow, eds., *The Kennedy Tapes: Inside the White House During the Cuban Missile Crisis* (Bellnap Press Harvard, 1997), 177.

5 Max Frankel, *High Noon in the Cold War: Kennedy, Kruschev, and the Cuban Missile Crisis*, 127.

6 Ernest R. May and Philip D. Zelikow, eds., *The Kennedy Tapes: Inside the White House During the Cuban Missile Crisis*, 182; and Max Frankel, *High Noon in the Cold War: Kennedy, Kruschev, and the Cuban Missile Crisis*, 98.

7 Ernest R. May and Philip D. Zelikow, eds., *The Kennedy Tapes: Inside the White House During the Cuban Missile Crisis*, 188.

8 Curtis LeMay and MacKinlay Kantor, *Mission With LeMay: My Story*, 380.

9 Robert McNamara to Author, August 19, 2005.

10 Max Frankel, *High Noon in the Cold War: Kennedy, Kruschev, and the Cuban Missile Crisis*, 97.

11 Ibid., 130.

12 Ibid., 163.

13 Thomas M. Coffey, *Iron Eagle: The Turbulent Life of General Curtis LeMay*, 425.

14 General Curtis E. LeMay with Major General Dale O. Smith, *America is in Danger* (NY: Funk & Wagnalls, 1968), 2.

15 Thomas M. Coffey, *Iron Eagle: The Turbulent Life of General Curtis LeMay*, 434.

16 Ibid., 436.

17 Ibid., 438.

18 Jane LeMay Lodge to Author, June 21, 2008.

19 Ibid.

20 *Newsweek*, January 4, 1965.

21 Anonymous source to Author, May 20, 2008.

22 Thomas M. Coffey, *Iron Eagle: The Turbulent Life of General Curtis LeMay*, 443.

23 Jane LeMay Lodge to Author, May 5, 2008.

24 General Curtis E. LeMay with Major General Dale O. Smith, *America is in Danger*, 69.

25 Ibid., xii.

26 Ibid., xv.

27 Ibid., 12.

CHAPTER FOURTEEN

1 Lewis Chester, Godfrey Hodgson, and Bruce Page, *American Melodrama: The Presidential Campaign of 1968* (NY: Viking Adult, 1969), 32.

2 Ibid, 652.

3 Ibid., 668.

4 Jane LeMay Lodge to Author, May 5, 2008.

5 Lewis Chester, Godfrey Hodgson, and Bruce Page, *American Melodrama: The Presidential Campaign of 1968*, 698.

6 Ibid., 699.

7 Theodore H. White, *The Making of the President, 1968* (NY: Atheneum, 1969), 429.

8 Ibid.

9 Ibid., 424.

10 *Time* Magazine, October 18, 1968.

11 Herman Wolk to Author, April 21, 2006.

12 Curtis E. LeMay Papers, Library of Congress, Washington, D.C., Container D-2.

13 *Wall Street Journal*, October 25, 1968.

14 Curtis E. LeMay Papers, Library of Congress, Washington, D.C., Container D-2.
15 Ibid.
16 Jane LeMay Lodge to Author, May 5, 2008.
17 Ralph Nutter to Author, April 8, 2008.
18 Jane LeMay Lodge to Author, March 31, 2008.
19 Charles Lodge to Author, June 5, 2008.
20 General Perry Smith to Author, May 20, 2008.
21 Jane LeMay Lodge to Author, April 2, 2008.
22 Ralph Nutter to Author, April 8, 2008.

INDEX